Praise for
Leading at a Higher Level

"At Southwest Airlines, we have always strived to lead at a higher level. We truly believe that profit is the applause you get for taking care of your internal and external customers. We have always insisted upon a happy, carefree, team-spirited—yes, even fun—working environment, which we think results in motivated employees who will do the right thing for their internal and external customers. Reading this book will make a positive difference in your organisation."

Colleen C. Barrett, *President Emeritus, Southwest Airlines*

"This is not just theory. It is the real stuff, tried in dozens of companies big and small. It represents the most concise, practical, and effective thinking on leadership around. Plainly said, this works."

Gary Crittenden, *Managing Director, Huntsman Gay Global Capital, former CFO of Citigroup and American Express*

"Leading at a higher level is a must today if leaders are to rebuild trust and credibility, as we are doing at Tyco. This book will teach you how."

Eric Pillmore, *Senior Vice President of Corporate Governance, Tyco International*

"*Leading at a Higher Level* translates decades of research and 30 years of global experience into simple, practical, and powerful strategies to equip leaders at every level to build organisations that produce bottom-line results. At Nissan, we have made these principles a core part of our leadership philosophy, better equipping our managers to bring out the great energies and talents of our employees."

Jim Irvine, *Vice President of Human Resources,*
⋯⋯⋯ North America

The concepts in *Leading at a Higher Level* have been used by high-performing organisations around the world, including:

Abbott Laboratories

AMF Bowling Worldwide, Inc.

Anthem Blue Cross and Blue Shield

Applebee's International, Inc.

Bayer AG

Big Lots Stores, Inc.

Biogen Idec Inc.

Bose® Corporation

Bowater® Incorporated

Burger King®

Callaway Golf Company

Caterpillar Inc.

Cellular One

Chick-fil-A®, Inc.

Children's Hospital

The Coffee Bean and Tea Leaf®

Comerica Incorporated

Compaq

CompUSA®

ConocoPhillips

Domino's Pizza

Dow Corning Corporation

Energy Northwest

Exxon Mobil Corporation

Fairmont Hotels & Resorts

FedEx Kinko's Office and Print Services

Fireman's Fund Insurance Company®

Foster Farms

Genentech, Inc.

Georgetown University

Hilton Hotels Corporation

Home Depot

Host Hotels & Resorts, (formerly known as Host Marriott)

Hyatt Corporation

Jack in the Box Inc.

Kennedy Space Center

Krispy Kreme Doughnut Corporation

L'Oréal

Mattel, Inc.

Marriott International

MCI, Inc.

Merck & Co., Inc.

The Michelin Group

Microsoft Corporation

Nabisco

Nissan Motor Co.

Northrop Grumman Corporation

Novartis AG

Pepperdine University

Polaris Industries

The Ritz-Carlton Hotel Company

Royal Caribbean Cruises Ltd.®

Safeco Corporation

San Diego Padres

S.C. Johnson & Son, Inc.

Six Continents Retail

Sony Corporation of America

Staples, Inc.

Toshiba Corporation

Toyota Motor Corporation

TRW Automotive Inc.

Tyson Foods, Inc.

UCLA

United States Postal Service®

UPS™

Verizon

Victoria's Secret

Wal-Mart Stores, Inc.

Washington State Criminal Justice Training Commission

WD-40 Company

Wells Fargo & Company

Wendy's International, Inc.

Yellow Pages (GTE)

LEADING AT A HIGHER LEVEL

Revised and Expanded Edition

LEADING AT A HIGHER LEVEL

Revised and Expanded Edition

Blanchard on How to Be a High-Performing Leader

The Founding Associates and Consulting Partners
of The Ken Blanchard Companies

*with an Introduction
by Ken Blanchard*

**Financial Times
Prentice Hall
is an imprint of**

Harlow, England • London • New York • Boston • San Francisco • Toronto
Sydney • Tokyo • Singapore • Hong Kong • Seoul • Taipei • New Delhi
Cape Town • Madrid • Mexico City • Amsterdam • Munich • Paris • Milan

PEARSON EDUCATION LIMITED

Edinburgh Gate
Harlow CM20 2JE
Tel: +44 (0)1279 623623
Fax: +44 (0)1279 431059
Website: www.pearsoned.co.uk

Original edition, entitled LEADING AT A HIGHER LEVEL, REVISED AND EXPANDED EDITION: BLANCHARD ON LEADERSHIP AND CREATING HIGH PERFORMING ORGANIZATIONS, 1st edition, by BLANCHARD, KEN, published by Pearson Education, Inc, publishing as FT Press, Copyright © 2010.

UK adaptation published by PEARSON EDUCATION LTD, Copyright © 2010.

This edition is manufactured in the United Kingdom and is authorised for sale only in the United Kingdom, Europe, the Middle East and Africa.

The right of Kenneth Blanchard to be identified as author of this work has been asserted by him in accordance with the Copyright, Designs and Patents Act 1988.

ISBN: 978-0-273-73618-9

British Library Cataloguing-in-Publication Data
A catalogue record for this book is available from the British Library

10 9 8 7 6 5 4
14 13 12 11

Typeset in 12pt Photina MT by 30
Printed in Great Britain by Henry Ling Limited., at the Dorset Press, Dorchester, DT1 1HD

Dedicated to all leaders in the world
who are trying every day to lead at a higher level.
May you keep your energy high and know
that what you are doing makes a difference.

CONTRIBUTING AUTHORS

Ken Blanchard

Marjorie Blanchard

Scott Blanchard

Madeleine Blanchard

Don Carew

Eunice Parisi-Carew

Kathy Cuff

Garry Demarest

Chris Edmonds

Fred Finch

Susan Fowler

Bob Glaser

Lael Good

Vicki Halsey

Laurence Hawkins

Judd Hoekstra

Fay Kandarian

Linda Miller

Alan Randolph

Jesse Stoner

Drea Zigarmi

Pat Zigarmi

CONTENTS

Contents

Contents

Contents

LIST OF ILLUSTRATIONS

Introduction

Several years ago, my wife Margie and I went on a safari in South Africa with some family and friends. We had been on a number of safaris over the past 20 years, but this time I saw some things differently. The jungle appeared more vicious, competitive, and territorial than ever before. If you've ever heard a lion roar, it sends chills up your back. When our long-time guide, Gary Clarke from Topeka, Kansas, imitates the lion's roar, he shouts, "It's mine, mine, mine, mine!" That's because when the lion roars, what he's really saying is, "This is my territory. Don't mess with me." In fact, lions will kill their sons if the sons challenge their fathers' control over their territory.

The reason I saw this more vividly than ever before is that I had decided on this trip that I was going to find out as much as I possibly could about Nelson Mandela. We had been at a dinner party where people around the table were asked to share what person—of anyone in the world—they would love to have dinner with. It was a quick decision for me. I said, "Nelson Mandela. I would love to have dinner with a man who was in prison for 28 years and treated cruelly, yet came out of that experience full of love, compassion, and reconciliation." On the trip, I began to read Mandela's autobiography, *Long Walk to Freedom*.

When I compared what I saw in the jungle with how Mandela had reacted to his treatment, I realised that in many ways we as human beings are just intelligent animals. And being intelligent animals, we can choose every day whether to be self-serving or serving. Jungle animals, like the lion, can't make that choice. They have to protect their territory. It's not in their nature to share with other species. And yet, just as Mandela did, we as human beings can make choices to live and lead at a higher level, to be serving rather than self-serving. But when you look at the leaders around the world—whether they're running countries, businesses, churches, educational institutions, or what have you—too many people are choosing to be self-serving rather than serving. Why is that? Because they don't have a different leadership role model. They have been conditioned to think about leadership only in terms of power and control. That's what this book is all about—a different leadership paradigm. We want to help individuals and organisations lead at a higher level.

Leading at a Higher Level

What is leadership? For years we defined leadership as an *influence process*. We believed that any time you tried to influence the thoughts and actions of others towards goal accomplishment in either your personal or professional life, you were engaging in leadership. In recent years, we have taken the emphasis away from goal accomplishment and have defined leadership as *the capacity to influence others by unleashing their power and potential to impact the greater good*. Why did we do that? Because when the definition of leadership focuses on goal accomplishment, one can think that leadership is only about results. Yet when we talk about leading at a higher level, just focusing on goal accomplishment is not enough. The key phrase in our new definition is "the greater good"—what is best for all involved. We think leadership is a high calling. Leadership should not be done purely for personal gain or goal accomplishment; it should have a much higher purpose than that.

What is a higher purpose? It is not something as internally focused and self-centred as making money. As Matt Hayes and Jeff Stevens contend in *The Heart of Business*, when it becomes obvious that profit, which is a legitimate goal, is the driving reason for being in business, everyone—stockholders, top managers, employees, customers, suppliers, and the community—quickly becomes self-serving. They focus on their own agenda and personal enrichment. Employee loyalty and passion often go out the window as the point of work becomes simply to get as much as you can for as little effort as possible.[1]

What is the answer to this dilemma? A higher purpose—a key element of what we will refer to throughout this book as a *compelling vision*. In Hayes and Stevens' terms, it is something outwardly focused, it requires sacrifice—in other words, it takes precedence over any short-term goal like profit—and it is intrinsically honourable.

Leaders can be successful in the short run if they emphasise only goal accomplishment. What tends to fall by the wayside is the condition of the human organisation. Leaders don't always take morale and job satisfaction into consideration—only results count. They forget what the point is. They don't have a higher purpose. In business, with that kind of leadership, it is a short leap to thinking that the only reason to be in business is to make money. An either/or is added to people and results. Leaders falsely believe that they can't focus on both at the same time.

When you are leading at a higher level, you have a both/and philosophy. The development of people—both customers and employees—is of equal importance to performance. As a result, the focus in leading at a higher level is on long-term results and human satisfaction. *Leading at a higher level*, therefore, is a process. We define it as *the process of achieving worthwhile results while acting with respect, care, and fairness for the well-being of all involved.* When that occurs, self-serving leadership is not possible. Why?

Self-serving leaders think that leadership is all about them and not about the best interests of those they serve. They forget about acting with respect, care, and fairness towards all involved. Everything is about their own self-interest. It's only when you realise that it's not about you that you begin to lead at a higher level.

Why Did We Write This Book?

In 2006 we wrote the original edition of this book for several reasons. First, our dream was that someday everyone will know someone who is leading at a higher level. Self-serving leaders will be a thing of the past, and leadership throughout the world will be composed of people who, as Robert Greenleaf said, "serve first and lead second."[2] We wrote this book to help make our dream a reality.

Second, the vision of The Ken Blanchard Companies is focused on leading at a higher level. This kind of leadership begins with a vision. Jesse Stoner and I wrote a book called *Full Steam Ahead!* about the power of visioning. To us, a compelling vision tells you *who you are* (your purpose), *where you're going* (your preferred picture of the future), and *what will drive your journey* (your values).

The purpose of The Ken Blanchard Companies is to help individuals and organisations lead at a higher level. Our mission statement reflects our new definition of leadership:

Unleash the power and potential of people and organisations for the greater good.

Our picture of the future is

- Everyone is trained to lead at a higher level.
- Every organisation is led by people leading at a higher level.

- People are motivated to lead at a higher level by observing people who lead at a higher level.

Our operating *values* are

- **Ethical Behaviour**: Doing the right thing
- **Relationships**: Developing mutual trust and respect
- **Success**: Operating a profitable and well-run organisation
- **Learning**: Always growing, enquiring, and developing

These values are ordered by rank. In other words, we won't do anything to improve the company's profitability that is unethical or that doesn't honour the relationships we have with our customers, our people, our suppliers, and our community. We realise that making money is not the higher purpose of our business.

You might say that this all sounds like Pollyanna—overly optimistic. That may be, but these are the standards we have set for ourselves. And these are the same high standards we want to help you and the people in your organisation reach through this book. Helping individuals and organisations lead at a higher level is our passion, both for your organisation and our own.

Finally, in many ways this book spells out our leadership point of view. Extensive research shows that effective leaders have a clear leadership point of view and are willing to share with others these beliefs about leading and motivating people. We hope reading this book will impact your leadership point of view.

How This Book Is Organised

Over the years, I have found that in organisations where leading at a higher level is the rule rather than the exception, people do four things well:

- They set their sights on the right target and vision.
- They treat their customers right.

- They treat their people right.
- They have the right kind of leadership.

This book is organised into four sections. Section I focuses on *the right target and vision* and integrates our work on the triple bottom line, the characteristics of a high-performing organisation, and the creation of a compelling vision.

Section II highlights *treating the customer right* and integrates our work on legendary service, raving fans, and customer mania. Today, everybody should realise that their customers are the reason that their organisation exists.

Section III focuses on *treating your people right*. This is where the rubber meets the road. If you don't empower your people and treat them right, they won't take care of your customers, and in the long run, you won't get your desired results. This is the longest section of the book, because your treatment of people is leadership in action. This is what The Ken Blanchard Companies has been focusing on for more than 30 years. In this section, we start with empowerment and then examine four leadership domains: self-leadership, one-on-one leadership, team leadership, and organisational leadership.

Section IV zeroes in on *the right kind of leadership*. Here we're not talking about leadership style; we're talking about character and intentionality. My travels over the years through organisations of all shapes and sizes have convinced me of two things: effective leadership starts on the inside, and the right kind of leadership is servant leadership. This is a leadership not based on false pride or fear, but one that's grounded in humility and focused on the greater good. With the right kind of leadership, leading at a higher level can become a reality.

This section also includes our thoughts on determining your leadership point of view. This turns the focus to you. Here we assist you in pulling together many of the concepts you have learned and help you integrate and apply that knowledge to your own leadership situation.

Writing this book has been a labour of love. Pulling together our best thinking from more than 30 years of working together, it truly is *Blanchard on Leadership*. With new chapters on culture and coaching, this second edition includes not only Margie's and my thinking, but also all the wonderful contributions of our founding associates—Don Carew, Eunice Parisi-Carew, Fred Finch, Laurie Hawkins, Drea Zigarmi, and Pat Zigarmi—and other fabulous consulting partners who have really made Blanchard "the home of the authors," including Scott Blanchard, Madeleine Homan Blanchard, Kathy Cuff, Garry Demarest, Chris Edmonds, Susan Fowler, Bob Glaser, Lael Good, Vicki Halsey, Judd Hoekstra, Fay Kandarian, Linda Miller, Alan Randolph, and Jesse Stoner.

We think everyone can lead at a higher level, whether at work, at home, or in the community. We hope that, regardless of your position, the size or type of your organisation, or the kind of customers or people you serve, you will learn some important information in this book. We also hope this book will help you lead at a higher level and create a high-performing organisation that not only accomplishes your desired results but is a welcome harbour for the people you touch. May good come out of your reading of this book.

Ken Blanchard
San Diego, California
Spring 2009

section I

SET YOUR SIGHTS
ON THE
RIGHT TARGET AND VISION

Chapter 1

Is Your Organisation High-Performing?

Don Carew, Fay Kandarian,
Eunice Parisi-Carew, Jesse Stoner,
and Ken Blanchard

Marksmen will tell you that when you aim at a target, you should go for the bull's eye. The reason is that if you miss the bull's eye, you're still on the target. But if all you do is aim for the target and you miss, you're nowhere. Don Shula, who co-authored *Everyone's a Coach*[1] with Ken Blanchard, always told his Miami Dolphins football team that the target they were aiming at was to win every game. Was that possible? Obviously not, but if you don't shoot for excellence, you never have a chance of getting there. That's probably why Shula's teams won more football games than teams of any other coach in the history of the NFL. His 1972 Dolphins is still the only team in history to go undefeated for an entire season. So the target you aim for has a lot to do with your performance.

Wall Street and the pressures of business today make many people think that the only target that counts is financial success. Yet few, if any, businesspeople would want their epitaph to include their company's bottom line—their stock price or profit margin. They might, however, want people to remember their contribution to the creation of a high-performing organisation.

Those who want to lead at a higher level need to understand that to create a high-performing organisation, they need to aim for the right target.

The Right Target: The Triple Bottom Line

In high-performing organisations, everyone's energy is focused on not just one bottom line, but three bottom lines—being the ***provider of choice***, the ***employer of choice***, and the ***investment of choice***. This triple bottom line is the right target and can make the difference between mediocrity and greatness.[2] The leaders in high-performing organisations know that their bottom line depends on their customers, their people, and their investors. These leaders realise the following:

> *Profit is the applause you get for taking care of your customers and creating a motivating environment for your people.*

Provider of Choice

Being the provider of choice is increasingly challenging. Competition is fierce as new competitors emerge unexpectedly. Customers are more demanding, with many more options at their fingertips. The world has changed in such a way that today the buyer, not the seller, is sitting in the driver's seat. These days, nobody has to convince anybody that the customer reigns. In fact, companies are motivated to change when they discover the new rule:

> *If you don't take care of your customers, somebody else will.*

In *Raving Fans®: Satisfied Customers Are Not Enough*,[3] Sheldon Bowles and Ken Blanchard argue that to keep your customers today, you can't be content just to satisfy them. You have to create raving fans—customers who are so excited about how you treat them that they want to tell everyone about you. They become part of your sales force. Let's look at a simple yet powerful example.

What's the most common wake-up call that you get in a hotel in America today? The phone rings at the allotted hour, but when you pick it up, no one is there. At least they got the machine to call your room at the designated hour. The second most common wake-up call greets you with a recording. But again, no one's there. Today if you pick up the phone on a wake-up call and a human being is on the other end—someone you can actually talk to—you hardly know what to say. A while back, one of our colleagues was staying at the Marriott Convention Hotel in Orlando. He asked for a 7:00 wake-up call. When the phone rang and he picked it up, a woman said, "Good morning; this is Teresa. It's 7 o'clock. It's going to be 75 and beautiful in Orlando today, but your ticket says you're leaving. Where are you going?"

Taken aback, our colleague stammered, "New York City."

Teresa said, "Let me look at the *USA Today* weather map. Oh, no! It's supposed to be 40 degrees and rainy in New York today. Can't you stay another day?"

Now where do you think our colleague wants to stay when he gets to Orlando? He wants to stay at the Marriott so that he can talk to Teresa in the morning! Raving fans are created by companies whose service far exceeds that of the competition and even exceeds customer expectations. These companies routinely do the unexpected and then enjoy the growth generated by customers who have spontaneously joined their sales force.

Employer of Choice

Being the employer of choice is equally challenging. With highly mobile, competent workers in demand, employers must find ways to attract and keep their best people. Good pay is no longer the only answer. It is true that some competent workers will go elsewhere for a higher wage; however, today's workers generally want more. They seek opportunities where they feel like their contributions are valued and rewarded—where they are involved and empowered, can develop skills, can see advancement opportunities, and can believe they are making a difference.

You will get little argument today if you tell managers that people are their most important resource. Some even argue that the customer should come second, because without committed and empowered employees, a company can never provide good service. You can't treat your people poorly and expect them to treat your customers well.

Several years ago, a friend of ours had an experience in a department store that illustrates this point well. He normally shops at Nordstrom but found himself in a competitor's store. Realising that he needed to talk to his wife, he asked a salesperson in the men's department if he could use their telephone. "No!" the salesperson said.

He replied, "You have to be kidding me. You can always use the phone at Nordstrom."

The salesperson said, "Look, buddy! They don't let *me* use the phone here. Why should I let *you?*"

People who are treated poorly tend to pass that attitude on to their customers.

Another reason that your people are so important today is because these days your organisation is evaluated on how quickly it can respond to customer needs and problems. "I'll have to talk to my boss" doesn't cut it any more. Nobody cares who the boss is. The only people customers care about are the ones who answer the phone, greet them, write up their order, make their delivery, or respond to their complaints. They want top service, and they want it fast. This means that you need to create a motivating environment for your people and an organisational structure that is flexible enough to permit them to be the best they can be.

Investment of Choice

Growing or expanding requires investment, regardless of whether the company is publicly owned, privately held, government, or non-profit. All organisations require funding sources, through stock purchases, loans, grants, or contracts. To be willing to invest, people must believe in the organisation's viability and performance over time. They need to have faith in the leadership, the quality of the people, the product and services, the management practices, and the organisation's resilience.

If an organisation's financial success is a function of revenue minus expenses, you can become more sound financially either by reducing costs or increasing revenues. Let's look at costs first, because in today's competitive environment, the prize goes to those who can do more with less. More organisations today are deciding that the only way to be financially effective is to downsize. There's no doubt that some personnel reduction is necessary in large bureaucracies where everyone just has to have an assistant, and the assistant must have an assistant. Yet downsizing is an energy drain, and it's by no means the only way to manage costs.

There's a growing realisation that another effective way to manage cost is to make all your people your business partners. For instance, in some companies, new people can't get a pay rise until they can read their company's balance sheet and understand where and how their individual efforts are impacting the company's profit-and-loss statement. When people understand the business realities of how their organisation makes and spends money, they are much more apt to roll up their sleeves and help out.

Traditionally, managers have been reluctant to share financial information. Yet these days, many organisations are responding with open-book management. That's because they realise the financial benefits of sharing previously sensitive data. For example, in working with a restaurant company, one of our consulting partners was having a hard time convincing the managing director of the merits of sharing important financial data with employees. To unfreeze the managing director's thinking, the consulting partner went to the firm's largest restaurant one night at closing time. Dividing all the employees—chefs, dishwashers, waiters and waitresses, receptionists—into groups of five or six, he asked them to come to an agreement about the answer to a question: "Of every pound that comes into this restaurant, how many pence do you think fall to the bottom line—money that can be returned to investors as profit or re-invested in the business?"

The least amount any group guessed was 40 pence. Several groups guessed 70 pence. In a restaurant, the reality is that if you can keep 5 pence in the pound, you get excited—10 pence, and you're ecstatic! Can you imagine the attitude among employees towards such things as food costs, labour costs, and breakage when they thought their company was a money machine? After sharing the actual figures, the manager was impressed when a chef asked, "You mean, if I burn a steak that costs us £3 and we sell it for £10, at a 5 per cent profit margin, we have to sell six steaks for essentially no profit to make up for my mistake?" He already had things figured out.

If you keep your people well informed and let them use their brains, you'll be amazed at how they can help manage costs.

This is particularly important in uncertain times. If you develop committed and empowered people, not only will they help manage costs, but they'll also increase your revenues. How? By providing legendary service that creates raving fan customers who will want to brag about you. These customers become part of your unofficial sales force or PR department, which increases your sales and/or visibility and makes your organisation more attractive as an investment. Now you are a leader of a high-performing organisation.

A High-Performing Organisation SCORES Every Time

Provider of choice, employer of choice, and investment of choice—the three elements of the triple bottom line—form the right target. If you aim for only one of the three elements, you won't hit the target, and your organisation won't be able to sustain high-performance. Once leaders understand the importance of the target, questions naturally arise, such as "What is a high-performing organisation?" and "What does a high-performing organisation that hits the target look like?"

To answer these questions, Don Carew, Fay Kandarian, Eunice Parisi-Carew, and Jesse Stoner conducted an extensive research project to define and identify the characteristics of a high-performing organisation.[4] Their first step was to define a "high-performing organisation." While many organisations rise quickly and then plateau or topple, some continue to thrive, somehow reinventing themselves as needed. The researchers focused on these kinds of organisations, creating the following definition:

High-performing organisations are enterprises that over time continue to produce outstanding results with the highest level of human satisfaction and commitment to success.

Because of their flexibility, nimbleness, and responsive systems, high-performing organisations (HPOs) remain not only successful and respected today but also are poised to succeed in the future. HPOs demonstrate results consistently over time.

The HPO SCORES™ Model

As a result of their research, Drs Carew, Kandarian, Parisi-Carew, and Stoner created the HPO SCORES model. SCORES is an acronym that represents the six elements evident in every high-performing organisation. A high-performing organisation scores—hits the target consistently—because it demonstrates strength in each of these six elements. The following pages give an overview of these elements.

S = *Shared Information and Open Communication*

In high-performing organisations, information needed to make informed decisions is readily available to people and is openly communicated. Sharing information and facilitating open communication builds trust and encourages people to act like owners of the organisation. Encouraging dialogue lessens the danger of territoriality and keeps the organisation healthy, agile, flexible, and fluid.

C = *Compelling Vision*

A compelling vision is the hallmark of a high-performing organisation. When everyone supports such an organisational vision—including purpose, a picture of the future, and values—it creates a deliberate, highly focused culture that drives the desired business results towards a greater good. In these organisations, people are energised by, excited about, and dedicated to such a vision. They have a noble sense of purpose that creates and focuses energy. Their personal values are aligned with the values of the organisation. They can describe a clear picture of what they intend to create. Everyone is aligned and going in the same direction.

O = *Ongoing Learning*

High-performing organisations are constantly focusing on improving their capabilities through learning systems, building knowledge capital, and transferring learning throughout the organisation. Organisational learning is different from individual learning. High-performing organisations engage in both. Everyone is always striving to get better, both individually and as an organisation.

R = Relentless Focus on Customer Results

No matter what industry they are in, high-performing organisations understand who their customer is and measure their results accordingly. They produce outstanding results, in part because of an almost obsessive focus on results. However, what is unique is the way in which they focus on those results: from the customer's viewpoint.

E = Energising Systems and Structures

The systems, structures, processes, and practices in high-performing organisations are aligned to support the organisation's vision, strategic direction, and goals. This makes it easier for people to get their jobs done. Energising systems and structures provide the platform for rapid response to obstacles and opportunities. The bottom-line test of whether the systems and structures are energising is to look at whether they help people accomplish their jobs more easily or make them more difficult.

S = Shared Power and High Involvement

In high-performing organisations, power and decision making are shared and distributed throughout the organisation, not guarded at the top of the hierarchy. Participation, collaboration, and teamwork are a way of life. When people feel valued and respected for their contributions, are allowed to make decisions that impact their lives, and have access to information to make good decisions, they *can* and *will* function as valuable contributors to the organisation's purpose and vision. In high-performing organisations, a sense of personal and collective power exists.

The HPO SCORES™ Model

Shared Power and High Involvement
Power and decision making are shared and distributed throughout the organisation and not guarded at the top of a hierarchy. Participation, collaboration, and teamwork are the way of life.

Shared Information and Open Communication
High-performing organisations employ a broad definition of what is relevant and necessary information. Information needed to make informed decisions is readily available to employees.

SHARED POWER and HIGH INVOLVEMENT

SHARED INFORMATION and OPEN COMMUNICATION

ENERGISING SYSTEMS and STRUCTURES

Employer of Choice • Provider of Choice
Unleashing Potential and Power
Investment of Choice

COMPELLING VISION: PURPOSE and VALUES

RELENTLESS FOCUS on CUSTOMER RESULTS

ONGOING LEARNING

Organisation Knowledge and Capabilities

Individual Learning

Energising Systems and Structures
Systems, structures, processes, and practices are aligned to support the organisation's purpose, values, strategic direction, and goals—which makes it easier for people to get their jobs done.

Compelling Vision
Organisational vision, including purpose and values, are clearly understood and passionately supported by all—which creates a deliberate, highly focused culture that drives the desired business results.

Relentless Focus on Results
High-performing organisations produce outstanding results, in part because of an almost obsessive focus on results. However, what is unique is the way in which they focus on those results—from the perspective of their customer.

Ongoing Learning
High-performing organisations are constantly focused on improving their capabilities through learning systems, building knowledge capital, and transferring learning throughout the organisation.

The six essential elements of the HPO SCORES™ Model operate interdependently to produce sustainable high performance and human satisfaction. Refer to the "High Performing Organisations: SCORES" article for more information on each of the elements and the research behind them.

Figure 1.1   The HPO SCORES™ Model

Leadership Is the Engine

If becoming a high-performing organisation is the destination, leadership is the engine. While the HPO SCORES model describes the characteristics of a high-performing organisation, leadership is what moves the organisation in that direction.

In high-performing organisations, the role of formal leadership is radically different from traditional organisations. High-performing organisations rely not on cultivating a great, charismatic leader, but on building a visionary organisation that endures beyond the leader. The role of leadership shifts from privileged status and power for its own sake towards a more complex, participative, long-term process. As this book will continually emphasise, once leaders establish the vision, they assume the attitude and behaviour of a servant leader.

In high-performing organisations, leadership practices support collabouration and involvement. Leadership is assumed at every level of the organisation. Top leaders live the organisation's values. They embody and encourage a spirit of enquiry and discovery. They help others think systematically. They act as teachers *and* lifelong learners. They are visible in their leadership and have the strength to stand firm on strategic business decisions and values. They keep everyone's energy focused on the bull's eye of excellence.

In high-performing organisations, leadership is not the province of formal leaders or a few peak performers alone; leadership emerges everywhere. Individuals with expertise come forward as needed throughout the organisation.

The HPO SCORES Quiz:
How Does Your Organisation Score?

To begin to see how your organisation scores, take a few moments to complete the following quiz. It is based on a few of the questions from the HPO SCORES Profile, an organisational assessment that was developed as part of a research project.[5] We've also included some supplemental questions on leadership.

HPO SCORES Quiz

On a scale of 1 to 7, to what extent do you disagree or agree with the following statements?

1 = Strongly disagree

2 = Disagree

3 = Slightly disagree

4 = Neutral

5 = Slightly agree

6 = Agree

7 = Strongly agree

Shared Information and Open Communication

___ 1. People have easy access to the information they need to do their job effectively.

___ 2. Plans and decisions are communicated so that they are clearly understood.

Compelling Vision: Purpose and Values

___ 1. Leadership in your organisation is aligned around a shared vision and values.

___ 2. The people in your organisation have passion around a shared purpose and values.

Ongoing Learning

___ 1. People in your organisation are actively supported in the development of new skills and competencies.

___ 2. Your organisation continually incorporates new learning into standard ways of doing business.

Relentless Focus on Customer Results

___ 1. Everyone in your organisation maintains the highest standards of quality and service.

___ 2. All work processes are designed to make it easier for your customers to do business with you.

Energising Systems and Structures

___ 1. Systems, structures, and formal and informal practices are integrated and aligned.

___ 2. Systems, structures, and formal and informal practices make it easy for people in your organisation to get their jobs done.

Shared Power and High Involvement

___ 1. People have an opportunity to influence decisions that affect them.

___ 2. Teams are used as a vehicle for accomplishing work and influencing decisions.

Leadership[6]

___ 1. Leaders think that leading is about serving, not being served.

___ 2. Leaders remove barriers to help people focus on their work and their customers.

How Does Your Organisation Score?

It is possible to receive a total of 14 points for each of the elements and for the supplemental questions on leadership.

Add the scores for each element to determine how strong your organisation is in that element:

Score 12 to 14 = High performing
Score 9 to 11 = Average
Score 8 or below = Opportunity for improvement

How Should I Use My Quiz Results?

Although this quiz may help you begin to determine if your organisation is high performing, it should not be used as an organisational analysis. The main purpose of the quiz is to guide your reading. While the sections and chapters of this book are sequenced for good reason, they may not be laid out in the order that most matters to you and your organisation today. If you scored 8 or below on any element of the HPO SCORES quiz, you might want to begin by focusing specifically on that area.

While it makes perfect sense to us to focus first on setting your sights on the right target and vision, it may make more sense for you to start with having the right kind of leadership. For example, some of our clients have a long history of having the right target and vision, but in recent years, some self-serving leaders have risen to the top and have been causing a gap between the espoused vision and values and the vision and values in action. Other clients have a real sense of the right target and vision, but a culture has emerged that is not treating their customers right. If that sounds familiar to you, you might want to start with Section II, "Treat Your Customers Right."

If you have no particular problem areas, we recommend that you start at the beginning and move through the planned sequence of sections as you learn how to create a high-performing organisation.

Chapter 2

THE POWER OF VISION

Jesse Stoner, Ken Blanchard,
and Drea Zigarmi

When leaders who are leading at a higher level understand the role of the triple bottom line as the right target—to be the provider of choice, employer of choice, and investment of choice—they are ready to focus everyone's energy on a compelling vision.

The Importance of Vision

Why is it so important for leaders to have clear vision? Because:

Leadership is about going somewhere.
If you and your people don't know
where you are going,
your leadership doesn't matter.

Alice learned this lesson in *Alice in Wonderland* when she was searching for a way out of Wonderland and came to a fork in the road. "Would you tell me, please, which way I ought to go from here?" she asked the Cheshire Cat. "That depends a good deal on where you want to go," the cat responded. Alice replied that she really did not much care. The smiling cat told her in no uncertain terms: "Then it doesn't matter which way you go."

Jesse Stoner conducted an extensive study that demonstrated the powerful impact of vision and leadership on organisational performance.[1] She collected information from the team members of more than 500 leaders. The results were striking. Leaders who demonstrated strong visionary leadership had the highest-performing teams. Leaders with good management skills but without vision had average team performance. Leaders who were identified as weak in vision and management skills had poor-performing teams.

The biggest impediment blocking most managers from being great leaders is the lack of a clear vision for them to serve. In fewer than 10 per cent of the organisations we have visited were members clear about the vision. This lack of shared vision causes people to become inundated with multiple priorities, duplication of efforts, false starts, and wasted energy—none of which supports the triple bottom line.

A vision builds trust, collaboration, interdependence, motivation, and mutual responsibility for success. Vision helps people make smart choices, because their decisions are being made with the end result in mind. As goals are accomplished, the answer to "What next?" becomes clear. Vision allows us to act from a proactive stance, moving towards what we want rather than reactively away from what we don't want. Vision empowers and excites us to reach for what we truly desire. As the late management guru Peter Drucker said, "The best way to predict your future is to create it."

Effective Versus Ineffective Vision Statements

A lot of organisations already have vision statements, but most of them seem irrelevant when you look at the organisation and where it's going. The purpose of a vision statement is to create an aligned organisation where everyone is working together towards the same desired ends.

The vision provides guidance for daily decisions so that people are aiming at the right target, not working at cross-purposes.

How do you know if your vision statement works? Here's the test: Is it hidden in a forgotten file or framed on a wall solely for decoration? If so, it's not working. Is it actively used to guide everyday decision making? If the answer is yes, your vision statement is working.

Creating a Vision That Really Works

Why don't more leaders have a vision? We believe it's a lack of knowledge. Many leaders—such as former president George H. W. Bush—say they just don't get the "vision thing." They acknowledge that vision is desirable, but they're unsure how to create it. To these leaders, vision seems elusive—something that is magically bestowed only on the fortunate few. Intrigued by the possibility of making vision accessible for all leaders, Jesse Stoner teamed up with Drea Zigarmi to identify the key elements of a compelling vision—one that would inspire people and provide direction. In "From Vision to Reality," Jesse and Drea identified three key elements of a compelling vision:[2]

- **Significant purpose**: What business are you in?
- **A picture of the future**: What will the future look like if you are successful?

- **Clear values**: What guides your behaviour and decisions on a daily basis?

A vision must include all three elements to be inspiring and enduring. Let's explore these elements with some real-world examples.

Significant Purpose

The first element of a compelling vision is a significant purpose. This higher purpose is your organisation's reason for existence. It answers the question "Why?" rather than just explaining what you do. It clarifies, from your customers' viewpoint, what business you are *really* in.

CNN is in the "hard spot news-breaking business." Their customers are busy people who need breaking news on demand. Their business is to provide hard news as it unfolds—not to provide entertainment. According to CNN, the typical family today is too busy to sit in front of the television at 7 p.m. Dad has a second job, Mum is working late, and the kids are involved in activities. Therefore, CNN's purpose is to provide news 24 hours a day. This helps CNN employees answer the questions "What are my priorities?" and "Where should I focus my energy?"

Walt Disney started his theme parks with a clear purpose. He said, "We're in the happiness business." That is very different from being in the theme park business. Clear purpose drives everything the cast members (employees) do with their guests (customers). Being in the happiness business helps cast members understand their primary role in the company.

A wonderful organisation in Orlando, Florida, called Give Kids the World, is an implementation operation for the Make-A-Wish Foundation. Dying children who always wanted to go to Disney World, SeaWorld, or other attractions in Orlando can get a chance through Give Kids the World. Over the years, the organisation has brought more than 50,000 families to Orlando for a week at no cost to them. The organisation thinks having a sick child is a family issue; therefore, the whole family goes to Orlando.

When you ask the employees what business they are in, they tell you they're in the memory business—they want to create memories for these kids and their families.

On a visit to Give Kids the World, one of our colleagues passed a man who was cutting the grass. Curious about how widely understood the organisation's mission was, our colleague asked the man, "What business are you in here at Give Kids the World?" The man smiled and said, "We make memories."

"How do *you* make memories?" our associate asked. "You just cut the grass."

The man said, "I certainly don't make memories by continuing to cut the grass if a family comes by. You can always tell who the sick kid is, so I ask that youngster whether he or she or a brother or sister wants to help me with my chores."

Isn't that a wonderful attitude? It keeps him focused on servicing the folks who come to Give Kids the World.

Great organisations have a deep and noble sense of purpose—a significant purpose—that inspires excitement and commitment.

When work is meaningful and connected to what we truly desire, we can unleash a productive and creative power we never imagined. But purpose alone is not enough, because it does not tell you where you're going.

A *Picture of the Future*

The second element of a compelling vision is a picture of the future. This picture of the end result should not be abstract. It should be a mental image you can actually see. The power of imagery has been described by many sports psychologists, including Charles Garfield in *Peak Performance: Mental Training Techniques of the World's Greatest Athletes*. Numerous studies have demonstrated that not only does mental imagery enhance performance, but it enhances intrinsic motivation as well.[3]

CNN's picture of the future is not something vague like being the premier network news station or being "number one." It's a picture you can actually create a mental image of: "To be viewed in every nation on the planet in English and in the language of that region."

Walt Disney's picture of the future was expressed in the charge he gave every cast member: "Keep the same smile on people's faces when they leave the park as when they entered." Disney didn't care whether a guest was in the park two hours or ten hours. He just wanted to keep them smiling. After all, they were in the happiness business. Your picture should focus on the end result, not the process of getting there.

At Give Kids the World, their picture of the future is that in the last week of the lives of youngsters who have been there, they will still be laughing and talking to their families about their time in Orlando.

Some people mistakenly use the Apollo Moon Project as an example of a vision. It is a wonderful example of the power of creating a picture of the future, but it's not an example of a vision. In 1961, when President John F. Kennedy articulated a picture of the future—to place a man on the Moon by the end of the 1960s and bring him home safely—the United States had not even invented the technology to accomplish it. To achieve that goal, NASA overcame seemingly insurmountable obstacles, demonstrating the power of articulating a picture of the future. However, once the goal was achieved, NASA never re-created its spectacular achievement, because it was not linked to a significant purpose. There was nothing to answer the question "Why?" Was the purpose to "beat the Russians" or to "begin the Space Defence Initiative" or—in the spirit of *Star Trek*—"to boldly go where no one has gone before"? Because there was no clear purpose, there was no way to guide decision making going forward and answer the question "What next?" The second element—a picture of the future—is powerful, but it alone does not create an enduring vision.

Clear Values

The third element of a compelling vision is having clear values. High-performing organisations have clear values. Values define leadership and how employees act on a day-to-day basis while doing their work.

Values provide guidelines for how you should proceed as you pursue your purpose and picture of the future. They answer the questions "What do I want to live by?" and "How?" They need to be clearly described so that you know exactly what behaviours demonstrate that the value is being lived. Values need to be consistently acted on, or they are only good intentions. They need to resonate with the personal values of the members of the organisation so that people truly choose to live by them.

The values need to support the organisation's purpose. Because CNN is in the journalism business, not the entertainment business, its values are "to provide accurate, responsible journalism and to be responsive to the news needs of people around the world." These values help reporters and producers make on-the-spot decisions about news coverage and would be quite different if CNN were in the entertainment business.

Robert Johnson founded Johnson & Johnson for the purpose of alleviating pain and disease. The company's purpose and values, reflected in its credo, continue to guide the company. Using its values to guide its decision making, Johnson & Johnson quickly recalled all Tylenol capsules throughout the United States during a 1982 tampering incident that was localised in the Chicago area. The immediate cost was substantial, but not knowing the extent of the tampering, the company didn't want to risk anyone's safety. In the end, Johnson & Johnson's triple bottom line was served, demonstrated by the company's long-term gains in reputation and profitability.

Most organisations that do have values either have too many values or have not rank-ordered them.[4] Research done by Ken Blanchard and Michael O'Connor shows that people can't focus on more than three or four values that really impact behaviour. They also found that values must be rank-ordered to be effective. Why? Because life is about value conflicts. When these conflicts arise, people need to know which value they should focus on.

The Disney theme parks have four rank-ordered values: safety, courtesy, the show, and efficiency. Why is safety the highest-ranked value? Walt Disney knew that if guests were carried out of one of his parks on a stretcher, they would not have the same smiles on their faces leaving the park as they had when they entered.

The second-ranked value, courtesy, is all about the friendly attitude you expect at a Disney park. Why is it important to know that it's the number-two value? Suppose one of the Disney cast members is answering a guest question in a friendly, courteous manner, and he hears a scream that's not coming from a roller coaster. If that cast member wants to act according to the park's rank-ordered values, he will excuse himself as quickly and politely as possible and race towards the scream. Why? Because the number-one value just called. If the values were not rank-ordered and the cast member was enjoying the interaction with the guest, he might say, "They're always yelling in the park," and not move in the direction of the scream. Later somebody could come to that cast member and say, "You were the closest to the scream. Why didn't you move?" The response could be, "I was dealing with our courtesy value." Life is a series of value conflicts. There will be times when you can't act on two values at the same time.

For a vision to endure, you need all three elements—a significant purpose, a picture of the future, and clear values—to guide behaviour on a day-by-day basis. Martin Luther King, Jr outlined his vision in his "I Have a Dream" speech. By describing a world where his children "will not be judged by the colour of their skin but by the content of their character," he created powerful and specific images arising from the values of brotherhood, respect, and freedom for all—values that resonate with the founding values of the United States. King's vision continues to mobilise and guide people beyond his lifetime because it illuminates a significant purpose, provides a picture of the future, and describes values that resonate with people's hopes and dreams.

A Compelling Vision Creates a Culture of Greatness

A compelling vision creates a strong culture in which the energy of everyone in the organisation is aligned. This results in trust, customer satisfaction, an energised and committed workforce, and profitability. Conversely, when an organisation does not live up to its stated values, employee and customer trust and commitment erode, negatively impacting all aspects of the bottom line. For example, Ford lost credibility and market share when its stated value—"Quality Is Job One"—was tested by its hesitation to take responsibility in the recall of the defective Firestone tyres on its Explorer four-wheel drive vehicle in 2000.[5]

Vision Is the Place to Start

Research clearly demonstrates the extraordinary impact of a shared vision, or core ideology, on long-term financial performance. The cumulative stock returns of the HPOs researched by Collins and Porras were 6 times greater than the "successful" companies they examined and 15 times greater than the general market over a 50-year period of time![6] For this reason, vision is the place to start if you want to improve your organisation's HPO SCORES and hit the target.

Research has demonstrated time and again that an essential characteristic of great leaders is their ability to mobilise people around a shared vision.[7]

If it's not in service of a shared vision, leadership can become self-serving. Leaders begin to think their people are there to serve them, instead of the customer. Organisations can become self-serving bureaucracies where leaders focus their energies on recognition, power, and status, rather than the organisation's larger purpose and goals. The results of this type of behaviour have been all too evident recently at Enron, WorldCom, and others.

Once leaders have clarified and shared their vision, they can focus on serving and being responsive to the needs of the people, understanding that the role of leadership is to remove barriers and help people achieve the vision. The greatest leaders mobilise others by coalescing people around a shared vision. Sometimes leaders don't get it at first, but the great ones eventually do.

Louis Gerstner, Jr is a perfect example. When Gerstner took the helm of IBM in 1993—amidst turmoil and instability as the company's annual net losses reached a record $8 billion—he was quoted as saying, "The last thing IBM needs is a vision." A lot of people asked us what we thought about that statement. Our reply was, "It depends on how he defines vision. If he means a 'pie-in-the-sky' dream, he's absolutely right. The ship is sinking. But if all he's doing is plugging the holes, the ship isn't going anywhere." We were amused to read an article in *The New York Times*[8] two years later. In that article, Gerstner conceded that IBM had lost the war for the desktop operating system, acknowledging that the acquisition of Lotus signified that the company had failed to plan properly for its future. He admitted that he and his management team now "spent a lot of time thinking ahead." Once Gerstner understood the importance of vision, an incredible turnaround occurred. It became clear that the company's source of strength would be in integrated solutions and resisted pressures to split the company. In 1995, delivering the keynote address at the computer industry trade show, Gerstner articulated IBM's new vision—that network computing would drive the next phase of industry growth and would be the company's overarching strategy. That year, IBM began a series of acquisitions that positioned services to become the company's fastest-growing segment, with growth at more than 20 per cent per year. This extraordinary turnaround demonstrated that the *most important thing* IBM needed was a vision—a shared vision.

If an organisation's vision is compelling, the triple bottom line is served. Success goes way beyond mere financial rewards. Vision generates tremendous energy, excitement, and passion, because people feel they are making a difference. They know what they are doing and why. There is a strong sense of trust and respect. Managers don't try to control, but rather let others assume responsibility, because people know they are part of an aligned whole. People assume responsibility for their own actions. They take charge of their future, rather than passively waiting for it to happen. There is room for creativity and risk taking. People can make their contributions in their own way, and those differences are respected, because people know they are in the same boat— all part of a larger whole going "full steam ahead!"

Vision Can Exist Anywhere in an Organisation

You don't have to wait for an organisational vision to begin. Vision is the responsibility of every leader at every level of the organisation. It's possible for leaders of departments or teams to create shared visions for their departments even when the rest of the organisation doesn't have one. Consider our work helping a tax department in a Fortune 500 company. The leader of the department stated:

> "We began to understand our own and each others' hopes and dreams and discovered how close they were. We found ways to work together more effectively and began to enjoy work a lot more. We discovered what business we were really in: 'Providing financial information to help leaders make good business decisions.' As a result, we began to partner more effectively with business leaders. Our department gained more credibility in the company, and other departments began asking us what we had done to make such a turnaround. They became interested in creating a vision for their own department. It was contagious."

Too often, leaders complain that they can't have a vision because the larger organisation doesn't have one. Again, it's not necessary to wait. The power of vision will work for you and your team, regardless of your level in the organisation.

Make Your Vision a Reality

In their book *Full Steam Ahead! Unleash the Power of Vision in Your Company and Your Life,* Ken Blanchard and Jesse Stoner define vision as "knowing who you are, where you're going, and what will guide your journey."[9] *Knowing who you are* means having a significant purpose. *Where you're going* means having a picture of the future. *What will guide your journey* are clear values. However, vision alone is not enough. For a leader to ensure that the vision becomes a reality—a shared vision that mobilises people—Ken and Jesse identify three important guidelines that people must follow: how the vision is created, how it's communicated, and how it's lived.

How It's Created

The process of creating the vision is as important as what the vision says. Instead of simply taking the top management to a retreat to put the vision together and then announcing it to others, encourage dialogue about the vision. While the initial responsibility for drafting an organisational vision rests with the top management, the organisation needs to put in place mechanisms to give others an opportunity to help shape the vision—to put their thumbprint on it.

For a departmental or team vision, it's possible to craft the vision as a team. Although leaders must have a sense of where they're going, it's important that they trust and utilise the knowledge and skills of the people on the team to get the best vision.

Regardless of how you initially draft the vision, it's important that you get input from those it affects before you finalise it. Ask people these questions: "Would you like to work for an organisation that has this vision? Can you see where you fit in the vision? Does it help you set priorities? Does it provide guidelines for making decisions? Is it exciting and motivating? Have we left anything out? Should we delete anything?" Involving people will deepen their understanding and commitment and create a better vision.

How It's Communicated

Creating a vision—for your organisation or department, for your work, and for your life—is a journey, not a one-time activity.

In some organisations, a vision statement may be found framed on the wall, but it provides no guidance or, worse, has nothing to do with the reality of how things actually are. This turns people off. Visioning is an ongoing process; you need to keep it alive. It's important to keep talking about the vision and referring to it as much as possible. Max DePree, the legendary former chairman of Herman Miller and author of *Leadership Is an Art*, said that in his visionary role, he had to be like a primary school teacher. He had to keep on saying it over and over and over until people got it right, right, right! The more you focus on your vision, the clearer it will become, and the more deeply you will understand it. In fact, aspects of what you thought was the vision may change over time, but its essence will remain.

How It's Lived

The moment you identify your vision, you need to behave as if it were happening right now. Your actions need to be congruent with your vision. As others see you living the vision, they will believe you are serious, and this will help deepen their understanding and commitment. Two strategies will support your efforts to live your vision:

- **Always focus on your vision.** Your vision should be the foundation for your organisation. If an obstacle or unforeseen event throws you off-course, you may have to change your short-term goals, but your vision should be long-lasting. Change is bound to happen. Unforeseen events are bound to occur. Find a way to reframe what is happening as a challenge or opportunity on the road to living your vision.

- **Show the courage of commitment.** True commitment begins when you take action. There will be fears; feel them and move ahead. It takes courage to create a vision, and it takes courage to act on it. In the words of Goethe, "Whatever you can do, or dream you can, begin it. Boldness has genius, power, and magic in it."

Vision and Leadership

Vision always comes back to leadership. People look to their formal leaders for vision and direction. While leaders should involve people in shaping direction, the ultimate responsibility for ensuring and maintaining a vision remains with the leaders and cannot be delegated to others. Creating a vision is not an activity that can be checked off a list. It's one of the most critical ongoing roles of a successful leader. It means the difference between high and average performance, whether it's an entire organisation, a department, or a team.

Once a vision is agreed upon, it is up to the leader to ensure that people respond to the vision. The leader's job is to support people in accomplishing the vision by removing barriers; by ensuring that policies, practices, and systems make it easier for them to act on the vision; and by holding themselves, their peers, and their people accountable for acting consistently with the vision. This way people serve the vision, not the leader.

Vision calls an organisation to be truly great, not merely to beat the competition and get big numbers. A magnificent vision articulates people's hopes and dreams, touches their hearts and spirits, and helps them see how they can contribute. It aims everyone in the right direction.

COMPANION **ONLINE** RESOURCE

Visit **www.LeadingAtAHigherLevel.com** to access the free virtual conference titled *Set Your Sights on the Right Target and Vision.* Use the password "Target" for your FREE access.

section II

TREAT
YOUR CUSTOMERS
RIGHT

Chapter 3

SERVING CUSTOMERS
AT A
HIGHER LEVEL

Ken Blanchard, Kathy Cuff, Vicki Halsey,
and Jesse Stoner

The second step in leading at a higher level is to treat your customers right. While everybody seems to know that, organisations with exceptional service are rare. When an organisation delivers with such excellence and consistency that its service reputation becomes a competitive edge, that's Legendary Service.

Getting Legendary SCORES from Your Customers

In Chapter 1, "Is Your Organisation High Performing?," we discussed HPO SCORES; one of the key elements was *relentless focus on customer results*. In high-performing organisations, everyone passionately holds and maintains the highest standards for quality and service from their customers' perspective. These organisations use the customer experience to evaluate how well they are doing in every aspect of the organisation. Processes are designed with the customer in mind. Those who are in contact with the customer can make decisions. Accountability is to the customer. In high-performing organisations, everything starts and ends with the customer. This is a radical shift from organisations whose business design puts the customer as the end receiver of the chain. For example, at the renowned Golden Door Spa, all systems are set up to wow the customer. Employees know that their job is to exceed expectations and to back up the key frontline person at that moment. Customer needs and trends drive innovation, new products, and services. High-performing organisations design work processes from the customer backwards to ensure a flow that makes sense from a customer's perspective. Internal cross-functional relationships and structures are organised around customer needs. High-performing organisations ensure that they can respond quickly to customer needs and adapt to changes in the marketplace. They anticipate trends and get in front of them. Innovations in processes are developed to make it easier for customers to do business. This creates constant innovation in operating practices, market strategies, products, and services.

In high-performing organisations, management has regular face-to-face contact with customers—not only with devoted customers, but also with those who are frustrated, angry, or not using the organisation's products and services. Leaders are passionate about developing sophisticated knowledge of customers and sharing the information broadly throughout the organisation. Working with the people they serve and listening intently allows high-performing organisations to respond rapidly and flexibly to changing conditions.

Connecticut's Trader Joe's Grocery exceeds expectations by making sure customers get the best of what they want. One of the HPO SCORES researchers, Fay Kandarian, had an experience with this when she brought red tulips to the checkout line. The assistant checked the tulips before ringing them up and suggested looking for a fresher bunch. Together they went to look at other tulips, and after checking for colour preference, the assistant picked out the freshest-looking tulips, which were pink and white. After ringing up the new tulips, the assistant said, "Since I need to throw away these red tulips, I'll give them to you to enjoy for the few days they will last." This is another example of how high-performing organisations encourage those who touch the customer to create the best possible customer experience and act on their ideas.

Nordstrom's core ideology, "service to the customer above all else," was a way of life for the company long before customer service programmes became stylish.[1] Planning starts with the customer, and execution focuses on the customer. For example, planning the sales environment exceeds the effort put into planning sales advertising. To ensure customer comfort, sales planning may involve valet parking, extra fitting rooms, and additional sales staff. A key aspect of the orientation of new associates is teaching them how to say "no problem" and mean it. To ensure that their frontline people put all their initiative into serving customers, Nordstrom's rule of thumb and main guideline for employees is that they should always use their best judgement. In fact, that is the only rule that is really enforced. Combining the service ethic with best judgement has resulted in legendary tales of clothes being pressed, Macy's packages being wrapped, outfits being personally delivered, and two different-sized shoes being sold as a pair to fit a customer's different-sized feet. The result? Customers are dedicated to Nordstrom with almost as much passion as Nordstrom's long-term associates, who also enjoy profit sharing year after year.

Creating Legendary Service

High-performing organisations that have relentless focus on customer results deliver Legendary Service. As we discussed, Legendary Service goes beyond merely good customer service—and it doesn't happen by accident. It begins with leaders who believe that outstanding service is a top priority. We call them service champions—inspirational leaders who create passion and momentum in others to better serve their customers. These leaders follow up their inspiring words with actions, creating systems and processes that support their belief that service is vitally important.

According to Kathy Cuff and Vicki Halsey, the designers of Blanchard's Legendary Service programme, exceptional service starts with leaders serving their people at the highest level, so that people on the front line can in turn serve their customers at the highest level. Creating Legendary Service is everyone's job—not just the people standing at the cash register or dealing directly with customers.

Legendary Service consists of five basic elements:

I **Ideal service**: Consistently meeting or exceeding the customers' needs on a day-to-day basis by acting on the belief that service is important.

C **Culture of service**: Creating an environment that focuses on serving customers—both internal and external—at the highest level.

A **Attentiveness**: Listening in a way that allows you to know your customers and their preferences.

R **Responsiveness**: Demonstrating a genuine willingness to serve others by paying attention to and acting on their needs.

E **Empowerment**: Sharing information and tools to help people meet customer needs or exceed customer expectations.

Together, these elements spell I CARE, which is fitting, because great customer service hits people at an emotional level and creates a connection. We've all experienced the shop assistant who takes our money and bags our goods, but leaves us feeling cold. One of our consulting partners describes it this way:

> "I was at this little family-owned pet shop, buying a collar for my puppy. You'd never know the lady behind the counter was trying to build business. Her face and mood were as flat as a pancake. I said, 'I wanted to support my community pet shop instead of going to the chain store.'

Instead of smiling, she frowned and said, 'They'll reel you in based on cheap food, but they won't keep you.' And I thought, *Hey, you're not keeping me either, lady.*"

Compare that experience with the Legendary Service received by Milt Garrett, a resource trainer who has worked with us over the years. At the end of a week of training, Milt and his wife, Jane, took a walk on Friday night. Jane said to him, "Milt, you missed my anniversary this week."

Surprised, Milt said, "What anniversary?"

"Five years cancer-free," said Jane. Five years ago, Jane had had a mastectomy. She and Milt celebrated every year that she was cancer-free.

Milt felt awful. He couldn't believe he had forgotten. The week before, when he and Jane had been talking one night, they'd decided that she needed a new car. Since their son was still in college in Australia, they'd decided to wait a year until he graduated. That night, Milt said to himself, "Why am I waiting? I am so lucky that Jane is still in my life."

The next morning, he called the Saturn dealership in Albuquerque and talked to one of their salespeople, whose name was Billy Graham. (No, we're not kidding.) Milt explained the situation to Billy, saying that his kids had told him Jane really wanted a white car. "Could you get me a white Saturn by next Saturday when I get back home from training?" Milt asked.

Billy told Milt that white Saturns were hard to get. "But if you'll come in next Saturday, I'll have one ready," he said.

The next Saturday morning Milt told Jane that he was running a bunch of errands, but he invited her to come with him so that they could go out to lunch. During their drive, they passed the Saturn dealership. Milt told Jane he had to stop in for some materials, because he was giving a speech about Saturn to the Chamber of Commerce. When they entered the dealership, they saw only one car: a white Saturn in the centre of the showroom.

"Milt, that's the kind of car I'd love to have!" Jane said. She ran over to the Saturn and, with a big grin on her face, got in. When she got out of the car and walked around to the front of it, she let out a scream and began to cry. Milt had no idea what had happened. When he got to the front of the car, he saw a beautiful sign on the hood of the car that read:

> Yes, Jane, this is your car!
> Congratulations on five years cancer-free.
> Love,
> Milt, Billy, and the whole Saturn staff

When Billy saw them coming, he got everyone out of the showroom and into the parking lot so that Milt and Jane could be alone. As they were crying in each other's arms, all of a sudden they heard applause. They looked up to see everyone giving them a hand.

The people at the Saturn dealership in Albuquerque took Legendary Service seriously and lived it on an ongoing basis. Saturn became known for these kinds of stories. For example, a pregnant woman bought a Saturn from a dealership in San Diego. She loved the car, but three months later, she learned she was expecting twins. The car wasn't big enough, so she called the dealership and told them about her situation. They told her that they would give her money back and help her find another car that better met her needs.

Legendary Service inspires customers to tell stories about your company. When customers tell positive stories about you and your level of service, you cannot ask for better publicity.

Recovering quickly from your mistakes will also make your customers want to brag about your service. If you make a mistake with a customer, do whatever you need to fix the problem and create or win back a devoted customer. Legendary Service is not about arguing over who is right or finding someone else to blame—it's about fixing the problem for the customer. Research has shown that 95 per cent of the time customers will continue to do business with you if you can solve their concern on the spot.[2]

For example, a hotel in Southern California had a history of poor guest ratings. When foreign owners took over the hotel, they felt the poor ratings were mainly because of the ageing, dilapidated condition of the property. They decided to put millions of dollars into refurbishing the hotel. Management decided not to tell the customers about the renovations, which would take nine months to a year. They felt that if the customers knew the extent of the renovations, they would move their meetings to other locations. Given that strategy, the general manager brought all the hotel workers together and told them this:[12]

> "It will be tough around here for the next 12 months or so. The noise and inconvenience may not be popular with our guests. Do whatever it takes to recover from any inconvenience caused by our remodeling. If you want to send someone a bottle of champagne, do so. If you want to hire a babysitter for them, do it. Do whatever it takes to recover from this trying situation."

With that recovery strategy in place, the hotel entered the remodelling phase. To the amazement of management, during the renovations, their guest ratings were the highest they had ever received. Even though things were bad for the guests, their memories of their experience with the hotel were formed by the customer-orientated staff who recovered quickly when things went wrong for guests. Management had empowered their front-line people to be all-out recovery experts. The results showed in highly satisfied customers.

If you empower people to do what's necessary to serve the customers' best interests to begin with, you are more likely to exceed customer expectations and minimise the need to recover. Most businesses believe that only a small per centage of customers are out to take advantage of them, while the vast majority are basically honest and loyal. That's why Nordstrom decided to train its customer contact people to use the phrase "no problem" as their first response to customer concerns. Yet because many business-es set policies, procedures, and practices to try to catch the small per centage of unethical customers, they miss servicing the hon-est majority. Have you ever attempted to try on clothes that have so many safety gadgets that it's almost impossible? There are risks to providing Legendary Service, but the gains can far outweigh the drawbacks, particularly when your customers start acting like part of your sales force. That's when you know you're treat-ing your customers right. As Sheldon Bowles and Ken Blanchard contend, your customers are now raving fans.

Serving Customers at a Higher Level

In their book *Raving Fans*, Sheldon and Ken write that there are three secrets to treating your customers right and turning them into raving fans: Decide, Discover, and Deliver Plus One Per cent.[3]

Decide What You Want Your Customer Experience to Be

If you want Legendary Service, you don't just announce it. You have to plan for it. You have to decide what you want to do. What kind of experience do you want your customers to have as they interact with every aspect of your organisation? Some people would argue that you should ask your customers first. While you do want input from your customers, they often are limited to cer-tain things they like and don't like. They don't know what the possibilities are beyond their own experience. They don't have the big picture. It's important that *you* determine from the beginning what you want your customers' experience to be. This doesn't mean that customers' opinions aren't important. In *Full Steam Ahead!*, Ken Blanchard and Jesse Stoner describe how the needs of your customers should determine the Law of the Situation— what business you are really in. Understanding what your cus-tomers really want when they come to you helps you determine what you should offer them.

A good example of how this works is Domo Gas, a full-service petrol station chain in Western Canada cofounded by Sheldon Bowles. The customer service vision that Sheldon and his cofounders imagined was an Indianapolis 500 pit stop. They dressed all their attendants in red jumpsuits. When a customer drove into one of Sheldon's stations, two or three people ran out of the kiosk and raced towards the car. As quickly as possible, they looked under the hood, cleaned the windscreen, and pumped the gas. A California station that got excited about the concept gave customers a cup of coffee and a newspaper and asked them to step out of their cars while the interior was vacuumed. As customers pulled away, they were given flyers that said, "P.S. We also sell petrol."

In deciding what experience you want your customers to have, you are creating a picture of what things would look like if everything were running as planned. World-class athletes often picture themselves breaking a world record, pitching a perfect game, or making a 99-yard punt return. They know that power comes from having a clear mental image of their best potential performance. Developing a clear picture of how you want to serve your customers is almost like producing a movie in your mind.

We had a chance to work with the top management and heads of dealerships for Freightliner, a leading manufacturer of large trucks. Jim Hibe, the president at the time, spearheaded the creation of a new picture of service for their dealerships—one that permitted them to go way beyond their competition. In preparation for their key annual conference, Freightliner produced a 30-minute video that illustrated two hypothetical dealerships. The first, called Great Scott Trucking, typified the present mode of operating for many of the dealerships: limited hours (8 to 5 Monday through Friday and 9 to 12 on Saturday); uncommitted employees; few, if any, extras (like doughnuts and coffee for truckers waiting for their vehicles); and so on. When you entered the dealership, everything seemed to be organised to serve the policies, rules, and regulations and not the customers. For example, suppose the manager comes in about 11:45 on Saturday. Seeing a long line in the parts department, he says, "Make sure you shut her down at 12. The line will make for a good Monday."

The other hypothetical dealership, called Daley Freightliner, was a customer-centred operation with 24-hour service. Seven days a week, committed and trained employees were willing to go the extra mile and provide all kinds of services for the truckers. They had a lounge with recliners and a huge TV showing movies. There was a quiet, dark room with bunk beds in case the truckers wanted to sleep. Employees drove repaired trucks to the front rather than making the drivers retrieve them from the back.

Many of the dealerships were closer to Great Scott Trucking than they were to Daley Freightliner. So when the conference opened with the video, it made some people squirm. But it beautifully depicted the new service vision for all to see and experience. Throughout the conference, dealers who were closest to the positive image shared their success stories. That programme was an excellent way to convey a customer service vision.

The Moments of Truth concept that Jan Carlzon used to create a customer-focused culture when he was president of the Scandinavian Airlines System (SAS) is most helpful in deciding what you want your customer experience to be. A Moment of Truth can be described as follows:

> Any time a customer comes in contact with anyone in our organisation in a way that they can get an impression. How do we answer the phone? How do we check people in? How do we greet them on our planes? How do we interact with them during flights? How do we handle baggage claim? What happens when a problem occurs?

For Carlzon and other great service providers, Moments of Truth could cover every detail, including coffee stains. When he was chairman of People Express Airlines, Donald Burr contended that if the flip-down trays were dirty, customers would assume that the plane's engines were not well maintained either.[4] When looking for a place to stay after a long day's drive, how many people would choose a motel with a sign that has some burned-out lights?

While most of our examples have focused on external customers, it is important to recognise that everyone has a customer. An external customer is someone outside your organisation who you serve or provide with a service. A person who takes orders at a quick-service restaurant is a good example of someone who serves external customers. An internal customer is someone within your organisation who may or may not serve external customers.

For example, people who work in the human resources field have mainly internal customers. And some people, like those in the accounting department, have both external and internal customers. They send bills and invoices to external customers, and they provide reports and information to internal customers. The point is, everyone has a customer.

Great customer service organisations analyse every key interaction they have with customers, whether they are external or internal, and they determine how they would like that scenario to play out. One of the ways to think about that is to suppose that word has gotten out about how fabulously you are serving customers. Ecstatic customers are running all over the place, bragging about you. A well-known television programme gets word of this and decides to send a crew in to film what is going on in your organisation. Who would you want them to talk to? What would your people tell them? What would these folks see?

Creating raving fans starts with a picture—an image of what kind of experience you want your customers to have. Analysing your Moments of Truth for each department and deciding how you want them played out is a good start. This will serve as your guide as you target new customers and adjust to changing conditions.

Discover What Your Customers Want

After you decide what you want to happen, it's important to discover any suggestions your customers may have that will improve their experience with your organisation. What would make their experience with you better? Ask them! But ask them in a way that stimulates an answer. For example, how many times have you been eating at a restaurant when the restaurant manager comes over and says, "How is everything tonight?" Isn't your usual response, "Fine"? That gives the restaurant manager no information. A better conversation would be, "Excuse me. I'm the restaurant manager. I wonder if I could ask you a question. Is there anything that we could have done differently tonight that would have made your experience with us better?" That question invites an answer. If the customer says "No," you can follow it up with a sincere "Are you sure?"

High-performing organisations regularly solicit customer and market feedback.

Organisations that provide Legendary Service are masters of listening to their customers. When a customer tells you something, you have to listen *without being defensive*. One reason people get uptight when they listen to customers is because they think they always have to do what the customer wants them to do. They don't understand that listening has two parts. As Steve Covey says, "Seek first to understand." In other words, listen for understanding. Try saying, "That's interesting. Tell me more. Could you be more specific?"

The second aspect of listening is deciding if you want to do anything about what you heard. You have to separate that from the understanding aspect of listening. And it is important to realise that you don't have to decide right after you understand what the person is suggesting. You can do it later, when you have some time to think about it or talk it over with others. Realising that you have time to think something over will make you less defensive and a better listener. First listen to understand, and then decide what you want to do about what you've heard.

In the mall, one of our colleagues saw an example of defensive listening. He was walking behind a woman who had an eight- or nine-year-old son. As they walked past the bicycle shop, the kid looked over and saw a beautiful red bicycle outside the shop. He stopped in his tracks and said to his mother, "Boy, would I like a bike like that." His mother nearly went crazy and started screaming: "I can't believe it! I just got you a new bike for Christmas! Here it is March, and you already want another one! I'm not buying you another $%&*^ thing!" Our colleague thought the mother would nail this kid's head to the cement. Sadly, she didn't distinguish the need to separate listening for understanding from deciding. If she had said to the kid, "Honey, what do you like about that bike?" he might have said, "See those streamers coming out of the handlebars? I really like them." And those streamers could have been a cheap birthday present. After listening to what he liked about the bike, the mother could have said, "Honey, why do you think I can't get you that bike?" The kid was no fool. He probably would have said, "I just got one for Christmas."

Listening without being defensive is also helpful if you make a mistake with a customer. Defending what you've done will only irritate the customer. When customers are upset, all they want is to be heard. In fact, we have found that if people listen to a complaining customer in a non-defensive, attentive way and then ask, "Is there any way we could win back your loyalty?," more often than not the customer will say, "You've already done it. You listened to me."

If a customer makes a good suggestion or is upset about something that makes sense to change, you can add that suggestion to your customer service picture. For example, we got a letter from a man who owns three quick-service restaurants in the Midwest. Some of the restaurant's elderly customers suggested that, during certain parts of the day, the restaurant should use table-cloths, have staff take orders at the tables, and deliver the food to the customers at their tables. After thinking about it, the owner realised it was a pretty good idea. Now, between 4 and 5:30 in the afternoon, the tables have tablecloths and candles, and the people behind the counter come out and wait on the customers. The elderly are pouring in to his restaurants during those hours.

When you put together what you want your customers to experience with what they want to have happen, you will have a fairly complete picture of your desired customer service experience.

Deliver Your Ideal Customer Service Experience

You now have a clear picture of the experience you want your customers to have that will satisfy and delight them and put smiles on their faces. Next you must figure out how to get your people excited about delivering this experience, plus a bit more.

As we emphasised in Chapter 2, "The Power of Vision," the responsibility for establishing a shared vision rests with the senior leadership. And that responsibility includes strong images of what excellent customer service looks like. Once your desired customer experience is set and people are committed to it, the implementation aspect of leadership begins. It is during implementation that most organisations get into trouble. The traditional pyramid is kept alive and well, leaving customers uncared for at the bottom of the hierarchy. All the energy in the organisation moves up the hierarchy as people try to please and be responsive to their bosses, instead of focusing their energy on meeting the needs of their customers. Now the bureaucracy rules, and policies and procedures carry the day. This leaves unprepared and uncommitted customer-contact people to quack like ducks.

Wayne Dyer, the great personal-growth teacher, said years ago that there are two kinds of people: ducks and eagles. Ducks act like victims and go "Quack! Quack! Quack!" Eagles, on the other hand, take the initiative and soar above the crowd. As a customer, you can always identify a bureaucracy if you have a problem and are confronted by ducks who quack: "It's our policy. I don't make the rules; I just work here. Do you want to talk to my superviser? Quack! Quack! Quack!"

Implementation is all about equipping people throughout the organisation to act and feel like owners of the vision. It's about allowing people to take a proactive role in carrying out the organisation's vision and direction so that they can soar like eagles and deliver great customer service rather than quack like ducks.

Our colleague's experience trying to hire a car in New York is a perfect example of this phenomenon. He is a trustee emeritus at Cornell University. A while back, he was heading to a meeting in Ithaca, New York, the small upstate town where Cornell is located. He wanted to hire a car that he could drop off at Syracuse, which was about an hour and a half away. Those who travel enough know that if you drop off a car at a different place than where you hired it, the company charges a big drop-off fee. You can avoid that drop-off fee if you hire a car that came from where you are going. Knowing this, our colleague asked the woman behind the counter, "Do you have a Syracuse car?"

She said, "You're lucky. I do." Then she went to the computer and prepared his contract.

Our colleague is not a particularly detail-orientated person, but as he was signing his contract, he noticed a $75 drop-off fee. He said, "What's that $75 drop-off fee?"

She said, "I didn't do it. Quack! Quack!"

He said, "Who did?"

She said, "The computer. Quack! Quack!"

He said, "How do we tell the computer it was wrong?"

"I don't know. Quack! Quack!"

He said, "Why don't you just cross it out?"

She said, "I can't. My boss will kill me. Quack! Quack!"

"You mean I have to pay a $75 fee because you have a mean boss?" he asked.

"I remember one time—quack! quack!—my boss let me cross it out."

"When was that?"

"When the customer worked for Cornell. Quack! Quack!"

He said, "That's great. I'm on the Cornell board of trustees!"

She asked, "What does the board do? Quack! Quack!"

"We can fire the president."

"What's your employee number? Quack! Quack!"

"I don't have one."

"What should I do? Quack! Quack!"

It took our colleague 20 minutes of psychological counselling to get out of this drop-off fee. He used to get angry at these front-line people but doesn't any more because he realises that it's not really their fault.

Who do you think this woman worked for, a duck or an eagle? Obviously, a duck. If she worked for an eagle, the eagle would eat the duck. We call the supervisory duck the head mallard, because they just quack higher up the bureaucracy. They tell you all the rules and regulations and laws that apply to your situation. Who do you think the supervisory duck works for? Another duck, who works for whom? Another duck, who works for whom? Another duck. And who sits at the top of the organisation? A great big duck. Have you ever been hit by an eagle turd? Obviously not, because eagles soar above the crowd. It's the ducks that make all the mess.

How do you create an organisation where ducks are busted and eagles can soar?

The traditional pyramid hierarchy must be turned
upside down so that the frontline people
who are closest to the customers are at the top.

Here the frontline people can be **responsible**—able to respond to their customers. In this scenario, leaders **serve** and are **responsive** to people's needs, training and developing them to soar like eagles so that they can accomplish established goals and live according to the vision you have of the customer experience.

Figure 3.1   The Implementation Role of Leadership

If the leaders in an organisation do not respond to the needs and desires of their people, these folks will not take good care of their customers. But when the frontline customer-contact people are treated as responsible owners of the vision, they can soar like eagles and create raving fans rather than quack like ducks.

Permitting People to Soar

One of our consulting partners experienced an eagle incident when he went to Nordstrom one day to get some perfume for his wife. The woman behind the counter said, "I'm sorry; we don't sell that perfume in our store. But I know where I can get it in the mall. How long will you be in our store?"

"About 30 minutes," he said.

"Fine. I'll go get it, bring it back, gift wrap it, and have it ready for you when you leave." This woman left Nordstrom, went to another store, got the perfume our colleague wanted, came back to Nordstrom, and gift wrapped it. You know what she charged him? The same price she paid at the other store. So Nordstrom didn't make any money on the deal, but what did they make? A raving fan.

Ken had a beautiful example of the different experiences you can have with organisations depending on whether they are duck ponds or they permit people to soar like eagles. Several years ago, he was heading to the airport for a trip that would take him to four different cities during the week. As he approached the airport, he realised that he had forgotten his driver's licence and didn't have a passport with him either. Not having time to go back home to get them and make the flight, he had to be creative.

Only one of Ken's books, *Everyone's a Coach*, which he wrote with Don Shula, has his picture on the cover.[5] So when Ken got to the airport, he ran into the bookshop; luckily, it had a copy of that book. Fortunately, his airline was Southwest Airlines. As Ken was checking in his bag, the porter asked to see some identification. He said, "I feel bad. I don't have a driver's licence or passport. But will this do?" And he showed him the cover of the book.

The man shouted, "The man knows Shula! Put him in first class!" (Of course, Southwest doesn't have first class.) Everybody out by the check-in desk started to high-five Ken. He was like a hero. Then one of the baggage handlers said, "Why don't I go in the terminal with you? I know the folks in security. I think I can get you through there, too."

Why did that happen? Herb Kelleher—who cofounded Southwest—and colleagues Colleen Barrett and Gary Kelly, who followed him in the executive suite, not only want to give customers the lowest possible price, but they also want to give them the best possible service. They set up the whole organisation to empower everyone—right down to the frontline baggage check folks—to make decisions, use their brains, and be customer maniacs so that they could create raving fans. These customer-focused leaders feel that policies should be followed but that people can use their brains in interpreting them. Why do they ask for identification at the airport? To make sure that the person getting on the plane is the same person as the name on the ticket. That was an easy decision for the Southwest Airlines frontline person.

Wallowing in a Duck Pond

The next airline Ken had to fly on before his office could overnight his driver's licence was one of the airlines that always seems to be in financial trouble. The baggage handler at the check-in desk looked at Ken's picture on the book and said, "You've got to be kidding me. You'd better go to the ticket counter."

When Ken showed the book to the woman at the ticket counter, she said, "You'd better talk to my superviser." Ken was moving up the hierarchy fast. He thought maybe pretty soon he would get to the mayor and then finally to the governor. Quack! Quack! Quack! In this troubled airline, the hierarchy was alive and well. All the energy was moving away from pleasing the customers and towards serving the hierarchy—following the policies, procedures, rules, and regulations to the letter.

Giving Your People Wings

Horst Schultze, one of the founders of the Ritz-Carlton Hotels, retired a few years ago as president and CEO. During his reign, after orientation and extensive training, every employee was given a $2,000 discretionary fund that they could use to solve a customer problem without checking with anyone. They didn't even have to tell their boss. Horst loved to collect stories about people using this empowerment to make a difference. One of our favourites is about a businessman who was staying at one of the Ritz-Carlton properties in Atlanta. That day he had to fly from Atlanta to Los Angeles and then from Los Angeles to Hawaii, because the next day at 1:00, he was making a major speech to his international company. He was a little disorganised as he was leaving. On his way to the airport, he discovered that he'd left behind his laptop computer, which contained all the PowerPoints he needed for his presentation. He tried to change his flights, but he couldn't. So he called the Ritz-Carlton and said, "This is the room I was in, and this is where my computer was. Have

Housekeeping get it and overnight it to me. They have to guarantee delivery by 10 tomorrow morning, because I need it for my 1 o'clock speech."

The next day Schultze was wandering around the hotel, as he often did. When he got to Housekeeping he said, "Where's Mary?" Her coworkers said, "She's in Hawaii." He said, "Hawaii? What's she doing there?"

He was told, "A guest left his computer in his room, and he needs it for a speech today at one o'clock—and Mary doesn't trust overnight courier services." Now you might think that Mary went for a vacation, but she came back on the next plane. And what do you think was waiting for her? A letter of commendation from Horst and high fives around the hotel. That's really empowering people and giving them wings.

You might wonder if this story is true. The answer is yes. If you create an environment where the customers rule and your people can use their brains to take care of customer needs, stories like this become commonplace, even legendary. People who spread these stories—including your customers—sometimes love to embellish them. For example, a well-known story developed about Nordstrom's "no questions asked" return policy. It was rumoured that somebody returned snow tyres to Nordstrom and, even though they didn't sell them, the store took them back. When cofounder Bruce Nordstrom was asked about this, he laughed, because Nordstrom actually does sell snow tyres—in its Alaska store.

Creating Legendary Service Requires Gung Ho People

When Ken Blanchard and Sheldon Bowles published *Raving Fans*, a lot of excitement was generated around the importance of customer service. The most frequent question leaders asked, though, was "How can you create Legendary Service when you have uncommitted, unmotivated people?" Answering that question led Ken and Sheldon to write *Gung Ho!*.[6] They found that there are three requirements for turning on the people in any organisation.

First, people need to have *worthwhile work*. To make the world a better place, people need a higher purpose and shared values that guide all plans, decisions, and actions. Worthwhile work gets people up in the morning with a spring in their step.

Second, people need to *be in control of achieving the goal*. When people know why they are working and where they're going, they want to bring their brains to work. Being responsible demands people's best and allows them to learn and act like owners.

Third, to continue to generate energy, people need to *cheer each other on*. Of all the things we've taught over the years, we can't overemphasise the power of catching each other doing things right and accentuating the positive.

In many ways, Chapter 2 was all about *worthwhile work*. *Being in control of achieving the goals* and *cheering each other on* turn our focus to Section III, "Treat Your People Right," the third practice that is characteristic of organisations where leading at a higher level is alive and well. The next chapter, "Empowerment Is the Key," zeroes in on *being in charge of achieving the goal*.

COMPANION **ONLINE** RESOURCE

Visit **www.LeadingAtAHigherLevel.com** to access the free virtual conference titled *Treat Your Customers Right*. Use the password "Customers" for your FREE access.

section III

TREAT YOUR PEOPLE RIGHT

Chapter 4

EMPOWERMENT IS THE KEY

Alan Randolph and Ken Blanchard

How do the best-run companies in the world beat the competition day in and day out? They treat their customers right and have a workforce that is excited about their vision and motivated to serve customers at a higher level. So how do you create this motivated workforce? The key is **empowerment**.

Empowerment means letting people bring their brains to work and allowing them to use their knowledge, experience, and motivation to create a healthy triple bottom line. Leaders of the best-run companies know that empowering people creates positive results that are just not possible when all the authority moves up the hierarchy and managers shoulder all the responsibility for success.

People already have power through their knowledge and motivation.
The key to empowerment is letting this power out.

Ideally, people's power will be focused not only on organisational outcomes—such as outstanding customer service and financial goals—but also on the greater good.

We believe organisations work best when they can depend on individual contributors who take the initiative to go beyond problem spotting to problem solving. Yet, because most of us have experienced only hierarchical organisations, we all have much to learn about moving to a culture of empowerment.

What Is Empowerment?

Empowerment is the process of unleashing the power in people—their knowledge, experience, and motivation—and focusing that power to achieve positive outcomes for the organisation. Creating a culture of empowerment consists of only a few key steps, yet because they challenge most people's assumptions, these steps are often difficult for managers and direct reports alike.

Empowerment requires a major shift in attitude.
The most crucial place that this shift must occur is in
the heart of every leader.

For empowerment to succeed, leaders must take a leap of faith and fight the battle against habit and tradition. For example, most managers continue to define empowerment as "giving people the power to make decisions." Perhaps this misguided definition explains why so many companies have difficulty engaging the minds and hearts of their people. Defining empowerment as "the manager giving power to the people" still regards the manager as controller and misses the essential point: namely, that *people already possess a great deal of power*—power that resides in their knowledge, experience, and internal motivation. We prefer the following definition:

Empowerment is the creation of an organisational
climate that releases the knowledge, experience,
and motivation that reside in people.

Unfortunately, this is easier said than done. Other players can block this release of power, and a strong force of past history often inhibits the shift to empowerment.

Direct reports, too, misunderstand empowerment. Many of them feel that if they are empowered, they will be given free rein to do as they please and make all the key decisions about their jobs. Direct reports often fail to grasp that the price of freedom is sharing risks and responsibilities. This is particularly true in a post-Sarbanes-Oxley environment of accounting oversight and corporate responsibility.[1] Indeed, an empowerment culture requires much greater accountability from direct reports than a hierarchical culture does. Yet it is precisely this frightening increase in responsibility that engages people and gives them a sense of fulfillment. The opportunities and risks of empowerment invigorate direct reports and managers alike.

The Power of Empowerment

Does empowerment work in the real world? You bet it does! Several researchers have found that when people are empowered, their organisations benefit overall. For example, Edward Lawler found that when people are given more control and responsibility, their companies achieve a greater return on sales (10.3 per cent) than companies that do not involve their people (6.3 per cent).[2] Trader Joe's is a niche retailer in the food industry well known for pushing decision making to the store level. Over an eight-year period its annual sales growth increased from 15 per cent to 26 per cent, sales per store increased 10 per cent per year, and the number of stores increased by almost 100 per cent. In addition, overall sales volume increased in excess of 500 per cent. While other factors contributed to these increased sales, empowered employees were deemed a major element of Trader Joe's success.[3]

Not only is there clear evidence of a positive relationship between empowerment and performance, but scholars such as Thomas Malone believe that empowerment is essential for companies that hope to succeed in the new knowledge-based economy.[4]

How Past History Blocks Change to Empowerment

Most people have a history of working under external guidance and control. The following questions are all too familiar to us.

At school: "What does the teacher want me to do to get good marks?"

At work: "What does my boss want me to do?"

Having spent our lives in a framework of hierarchical thinking, we are far less accustomed to dealing with questions like these.

At school: "What do I want to learn from this class?"

"How will I know I have learned something I can use?"

At work: "What do I need to do to help my company succeed?"

These are the kinds of questions that arise—and require answers—when an organisational culture begins to support empowerment. President Kennedy made a call for these kinds of questions when he challenged Americans: "Ask not what your country can do for you; ask what you can do for your country."[5]

Many of us possess hard-earned parenting, teaching, and managing skills that fulfil role expectations based on an assumption of hierarchical responsibility. Indeed, we feel it is our responsibility as parents, teachers, or managers to tell people what to do, how to do it, and why it needs to be done. We feel it would be avoiding our responsibility to ask children, students, or direct reports such questions as these:

"What do you think needs to be done, and why is it important?"

"What do you think your goals should be?"

"How do you think you should go about achieving your goals?"

Because managers know they will still be held accountable for outcomes, many are reluctant to relinquish control to direct reports. This reluctance points to one of the main sources of resistance to empowerment: managers who feel their control is threatened by empowerment. Ironically, it is through the development of self-directed individuals and teams as a replacement for the hierarchy that managers can most easily assume their new and more empowering roles as coaches, mentors, and team leaders.

Tapping People's Power and Potential: A Real-World Example

While there is a learning curve from a hierarchical to an empowerment culture, the benefits can be well worth the effort, as the following case study shows.

A management team of a large organisation was struggling with a severe traffic problem on the road leading to its location. The road crossed four miles of protected wetlands, so it could not be widened without significantly impacting the environment. Each morning, the traffic leading to the site was backing up the entire four-mile length of the road, adding an hour to commuting time. The resulting delay and aggravation caused a significant drop in productivity.

Three years earlier, the management team had hired traffic consultants to solve the problem. Their work focused on a future widening of the road and looked promising, but their attempts to devise short-term solutions failed miserably. As a last resort, management decided to assemble a team of engineers, clerical personnel, line workers, and union representatives to address short-term solutions. This team met twice a week for a month. At the end of that time, the team provided a series of practical recommendations.

The simplicity of the team's recommendations surprised management. For example, the team suggested that trucks be prohibited from making deliveries to the site between the hours of

6 a.m. and 9 a.m. Since there were many deliveries to the site at this time, this recommendation immediately removed some of the slowest, most cumbersome traffic clogging the road. Other recommendations also contributed to easing the problem. The result was almost instantaneous improvement in the traffic flow.

At the outset, management had doubted that this team could solve the problem. After all, experts had been studying the dilemma for three years. Yet in turning to their own people, they tapped into a hidden reservoir of knowledge, experience, and motivation—and found a solution.

Learning the Language of Empowerment

Moving to an empowerment culture requires learning a new language. To understand the differences between the command-and-control structure and the culture of empowerment, consider the following words and phrases:

Hierarchical Culture	Empowerment Culture
Planning	Visioning
Command and control	Partnering for performance
Monitoring	Self-monitoring
Individual responsiveness	Team responsibility
Pyramid structures	Cross-functional structures
Work flow processes	Projects
Managers	Coaches/team leaders
Employees	Team members
Participative management	Self-directed teams
Do as you are told	Own your own job
Compliance	Good judgement

As you compare the words in the two lists, the differences in attitude, expectations, and associated behaviours become clear. For example, *planning* suggests a step-by-step, controlled process, while *visioning* suggests a more holistic and inclusive approach. *Command and control* suggests that the manager tells us what to think and do, while *partnering for performance* suggests that how we achieve the vision is left open for discussion and input by everyone involved. *Monitoring* suggests that someone—usually the manager—should check on each individual's performance and provide performance evaluations and feedback, while *self-monitoring* suggests that everyone possesses requisite goal clarity and measurement skills, as well as access to relevant data. Thus armed, they can check their own performance and make the behaviour adjustments they need to stay on goal. *Do as you are told* exemplifies the external commitment attitude. Once you are told what to do, you can do it, but please don't use your intellect or judgement, and don't be too concerned about results—that's the manager's job. On the other hand, *own your own job* exemplifies the internal commitment attitude: You care about results and use your own intellect and judgement to decide how to achieve individual, team, and company success.

This final example may best clarify the key distinction between a culture of empowerment and a hierarchical culture. In the latter, individuals do what they are told—to a fault. Even when they know a task is not being done in the best way, or that it may be altogether the wrong task, they may continue to do it in a spirit of malicious compliance. Why? Because that is what they are rewarded for and what they are expected to do under hierarchical management.

In a culture of empowerment, individuals respond differently. They take the risk of challenging tasks and procedures that they feel are not in the best interest of the organisation. They are driven by a sense of pride in their jobs and a feeling of ownership of the results. People think about what makes sense in the situation and act in ways that both serve the customer and achieve the organisation's goals.

The Three Keys to Empowerment

The journey to empowerment needs strong leadership to support this change. In their book *Empowerment Takes More Than a Minute*, Ken Blanchard, John Carlos, and Alan Randolph contend that to guide the transition to a culture of empowerment, leaders must use three keys: sharing information, declaring the boundaries, and replacing the old hierarchy with self-directed individuals and teams.[6]

The First Key to Empowerment:
Share Information with Everyone

One of the best ways to build a sense of trust and responsibility in people is by sharing information. Giving team members the information they need enables them to make good business decisions. Sharing information sometimes means disclosing information that is considered privileged, including sensitive and important topics such as future business plans and strategies, financial data, and industry issues or problem areas. Providing people with more complete information communicates trust and a sense of "we're in this together." It helps people think more broadly about the organisation and the interrelationships of various groups, resources, and goals. By having access to information that helps them understand the big picture, people can better appreciate how their contribution fits in and how their behaviour impacts other aspects of the organisation. All of this leads to responsible, goal-related use of people's knowledge, experience, and motivation. While this runs counter to hierarchical management, it is based on the following premise:

People without accurate information cannot act responsibly; people with accurate information feel compelled to act responsibly.

In an example close to home, The Ken Blanchard Companies, like many businesses, was negatively impacted by the events of

September 11, 2001. In fact, the company lost $1.5 million in sales that month. To have any chance of ending the fiscal year in the black, the company would have to cut about $350,000 a month in expenses.

The leadership team had some tough decisions to make. One of the leaders suggested that the staffing level be cut by at least 10 per cent to stem the losses and help get the company back in the black—a typical response in most companies.

As with any major decision, members of the leadership team checked the decision to cut staff against the rank-ordered organisational values of ethical behaviour, relationships, success, and learning. Was the decision to let people go at such a difficult time ethical? To many, the answer was no. There was a general feeling that because the staff had made the company what it was, putting people out on the street at a time like this just was not the right thing to do. Did the decision to let people go honour the high value that the organisation placed on relationships? No, it did not. But what could be done? The company could not go on bleeding money and be successful.

Knowing that "no one of us is as smart as all of us," the leadership team decided to draw on the knowledge and talents of the entire staff. At an all-company meeting, the books were opened to show everyone how much the company was bleeding, and from where. This open-book policy unleashed a torrent of ideas and commitment. Small task forces were organised to look for ways to increase revenues and cut costs. This participation resulted in departments throughout the company finding all kinds of ways to minimise spending and maximise income. As the company's Chief Spiritual Officer, Ken Blanchard cheered people on by announcing they would all go to Hawaii together when the company got through the crisis. People smiled politely, although many had their doubts.

Over the next two years, the finances gradually turned around. By 2004, the company produced the highest sales in its history, exceeding its annual goal. In March 2005, the entire company—350 people strong—flew to Maui for a four-day celebration.

When important information is shared with people, they soon act like owners. They begin to solve problems creatively, which makes celebrating the wins even more special. On the other hand, leaders who are unwilling to share information will never have their people as partners in running a successful, empowered organisation.

Sharing Information Builds Trust

Another powerful benefit of information sharing is raising the level of trust in the organisation. Bureaucratic organisations typically are close to bankruptcy in terms of trust—direct reports do not trust managers, and managers do not trust direct reports. As a result, people exert enormous energy trying to protect themselves from each other. It's important to share information, even if the news is bad. If no decisions have been made, share information about what is being discussed. By sharing information about market share, true costs, potential layoffs, and real company performance—in other words, opening the books for everyone to see—management begins to let people know they are trusted, and people will return that trust to managers.

One top-level manager told us he was initially scared to share such sensitive information, but when he took the risk, people responded with a more mature understanding and a sense of appreciation for being included. "It created such a sense of ownership," the manager commented, "far more than I could have imagined. People began to come forward with ideas to save money by changing their jobs and by reorganising departments—ideas that previously had been met with great fear when proposed by management."

Sharing Information Promotes Organisational Learning

One of the most powerful ways to share information is through organisational learning, one of the key elements of high-performing organisations.[7] What we're talking about here goes beyond merely acquiring information; it means actually learning from that information and applying that knowledge to new situations.

High-performing organisations **seek knowledge** by constantly scanning the environment, checking the pulse of their customers, tracking their competition, surveying the marketplace, and following global events. They collect data continuously and use it to make corrections and develop new approaches. High-performing organisations also seek knowledge about internal performance. They treat mistakes and failures as important data, recognising that they often can lead to breakthroughs. This is why Hewlett-Packard's "HP Way" includes the statement "We reserve the right to make mistakes."[8]

High-performing organisations **transfer knowledge** by encouraging dialogue, questioning, and discussion. This runs counter to traditional organisations, where people hoard information as a way to protect themselves and establish a power base. High-performing organisations make information easy to access. They know that when data is unavailable or not easily retrieved, people have a harder time learning and lose opportunities. They create structures such as cross-functional teams that teach people how to transfer the knowledge they've gained, because they know that knowledge sharing is critical to success.

New car developers at Ford Motor Company learned this the hard way when they set out to understand why the original Taurus design team was so successful. Unfortunately, no one could tell them. No one remembered or had recorded what made that effort so special. The knowledge gained in the Taurus project was lost forever.[9]

High performing organisations continually look for ways to **incorporate knowledge into new ways of doing business**. When you don't recognise or share knowledge, you can't apply it directly to work. In the words of Michael Brown, former chief financial officer of Microsoft:[10]

The only way to compete today is to make your intellectual capital obsolete before anyone else does.

The Second Key to Empowerment:
Create Autonomy Through Boundaries

In a hierarchical culture, boundaries are really like barbed-wire fences. They are designed to control people by keeping them in certain places and out of other places. In an empowered culture, boundaries are more like rubber bands that can expand to allow people to take on more responsibility as they grow and develop.

Unlike the restrictive boundaries of a hierarchical culture, boundaries in an empowerment culture tell people where they *can* be autonomous and responsible, rather than telling them what they *can't* do. Boundaries are based on people's skill level. For example, people who lack the skills to set budgets are given a boundary—a spending limit—before they are given more responsibility. In an empowerment culture, they also are given the training and skill development needed to enable greater autonomy. One of the most paradoxical aspects of creating a culture of empowerment is that managers must start by creating *more* rather than *less* structure.

Like the lines on a tennis court, the boundaries in an empowerment culture help people keep score and improve their game.

A good example of boundary setting came up recently for a superviser we know who was frustrated by the amount of time he spent performing tasks that, although important from an administrative viewpoint, did not maximise his talents and skills. One of his most frustrating tasks was ordering small tools and materials for the team each time a team member came to him with a request. In a spirit of empowerment, he taught them how to place the orders themselves and allowed them to submit small orders directly without his approval. Initially, he placed a boundary on the purchases—a cost limit of $100—but he later widened the boundary as the team's (and his) comfort level grew. Because they had the authority to order needed supplies without the delay of their superviser's approval, the team members felt great. The cost of supplies decreased by 20 per cent as people took more care in ordering only those materials they really needed.

Boundaries help people clarify the big picture as well as the little picture. As we saw in Chapter 2, "The Power of Vision," organisations need to **create a compelling vision** that motivates and guides people.

The organisational vision is the big picture.
Boundaries help people see how their piece
of the puzzle fits into that picture.

Declaring the boundaries translates the big picture into specific actions. It allows people to **set goals** that help the organisation achieve that big picture. These goals are viewed not as ends, but rather as collaboratively set milestones of progress.

Declaring boundaries also requires that managers **clarify the new decision-making rules**. At first, team members may think that empowerment means, "We get to make all the decisions." Two reactions often follow. One is that team members are disappointed when managers continue to make strategic decisions and leave only the operational decisions to them. The other is that team members feel the urge to back off from decisions when they realise they will be held accountable for all the decisions they make—both the good and the bad.

Empowerment means that people have the freedom to act.
It also means that they are accountable for results.

In a culture of empowerment, managers continue to make strategic decisions. Team members get involved in making operational decisions as they become more comfortable assuming the inherent risks. As people gradually begin to assume responsibility for decisions and their consequences, managers must gradually pull back on their involvement in decision making. The new decision-making guidelines allow managers and team members to operate freely within their newly defined roles.

Declaring boundaries also calls managers to **create new performance appraisal processes**. The performance appraisal process found in most companies is almost inevitably disempowering in nature and must be restructured. Focus must shift away from the *appraisal* of the team member by the manager and towards *collaboration* between the team member and the manager. As a manager once told us, "The best person to assess an employee's performance and improvement is the employee himself or herself." Of course, this cultural shift is not easy. In Chapter 7, "Partnering for Performance," we'll discuss this transition to a new performance appraisal process in considerable detail.

As we stated earlier, declaring the boundaries requires that leaders **provide heavy doses of training**. To master the new skills of empowerment—negotiating performance plans, decision making, conflict resolution, leadership, budgeting, and technical expertise—people need regular training. Without this continuous learning, people cannot function in an evolving culture of empowerment. They have to unlearn bureaucratic habits and learn the new skills and attitudes needed in an empowered world. Ongoing learning is an integral part of a high-performing organisation, not an extra perk or necessary evil.

Moving from a hierarchical culture to a culture of empowerment should be a gradual process. People cannot handle too many changes at once, or large changes in one dose. We will discuss these issues further in Chapter 12, "Strategies for Leading a Change."

The Third Key to Empowerment: Replace the Old Hierarchy with Self-Directed Individuals and Teams

As people learn to create autonomy by using newly shared information and boundaries, they must move away from dependence on the hierarchy. But what will replace the clarity and support of the hierarchy? The answer is self-directed individuals and teams—highly skilled, interactive groups with strong self-managing skills.[11] Continual downsizing, which reduces the number of management layers and increases the spans of control for managers, is forcing companies to empower individuals and teams today. The result has been a decision-making void that must be filled if companies are to be successful.

---

*The perceived division between superior and subordinate is
no longer very useful in business organisations.
In fact, it works directly counter to success.
Success today depends on individual and team effort.*

Does success today really depend on empowered individuals and teams? Our work with organisations suggests that the answer to this question is a resounding yes. Here are two examples.

The Power of Self-Directed Individuals

The leaders of Yum! Brands—the world's largest restaurant company, with 850,000 employees in more than 100 nations—understand the power of self-directed individuals.[12] A significant part of training at Yum! now focuses on empowering people to take care of customer problems. If a waiter or waitress has a customer with a problem, the team member is encouraged to solve it immediately rather than talk to the manager. In fact, team members can decide how to take care of customers. That makes it a little crazier, but that's how Yum! likes it.

When Ken Blanchard spoke at a meeting of KFC (one of the companies that Yum! owns), he told the story of how Ritz-Carlton gives its frontline people a $2,000 discretionary fund to solve customer problems without checking with anyone. Yum! chairman and CEO David Novak—who is a great learner—loved the idea of giving people discretionary funds. He later told us, "Our customer mania programme now includes empowering team members to solve customer complaints right on the spot. They used to have to get the restaurant general manager to deal with problems. Now they can use up to $10 to respond to a customer issue.

"Some people in our organisation said, 'Hey, if we let our team members do that, we'll end up going broke, because we'll be giving away all our profits.' And yet we have the highest margin we've ever had in the company since we launched customer mania. So people aren't out there ripping us off. The half or 1 per cent who were doing it before are probably still doing it. But this policy has had an impact on team members. They feel respected and empowered; consequently, our customers see us as much more responsive."

A $10 discretionary fund in a quick-service restaurant is a lot of money. In Ritz-Carlton, which is a much higher-end operation, $2,000 is a lot of money. The point is, a discretionary fund becomes a competitive advantage when individuals who are closest to the customer are empowered to solve problems.

The Power of Self-Directed Teams

The case of the Allied Signal fibres plant in Moncure, North Carolina, illustrates the power of self-directed teams. The shift leaders (formerly called forepersons) were frustrated, angry, and confused about their role. The plant had recently restructured its manufacturing operations to work group teams. The shift leaders were told to back off and let the teams move towards self-management. Not only were the shift leaders frustrated, but morale among team members also was low. There was a decrease in production and an increase in cost per pound of products. Was the solution to go back to the old way of working? Some people wondered why not. The Moncure fibres plant had a history of excellent labour/management relationships. But leadership saw an opportunity for the organisation to move to a higher level if it could figure out how to do it right.

One shift leader, Barney, and two master facilitators, Dawn and Gloria, attended a course on building high-performing teams facilitated by one of the HPO SCORES researchers, Don Carew. Excited and enthusiastic, Dawn and Gloria returned to Moncure and convinced the plant leaders to implement team skills and team leadership training throughout the plant.

Don worked with the shift leaders and master facilitators to develop a one-day classroom training course to be given to each product team by their respective shift leader. The 24 shift leaders were trained to deliver this course. Over the next two years they provided the one-day initial training course to all 59 of the plant's teams. The formerly disillusioned shift leaders now had a whole new sense of purpose and a whole new set of skills. Their role had become clear: to focus on developing people and teams, both in a classroom setting and on the shop floor. The atmosphere in the plant changed from frustration to enthusiasm. Furthermore, productivity increased by 5 per cent, and costs decreased by 6 per cent.[13]

Dealing with the Leadership Vacuum

As they move towards empowerment, both managers and team members go through a stage of disillusionment and demotivation. During this time, team members often feel they lack competence, and managers are often just as lost as their people about what to do next. Even the top-level managers who initiated the empowerment process are often unclear about what to do. We call this phenomenon the *leadership vacuum*. Remember that both managers and team members are emerging from the grip of bureaucratic, hierarchical practices and assumptions. Both have been accustomed to operating in a hierarchy where managers make decisions and team members implement them. They have a lot to learn, and this learning is often fraught with periods of frustration.

Once people admit this lack of management knowledge, a dramatic transformation occurs. When managers begin to admit their confusion—but continue to hold on to a clear vision of empowerment and keep communication open and information flowing—things begin to change. Small flashes of empowerment begin to appear among individual performers and teams. One person might offer a suggestion to which others gravitate; then other ideas are expressed. Almost before anyone realises what is happening, leadership emerges from an unexpected source—team members. Over time, the glimmerings of empowerment become more frequent. The very leadership vacuum that has been so uncomfortable has actually drawn out team member talent and applied it to organisational problems. In the end, the leadership vacuum enhances the empowerment of people and organisations.

The journey to empowerment requires managers and direct reports alike to challenge some of their most basic assumptions about how organisations should operate. Simply announcing the destination is insufficient. People at all levels of the organisation must master new skills and learn to trust self-directed individuals and teams as decision-making entities. We discuss in detail the development of self-directed individuals in Chapter 6, "Self-Leadership: The Power Behind Empowerment," and Chapter 8, "Essential Skills for Partnering for Performance: The One Minute Manager®." Chapter 10, "Situational Team Leadership," discusses the development of high-performing teams. But first let's turn to Chapter 5, "Situational Leadership® II: The Integrating Concept," which explores the leader's role in empowering people.

Chapter 5

SITUATIONAL LEADERSHIP® II: THE INTEGRATING CONCEPT

The Founding Associates:
Ken Blanchard, Margie Blanchard,
Don Carew, Eunice Parisi-Carew,
Fred Finch, Laurence Hawkins,
Drea Zigarmi, and Pat Zigarmi

E mpowerment is the key to treating people the right way and motivating them to treat your customers right. Therefore, having a strategy to shift the emphasis from leader as boss and evaluator to leader as partner and cheerleader is imperative. But what, exactly, is the right strategy or leadership style?

For a long time, people thought there were only two leadership styles—autocratic and democratic. In fact, people used to shout at each other from these two extremes, insisting that one style was better than the other. Democratic managers were accused of being too soft and easy, while their autocratic counterparts were often called too tough and domineering.

We believe that managers who restrict themselves to either extreme are bound to be ineffective "half managers." Whole managers are flexible and can adapt their leadership style to the situation. Is the direct report new and inexperienced with the task at hand? Then more guidance and direction are called for. Is the direct report experienced and skilled? That person requires less hands-on supervision. The truth is, all of us are at different levels of development depending on the task we are working on at a particular time.

> *To bring out the best in others,*
> *leadership must match*
> *the development level*
> *of the person being led.*

Oversupervising or undersupervising—that is, giving people too much or too little direction—has a negative impact on people's development. That's why it's so important to match leadership style to development level. This matching strategy is the essence of Situational Leadership®, a leadership model originally created by Ken Blanchard and Paul Hersey at Ohio University in 1968. The revised model, Situational Leadership® II, has endured as an effective approach to managing and motivating people. It opens communication and fosters a partnership between the leader and the people the leader supports and depends on. This model can be summed up by a familiar phrase:

> *Different strokes for different folks.*

Situational Leadership® II is based on the beliefs that *people can and want to develop* and *there is no best leadership style* to encourage that development. You should tailor leadership style to the situation.

Matching Leadership Style to Development Level

The Situational Leadership® II model (see Figure 5.1) has four basic leadership styles: *directing (S1)*, *coaching (S2)*, *supporting (S3)*, and *delegating (S4)*. These correspond to the four basic development levels: *enthusiastic beginner (D1: low competence, high commitment)*, *disillusioned learner (D2: low to some competence, low commitment)*, *capable but cautious performer (D3: moderate to high competence, variable commitment)*, and *self-reliant achiever (D4: high competence, high commitment)*.

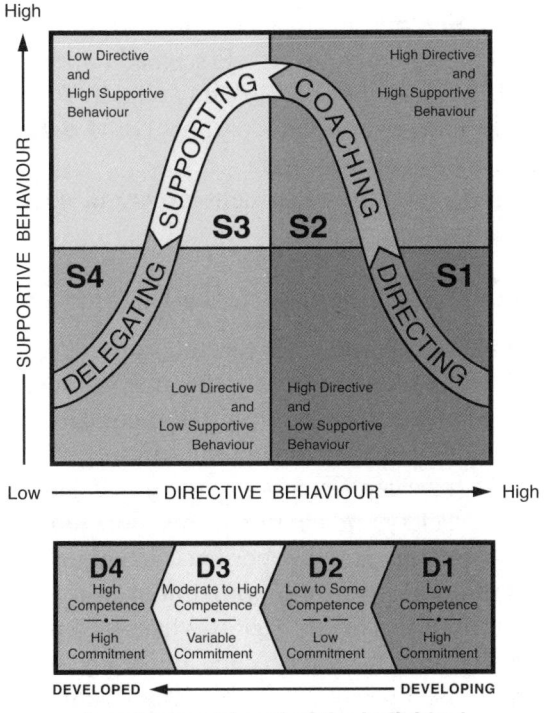

Figure 5.1   The Situational Leadership® II Model

Can you remember when you started learning how to ride a bicycle? Sometimes you were so excited that you couldn't sleep at night, even though you didn't know how to ride yet. You were a classic **enthusiastic beginner** who needed **direction**.

Remember the first time you fell off your bike? As you were picking yourself up off the pavement, you might have wondered why you wanted to learn to ride in the first place and if you would ever really master it. You had reached the **disillusioned learner** stage, and you needed **coaching**.

Once you could ride your bike with your mum or dad cheering you on, that confidence probably became shaky the first time you decided to take your bike out for a spin without your cheerleader and supporter close at hand. At this point, you were a **capable but cautious performer** in need of **support**. Finally, you reached the stage where your bicycle seemed to be a part of you. You could ride it without even thinking about it. You were truly a **self-reliant achiever**, and your parents could **delegate** to you the job of having fun on your bike.

Now, let's see how the development levels and leadership styles apply to the workplace.

Enthusiastic Beginners Need a Directing Style

Suppose you recently hired a 22-year-old salesperson. Three key responsibilities are required of an effective salesperson besides selling: service, administration, and team contribution. Having worked in the hotel industry during the summer, your new salesperson seems to have good experience in service. Since he was the treasurer of his society and captain of his school football team, it looks like he also has some experience in administration and team contribution. As a result, your initial training focus with him will be in the sales part of his job, where he is an **enthusiastic beginner**. In this area, he is excited and ready to learn, despite his lack of skills. Because of his high commitment to becoming a good salesperson, he is curious, hopeful, optimistic, and excited.

In this area of his job, a ***directing*** leadership style is appropriate. You teach your new employee everything about the sales process, from making a sales call to closing the sale. You take him on sales calls with you so that you can show him how the sales process works and what a good job looks like. Then you lay out a step-by-step plan for his self-development as a salesperson. In other words, you not only pass out the test, but you also are involved in teaching him the answers. You provide specific direction and closely supervise his sales performance, planning and prioritising what has to be accomplished for him to be successful. Teaching and showing him what experienced salespeople do—and letting him practise in low-risk sales situations—is the appropriate approach for this enthusiastic beginner.

Disillusioned Learners Need a Coaching Style

Now, suppose that your new employee has a few weeks of sales training under his belt. He understands the basics of selling but is finding it harder to master than he expected. You notice that his step has lost a little of its spring, and sometimes he looks a bit discouraged. While he knows more about sales than he did as a beginner and has flashes of real competence, he's sometimes overwhelmed and frustrated, which has put a damper on his commitment. A person at this stage is a ***disillusioned learner***. What's needed now is a ***coaching*** leadership style, which is high on direction and support. You continue to direct and closely monitor his sales efforts, but you now engage in more two-way conversations, going back and forth between your advice and his questions and suggestions. You also provide a lot of praise and support at this stage, because you want to build his confidence, restore his commitment, and encourage his initiative. While you consider your salesperson's input, you are the one who makes the final decisions, since he is learning on actual clients.

Capable But Cautious Performers Need a Supporting Style

Fast-forward a couple months. Now the young man you hired knows the day-to-day responsibilities of his sales position and has acquired some good sales skills. Yet he still has some self-doubt and questions if he can sell well *on his own*, without your help or the support of other colleagues. While you say he's competent and knows what he's doing, he is not so sure. He has a good grasp of the sales process and is working well with clients, but he's hesitant to be out there completely on his own. He may become self-critical or even reluctant to trust his own instincts. At this stage, he is a ***capable but cautious performer*** whose commitment to selling fluctuates from excitement to insecurity. This is when a **supporting** leadership style is called for. Since your direct report has learned his selling skills well, he needs little direction but lots of support from you to encourage his wavering confidence. Now is the time to stand behind his efforts, listen to his concerns and suggestions, and be there to support his interactions not only with clients, but also with others on your staff. You encourage and praise, but rarely do you direct his efforts. The supporting style is more collaborative; feedback is now a give-and-take process between the two of you. You help him reach his own sales solutions by asking questions that expand his thinking and encourage risk taking.

Self-Reliant Achievers Need a Delegating Style

As time passes, your former new salesperson becomes a key player on your team. Not only has he mastered sales tasks and skills, but he's also taken on challenging clients and has been successful with them. He anticipates problems and is ready with solutions. He is justifiably confident because of his success in managing his own sales area. Not only can he work on his own, but he also inspires others. At this stage, he is a ***self-reliant achiever*** in the sales part of his job. You can count on him to hit his sales goals. For a person at this level of development, a ***delegating*** leadership style is best. In this situation, it is appropriate to turn over responsibility for day-to-day decision making and problem solving to him by letting him run his own territory. Your job now is to empower him by allowing and trusting him to act independently. What you need to do is acknowledge his excellent performance and provide the appropriate resources he requires to carry out his sales duties. It's important at this stage to challenge your high-performing salesperson to continue to grow in his sales ability and cheer him on to even higher levels of sales.

Development Level Varies from Goal to Goal and Task to Task

As we implied in the preceding example, development level is not a global concept—it's task-specific. We could have tracked the salesperson's progress in service, administration, or team contribution, and it would have been a different journey. It's important not to pigeonhole people into any particular development level. In reality, development level applies not to the person, but to the person's competence and commitment to do *a specific goal or task*. In other words, an individual is not at any one development level overall. Development level varies from goal to goal and task to task. An individual can be at one level of development on one goal or task and be at a different level of development on another goal or task.

For example, Casey works in the consumer products industry. In the marketing part of her job, she is a genius when it comes to rolling out new products and opening new markets. She is clearly a ***self-reliant achiever***, as demonstrated by the success of her past marketing plans. However, when it comes to setting up a database to track demographics and buying patterns, Casey has little experience beyond e-mail and word processing. Depending on her motivation for the task, she could be an ***enthusiastic beginner*** or a ***disillusioned learner***.

This example shows that you need to use not only *different strokes for different folks*, but also *different strokes for the same folks*, depending on what goal or part of their job you are focused on at any given time.

To determine the appropriate leadership style to use with each of the four development levels, draw a vertical line up from a diagnosed development level to the leadership curve running through the four-quadrant model. As illustrated in Figure 5.2, the appropriate leadership style—the match—is the quadrant where the vertical line intersects the curved line.

Matching Leadership Style to Development Level

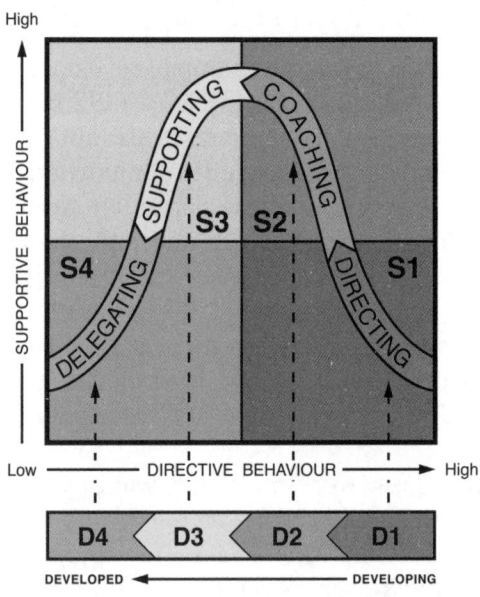

Figure 5.2   Matching Leadership Style to Development Level

Using this approach, the *enthusiastic beginner (D1)* would get a *directing (S1)* leadership style. The *disillusioned learner (D2)* would get a *coaching (S2)* leadership style. The *capable but cautious performer (D3)* would get a *supporting (S3)* leadership style, and the *self-reliant achiever (D4)* would get a *delegating (S4)* leadership style. In determining what style to use with what development level, just remember this:

> *Leaders need to do what the people they supervise*
> *currently can't do for themselves.*

The Importance of Meeting People Where They Are

Some people think that it's inconsistent to manage some people one way and other people in a different way. However, we don't define consistency as "treating everybody the same way." We define it as "using the same leadership style in similar situations." To those who argue that it's unfair to treat direct reports differently, we agree with US Supreme Court justice Felix Frankfurter:

> *There is nothing so unequal as the*
> *equal treatment of unequals.*

Friends of ours experienced the downside of equal treatment for unequals when their son was eight years old and in primary school. They got word from the school that he was way ahead of his class in reading but far behind in maths. Initially, they thought, "How can that be? How could a kid be so good at reading and so bad at maths?" But after they thought about it for a while, it made sense. Some kids are great in social studies but poor in science. People are good at some things and not others. When the father of the child in question understood the reality of the situation and how it was possible, he met with one of his son's teachers. We say "one of his son's teachers" because their son was in an open-style school with 110 kids in the class and 4 or 5 teachers working with them in a large, open space.

"Look, I don't want to cause any problems," he said, "but what I'd like to know is, why is our son doing so well in reading and so poorly in maths? How do you treat him differently in reading versus maths?"

The teacher said, "Over here on this wall we have a group of files. Each kid has his or her own reading file. When it's time for reading, the kids go get their reading files, come back to their desks, and continue to do their reading where they left off. If they have a question, they raise their hand, and one of us comes over and sees them."

Our friend asked, "How is that working with our son?"

The teacher said, "Super. He's one of our best readers."

Our friend said, "Keep it up. You're doing a great job teaching him reading."

What leadership style were they using with this youngster in reading? They were using a ***delegating*** leadership style. He picks out his folder; he decides when he needs help. Why was it working? Because the kid was a ***self-reliant achiever*** in reading. He loved it, and he had skills.

Our friend said, "Now tell me what you're doing with our son in maths."

The teacher said, "Over on the other wall we have a group of files for our maths curriculum. When it's time for maths, the kids go get their folders, bring them back to their desks, and continue to do their maths where they left off. If they have any problems, they raise their hand, and a teacher comes to see them."

Our friend said, "How is that working with our son?"

The teacher said, "Not very well. He's falling behind the class."

What leadership style were they using with the boy in maths? They were using a ***delegating*** leadership style, the same style they were using to teach him reading. In fact, that was the teaching style generally used in this open school. The problem with using a delegating style with this youngster in maths was that the kid was at a much lower development level in maths than he was in reading. He was a ***disillusioned learner***. He didn't have the competency. He didn't have the interest or the confidence. The teachers were leaving him alone.

Our friend knew all about Situational Leadership® II, so he said to the teacher, "Didn't they ever teach you in teacher education that with the same kid on a different subject you need to use a different leadership or teaching style?" Then our friend asked all the teachers in this open classroom, "Which one of you has the reputation of being a traditional teacher?" An older woman smiled. She had been a teacher for 35 years in this school system. Our friend had heard about her. Her close supervision of kids had given her a reputation for being too tough. Recognising that this was just what his kid needed, our friend asked her, "How would you deal with our son's maths problem? He's not doing very well." Before we tell you what she said, let us tell you a bit about this teacher. One of our associates had gone to the primary school where this teacher taught before she moved to the open school. In this school, the teacher had 30 eight- to nine-year-olds all by herself. The kids had to eat lunch in the classroom, because the school wasn't big enough to have a canteen. Our associate walked by her classroom one day at 12:15. The door was wide open, and 30 children were quietly sitting and eating their lunches while our teacher friend was playing Beethoven on the recorder. Our associate smiled when he saw this and said to himself, "That's what I call control."

Across the hall was the other teacher. The door to the classroom was shut, but our associate could see in through a window. The place looked like a zoo. Kids were running all over the place, up on the desks, while the teacher was dancing and hugging them. It looked like a fun place to be. Would that teacher be a good reading teacher for our friend's son? Absolutely, because the boy didn't need a reading teacher. If you don't need a manager, you might as well have a nice, warm, supportive one. Would this teacher be any good teaching the youngster maths? No, she wouldn't.

Now, back to the directive teacher's response to our friend. She said, "It would have been a lot easier if I'd had your son from the beginning. I think he's discouraged now, because it's harder than he thought it would be, and he's not doing well. So when it's time for maths, I would go over to him and say, 'It's time for maths.' Then I'd lead him by the hand over to his file. Sometimes I don't think he even gets his own file—he gets absent kids' files so he can goof them up. Then I would take him back to his desk, sit him down, and say, 'Do problems 1 to 3, and I'll be back in five minutes to check on you. If we work on this together, I know you'll get better at maths.'"

Our friend said, "You're brilliant. Would you take over his maths?" She did. Do you think their son got any better with her **coaching** style? You'd better believe it. Do you think he liked it? Not particularly. It is much easier to loosen up than tighten up. He had been used to working on his own. Even though working alone was not effective, he didn't welcome the sudden shift to close supervision. Yet if people don't know what they're doing and are discouraged, somebody has to direct and coach them. Notice that our effective maths teacher *clarified expectations and goals, observed and monitored performance,* and *gave him feedback.*

Luckily, there were only three months left in the school year. Why do we say luckily? Because it was difficult for this teacher to move from a **directing/coaching** style to a **supporting/ delegating** style. She was great at start-up work, but once the kids got the skills, she had problems letting the students take responsibility for their own learning. After three months, our friend's son was able to get out from under her. He moved on to a more humanistic, supporting teacher who could work with him now that he had the skills—like the warm, friendly teacher we described earlier. Teachers like these are absolutely super in their particular role, but you have to make sure they are working with the right kid at the right time. Both the directive teacher and the humanistic teacher would have been more effective if they could have used a variety of leadership styles. It's the same with managers and leaders. You have to be flexible enough to vary your leadership style depending on the skill level of your people; otherwise, your effectiveness will be limited.

All people have peak performance potential—you just need to know where they are coming from and meet them there.

The Three Skills of a Situational Leader

To become effective in using Situational Leadership® II, you must master three skills: ***diagnosis, flexibility***, and ***partnering for performance***. None of these skills is particularly difficult; each simply requires practice.

Diagnosis: The First Skill

As we stated earlier, to be an effective situational leader, you must determine the development level of your direct report. But how, exactly, do you do that? The key is to look at two factors—competence and commitment.

Competence is the sum of knowledge and skills that an individual brings to a goal or task. The best way to determine competence is to look at a person's performance. How well can your direct reports plan, organise, problem-solve, and communicate about doing a particular task? Can they accomplish the stated goal accurately and on time? Competence can be gained through formal education, on-the-job training, and experience, and it can be developed over time with appropriate direction and support.

The second factor to look for when diagnosing development level is **commitment**: a person's motivation and confidence about a goal or task. How interested and enthusiastic are your direct reports about doing a particular job? Are they self-assured? Do they trust their own ability to do the goal or task? If their motivation and confidence are high, your direct reports are committed.

Flexibility: The Second Skill

When you can comfortably use a variety of leadership styles, you have mastered the second skill of a situational leader: **flexibility**. As your direct reports move from one development level to the next, your style should change accordingly. Yet our research shows that most leaders have a preferred leadership style.[2] In fact, 54 per cent of leaders tend to use only one style, 35 per cent tend to use two styles, 10 per cent tend to use three styles, and only 1 per cent use four styles. To be effective, leaders must be able to use all four leadership styles.

Partnering for Performance: The Third Skill

The third skill of a situational leader is **partnering for performance**. Partnering opens communication between you and your direct reports and increases the quality and quantity of your conversations. When we first started to teach Situational Leadership® II, managers would leave our training excited and ready to apply and use the concepts. Yet we found that problems developed, because the people managers were applying the model to didn't understand what the managers were doing and often misinterpreted their intentions.

For example, suppose that you diagnosed one of your people as predominantly a self-reliant achiever. As a result, you decided basically to leave that person alone, but you didn't tell her why. After a while—when she hardly ever saw you any more—she could become confused. "I wonder what I've done wrong," she might think. "I never see my manager any more."

Suppose another one of your people is new, and you decide that he needs, at a minimum, a coaching style. As a result, you're in his office all the time. After a while, he might start to wonder, "Why doesn't my boss trust me? He's always looking over my shoulder."

In both cases, you might have made the right diagnosis, but since your people didn't understand your rationale, they misinterpreted your intentions. Through these kinds of experiences, we realised this:

> *Leadership is not something you do to people,*
> *but something you do with people.*

That's where partnering for performance comes in. This skill is about gaining your direct reports' permission to use the leadership style that is a match for their development level. As you will learn in the next chapter, "Self-Leadership: The Power Behind Empowerment," partnering for performance also allows people to ask their manager for the leadership style they need. Since partnering for performance involves this kind of give-and-take between leader and follower, we will wait until you fully understand Situational Self-Leadership before going into depth about partnering for performance in Chapter 7, "Partnering for Performance."

Effective Leadership Is a Transformational Journey

We call Situational Leadership® II the integrating concept because it was on this theory that The Ken Blanchard Companies was built. Over time, we realised that situational leadership applied not only when you were leading an individual, but also when you were leading a team, an organisation, and, most importantly, yourself. In fact, we have found that leadership is a four-stage transformational journey that includes self-leadership, one-on-one leadership, team leadership, and organisational leadership.[3]

Self-Leadership comes first, because effective leadership starts on the inside. Before you can hope to lead anyone else, you have to know yourself and what you need to be successful. Self-knowledge gives you perspective.

Only when leaders have had experience in leading themselves are they ready to lead others. The key to **one-on-one leadership** is being able to develop a trusting relationship with others. If you don't know who you are—or what your strengths and weaknesses are—and you are unwilling to be vulnerable, you will never develop a trusting relationship. Without trust, it is impossible for an organisation to function effectively. *Trust* between you and the people you lead is essential for working together.

The next step in the transformational journey of a leader is **team leadership**. As leaders develop a trusting relationship with people in the one-on-one leadership arena, they become trustworthy. This is great preparation for team development and building a *community*. Effective leaders working at the team level realise that to be good stewards of the energy and efforts of those committed to working with them, they must honour the power of diversity and acknowledge the power of teamwork. This makes the leadership challenge more complicated, yet the results can be especially gratifying.

Organisational leadership is the final stage in the transformational journey. Whether a leader can function well as an organisational leader—someone supervising more than one team—depends on the perspective, trust, and community attained during the first three stages of the leader's transformational journey. The key to developing an effective organisation is creating an environment that *values both relationships and results*.

One of the primary mistakes that leaders make today is that when they are called to lead, they spend most of their time and energy trying to improve things at the organisational level before ensuring that they have adequately addressed their own credibility at the self-, one-on-one, or team leadership levels.

As you take time at each of the leadership stops along your transformational journey, Situational Leadership® II will play a major role. The next chapter examines how the model applies to the first step of the transformational journey: self-leadership.

Chapter 6

SELF-LEADERSHIP: THE POWER BEHIND EMPOWERMENT

Susan Fowler, Ken Blanchard,
and Laurence Hawkins

As we discussed in Chapter 4, "Empowerment Is the Key," the traditional hierarchy of leadership is evolving into a new order: empowerment of individuals. When self-leaders can take the initiative to get what they need to succeed and leaders respond to those needs, the proverbial pyramid turns upside down, and leaders serve those who are being led. This puts the power into empowerment.

Managers must learn to let go of command-and-control leadership styles, because soon they will have no choice. In the 1980s, a manager typically supervised five people; in other words, the span of control was one manager to five direct reports. Today, companies have more lean-and-mean organisational structures, where spans of control have increased considerably. Now, it is common to find one manager for 25 to 75 direct reports. Add to that the emergence of virtual organisations—where managers supervise people they seldom, if ever, meet face to face—and an entirely different work landscape emerges. The truth is that most bosses today can no longer play the traditional role of telling their people everything they need to do, and when and how. Managers just don't have the time, and in many cases, their people know more about the work than they do. More than ever before, companies today rely on empowered individuals to get the job done.

A number of people are taking to this empowered environment like ducks to water. But some are becoming immobilised, unsure of how to take action without being told directly what to do by their manager. How can you get people to grab hold and run with the ball they're being handed?

Creating an Empowered Workforce

Just as leaders must move from command and control to partnering for performance, so too must those who are being led move from "waiting to be told" to taking the initiative to lead themselves. If the key role of situational leaders is to become partners with their people, the new role of people is to become partners with their leaders. This is what self-leadership is all about.

If empowerment is to be successful, organisations and leaders must develop self-leaders in the workforce who have the skills to take initiative.

People need to be trained in self-leadership. While many organisations teach managers how to delegate and "let go," there is less emphasis on developing individuals to solve problems and make decisions. Organisations on the leading edge have learned that developing self-leaders is a powerful way to positively impact the triple bottom line.

For example, one of our clients, Bandag Manufacturing, experienced the value of self-leadership after a major equipment breakdown. Rather than laying off the affected workforce, the company opted to train them in self-leadership. A funny thing happened. Direct reports began holding their managers accountable and asking them to demonstrate their leadership capabilities. They were asking managers for direction and support and urging them to clarify goals and expectations. Suddenly, managers were studying up on rusty skills and working harder.

When the plant's ramp-up time was compared to the company's other eight plants that had experienced similar breakdowns in the past, the California plant reached pre-breakdown production levels faster than any other in history. The manufacturer studied other measures, too. It concluded that the determining factor in the plant's successful rebound was the proactive behaviour of the workers, who were fully engaged and armed with the skills of self-leadership.

> *An organisation filled with self-leaders is an organisation with an empowered workforce.*

Creating Self-Leaders Through Individual Learning

Individual learning—one of the key elements of a high-performing organisation—is essential to self-leadership.[1] Organisations that do not encourage people to learn are less likely to be high-performing, because the skills of an organisation are no greater than the skills of its people. Unless its individuals learn, the organisation cannot learn.

In high-performing organisations, people are treated as appreciating assets who grow more valuable with experience and knowledge. High-performing organisations use formal training, mentoring, and on-the-job support to develop the skills and competencies of their people.

While self-leaders should be responsible for their own learning, they shouldn't bear the burden alone; management should support the development of knowledge and skills. Fortunately, examples of organisations that support individual learning and the development of self-leaders are plentiful. Yum! Brands—the parent company of Pizza Hut, Taco Bell, and KFC, among others—supports Yum! University. Here, employees learn the technical, business, and interpersonal skills that are related to creating customer mania.[2] Johnsonville Foods promotes continuous learning by encouraging all employees to attend any training course, regardless of its direct applicability to their current jobs.[3] GE's learning initiative broke down barriers to learning through cross-functional work on real applications.[4] Other examples abound.

Empowerment is what leaders give to their people.
Self-Leadership is what people do
to make empowerment work.

The Three Skills of a Self-Leader

You cannot invert the hierarchical pyramid and simply tell self-leaders to take responsibility. Self-leaders must be actively developed by teaching people skills and mental attitudes that foster empowerment.[5] In *Self Leadership and The One Minute Manager*, Ken Blanchard, Susan Fowler, and Laurence Hawkins teach the three skills of self-leadership: ***challenge assumed constraints***, ***celebrate your points of power***, and ***collaborate for success***.[6]

The First Skill of a Self-Leader: Challenge Assumed Constraints

The first skill of a self-leader is to **challenge assumed constraints**. What, exactly, do we mean by an assumed constraint?

An assumed constraint is a belief, based on past
experience, that limits current and future experiences.

The classic example of an assumed constraint is illustrated by the training of circus elephants. The trainer takes a baby elephant and ties him to a stake with a big, heavy chain. Although the baby elephant pulls and tugs, he can't break the chain. Eventually he stops trying. He is now a six-ton elephant with the Barnum & Bailey circus. He could easily pull the entire stake out of the ground—plus the stage—but he doesn't even try. His inability to move beyond the length of the chain isn't real; it's an assumed constraint.

Consider how the elephant's story relates to your own work experience. Do any of the following statements sound familiar? "Why should I bother? My boss won't approve anyway. They never listen to anyone's ideas around here. A woman has never held that position before. I've never been any good at that." These are all examples of assumed constraints that might be true at some level but are not the truth that should define your experience.

Indicators that an assumed constraint may be holding you hostage are negative internal dialogue, excuses, and blaming statements. At one time or another, most of us have assumed that because we did not have direct authority or position power, we could not be leaders or influence outcomes. This is one of the most common assumed constraints in the workplace. People who have become legendary for their effectiveness—from Bill Gates to Mother Teresa—are those who go beyond assumed constraints to reach their goals. For example, Mother Teresa—a minority Albanian who spoke broken English—did not begin her amazing career with a high position and authority. She used her personal power to achieve her goal of bringing dignity to the destitute. Fame and success followed.

This is not to say that all of us aren't constrained by outside forces, whether it's a lack of time, money, or position of authority. Yet self-leadership teaches that the constraints are not the problem; the problem is that we think these things are the only sources of power that are available to us. Every successful person can almost name the time and date when he or she decided to let go of an assumed constraint.

The Second Skill of a Self-Leader: Celebrate Your Points of Power

The second skill of a self-leader is to ***celebrate your points of power***. Everyone has points of power, although many are unaware of them.

People of all ages struggle with the mere notion of power. The abuse of power, the use of status and position to coerce others, and the egoism associated with people who have social and political power have turned people off to the acceptance of—let alone use of—power. Situational Self-Leadership teaches people that we all have points of power. In helping people recognise and accept their points of power, we suggest that "the sole advantage of power is the ability to do more good." Self-leaders can do more good for themselves, their families, their communities, their organisations, and their coworkers when they accept and tap into their power.

The five sources of power are *position power, personal power, task power, relationship power,* and *knowledge power* (see Figure 6.1).

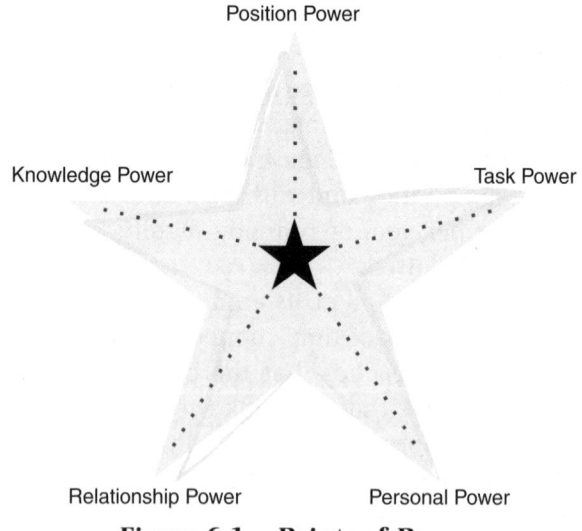

Position Power

Knowledge Power

Task Power

Relationship Power

Personal Power

Figure 6.1   Points of Power

Position power is the most recognised point of power. It is inherent in the authority of one's position. You have position power when your business card has a title printed on it that indicates you have the power to manage people or command resources.

Personal power comes from personal attributes such as strength of character, passion, inspiration, or wisdom. Personal power is further enhanced by strong interpersonal skills, such as an ability to communicate well and be persuasive. If people like to be around you, you have personal power.

Task power relates to a task or particular job. This is power you have in being able to help others with a process or procedure they need to do or, conversely, to block or delay others from doing a task. For example, an executive secretary for a president or CEO often has the power to influence who gets added to or deleted from the executive's agenda.

Relationship power comes from the power of association with others—through building a friendship, understanding a colleague, cultivating a relationship, or knowing someone who owes you a favour. If you are somebody who has position power, personal power, task power, or knowledge power, you potentially have relationship power.

Knowledge power comes from having special expertise or skills but is also evidenced by having certain degrees or certifications indicating special training. You can often transfer knowledge power from job to job or from company to company. We're all good at something, so we all have some form of knowledge power.

Everyone has some degree of each of these forms of power, and typically the distribution is uneven. We find that few people ever think about what points of power they have. Fewer still have asked others for their perceptions on this topic. If they did, they might be surprised at how others view them—their job, position, personality, and abilities.

Getting feedback on your points of power can be an enlightening experience. Chances are good that you'll be surprised and gratified by the responses you get. With raised awareness of and attention to your own power, you come to realise how to use your points of power to better advantage. You will probably also realise that while you have been taking some points of power for granted, you have been oblivious to others. The best way to increase your power base is to gather people around you who have points of power you don't have.

Don't buy into the assumed constraint that
position power is the only power that works.

Once you learn what your points of power are, you are ready to expand them. If you are strong in some points of power or weak in others, don't assume this will be true the rest of your life. For example, it wouldn't hurt a person with high knowledge power due to computer expertise but low personal power due to weak interpersonal skills to take a Dale Carnegie course on "How to Win Friends and Influence People." Assuming that people will never want to be around you is a life-limiting assumed constraint. The same can be said of people who have good interpersonal skills but lack technical skills. You're naïve to think that the computer will go away. So get with the programme, and ask someone to help you learn.

Using the Power of "I Need"

You can maximise your points of power when you combine them with two powerful words: "I need." Instead of directly stating what we need, many of us get trapped asking stupid questions, like the woman in the subway. Let us explain: A man got on a subway in New York City and discovered there was only one seat left. There was something on the seat he didn't want on his jeans, so he laid down his newspaper and sat on it. A few minutes later, a woman tapped him on the shoulder and said, "Excuse me, sir. Are you reading your newspaper?" The man thought that was one of the dumbest questions he'd ever heard. He couldn't help himself. He stood up, turned the page, sat back down on the paper, and replied, "Yes, ma'am, I am."

While that story is amusing, you might wonder if you ask any dumb questions. We all do. For example, suppose that a coworker is running around like a chicken with her head cut off, but you need some help. So you ask, "Are you busy?" That's a dumb question. Of course she's busy! So she says something like, "There just aren't enough hours in the day." You feel guilty, so you get flustered and leave her alone, not wanting to add to her burden.

The alternative to dumb questions is to simply state your needs to your coworker truthfully: "I need 15 minutes to discuss this project. If this isn't a good time, I could come back at 3 o'clock."

What makes the "I need" phrase so powerful? When you tell somebody you *want something*, that person's first thought is usually, "We all want things we can't have." However, when you use the "I need" phrase, you're coming from a position of strength. You've thought about what it will take to succeed, and you are requesting someone's help. Human beings love to feel needed. They love to think they can help you.

Don't be afraid to ask for what you need from people who have points of power you don't have. By being assertive in this way, you will eliminate "being a victim" from your vocabulary. Remember, if you ask for what you need, you will either win or break even. How excited would you be about going to Las Vegas if the worst you could do was win or break even? You would catch the next plane. If you ask for what you need and you get it, you win. If you ask and don't get it, you break even, because you didn't have it in the first place. Most people are afraid to ask for what they need for fear of rejection. Remember, when people say no to you, they are only turning down your idea. The only person who can turn you down is you.

"I need" is compelling. This is a key phrase when you begin to collaborate for success.

The Third Skill of a Self-Leader: Collaborate for Success

The third skill of a self-leader is to **collaborate for success**. This is where self-leaders take the initiative to get the direction and support they need to achieve their goals.

In Chapter 5, "Situational Leadership® II: The Integrating Concept," we introduced the four development levels and the appropriate leadership styles for each. Situational Self-Leadership turns the model upside down. Direct reports can now diagnose their own development levels on a particular goal or task and take the initiative to get from their managers the leadership style they need to succeed (see Figure 6.2).

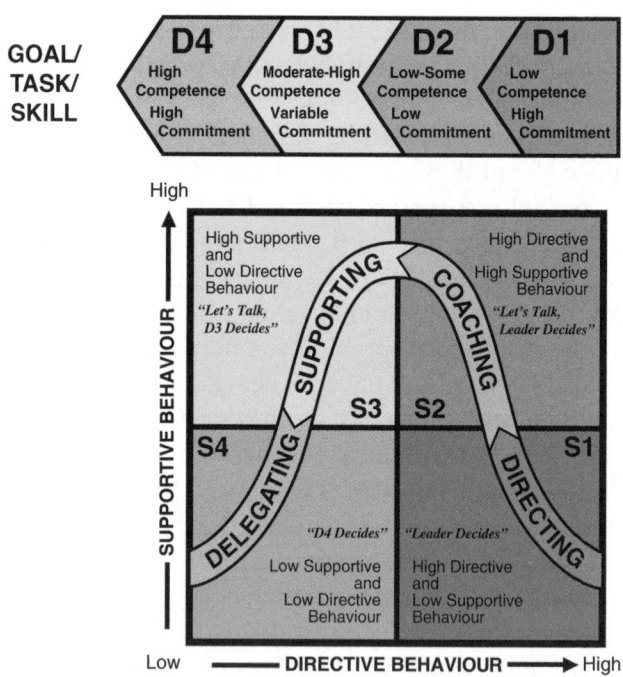

Figure 6.2   The Needs Model

To illustrate how this works, let's return to our example in Chapter 5 of the recently hired 22-year-old salesperson. Suppose that the first thing his manager did with him was train him in Situational Self-Leadership. Now when he and his manager set goals around his four key areas of responsibility—sales, service, administration, and team contribution—the young salesperson can *collaborate for success* by playing an active role in diagnosing his own development level. He can determine the leadership style he needs for each, rather than relying on his manager to do all the work. Not only will this increase his self-esteem and speed his journey to empowerment, but by being a good partner, he also will alleviate some of the management load for his boss. In the process, his manager can more easily invert the hierarchal pyramid and become more of a cheerleader and supporter than a director and controller.

Because the salesperson knows Situational Self-Leadership, he can diagnose himself as an *enthusiastic beginner (D1)* in the area of selling to existing clients. He knows that he has not yet demonstrated competence in this area and that he hasn't gained the knowledge and skills he needs to achieve his sales goals. Yet the thought of providing superior service to existing clients excites him, and his commitment is high. The salesperson should recognise that he needs a *directing (S1)* style, with high direction and low support. He should *collaborate for success* by asking his manager to teach him all about this part of the sales process, from making the first contact to completing the job.

In the area of administration—specifically, filing electronic reports—the salesperson realises that he is a *disillusioned learner (D2)* in need of *coaching (S2)*. His hotel job during the summer didn't give him a lot of computer training. After taking some beginning software classes, he thought he was on his way to computer literacy. Yet without the instructor at his side, his confidence is waning. The salesperson should admit to his manager that, while he's fairly comfortable with e-mail, he's so baffled by the spreadsheet programme that he finds himself mumbling to the computer monitor. Recognising that he needs a lot of direction and support in this area, the salesperson should **collaborate for success** by asking his manager for more computer training so that he can dialogue with the instructor as he learns. He also should ask his manager for lots of praise and support to build his confidence on the computer and encourage him to keep learning.

In the area of cold calling, the salesperson is having some trouble. He has been well trained in this area and knows the step-by-step process for cold calling. During his training and for the first few weeks afterwards, he had several successes. During the past couple of weeks, however, he's made hardly any sales through cold calls. His self-doubt has come roaring back, and he's beginning to wonder if he has what it takes to succeed in cold calling on his own. Remembering how excited and competent he felt about cold calling just a few weeks ago, he realises that he is a **capable but cautious performer (D3)** who needs a **supporting (S3)** leadership style. He should **collaborate for success** by asking his manager to listen to his concerns and questions and encourage his flagging confidence.

In the area of customer service, the salesperson knows full well he's a **self-reliant achiever (D4)**. Having worked in the hospitality industry, he brings all kinds of customer-pleasing skills to his new position, and delighting customers comes as naturally to him as breathing. He has already won the hearts of some of the company's biggest clients by anticipating their needs and delivering more than they ever dreamed of receiving. In this area, the salesperson should **collaborate for success** by letting his manager know that what would work best for him would be a **delegating (S4)** leadership style. He should ask his manager to let him do the day-to-day decision making in this area. He also should let his manager know that the best way to support him is to trust him to do his job well, provide him with the resources he needs, and challenge him to deliver even higher levels of raving fan service.

It is important to remember that the collaborating for success process doesn't have to be restricted to your manager. You can diagnose your development level and ask for the appropriate leadership style from any number of leaders. Remember that *a leader is anyone who can give you the direction and support you need to achieve your goal.* This is the perfect time for you to challenge your assumed constraints. Are you assuming that someone won't have the time or inclination to help you? Move beyond that constraint and ask the person anyway.

Now that you know about self-leadership, the next chapter introduces partnering for performance, the third skill of becoming an effective situational leader.

Chapter 7

PARTNERING FOR PERFORMANCE

Fred Finch and Ken Blanchard

A t its best, leadership is a partnership that involves mutual trust between two people who work together to achieve common goals. Both leader and follower influence each other. Leadership shifts between them, depending on the task at hand and who has the competence and commitment to deal with it. Both parties play a role in determining how things get done.

Partnering for performance, the third skill of effective situational leaders, provides a guide for creating such side-by-side leadership relationships. It is a process for increasing the quality and quantity of conversations between managers and direct reports—the people they support and depend on. These conversations not only help people perform better, but they also help everyone involved feel better about themselves and each other.

Establishing an Effective Performance Management System

An effective performance management system has three parts:

- **Performance plannings**. After everyone is clear on the organisational vision and direction, performance planning begins. During this time leaders agree with their direct reports about the goals and objectives they should be focusing on. At this stage it's okay for the traditional hierarchy to be alive and well, because if there's a disagreement between a manager and a direct report about goals, who wins? The manager, because that person represents the organisation's goals and objectives.

- **Performance coaching**. This is where the hierarchy is turned upside down on a day-to-day basis. Now leaders do everything they can to help direct reports be successful. Servant leadership kicks in at this stage. Managers work for their people, praising progress and redirecting inappropriate performance.

- **Performance review**. This is where a manager and direct report sit down and assess the direct report's performance over time.

Which of these three—performance planning, performance coaching, or performance review—do most organisations devote the greatest amount of time to? Unfortunately, it's performance review. We go into organisation after organisation, and people say to us, "You'll love our new performance review form." We always laugh, because we think most of them can be thrown out. Why? Because these forms often measure things nobody knows how to evaluate. For example, "initiative" or "willingness to take responsibility." Or "promotability"—that's a good one. When no one knows how to win during a performance review, they focus most of their energy up the hierarchy. After all, if you have a good relationship with your boss, you have a higher probability of getting a good evaluation.

Some organisations do a good job on performance planning and set very clear goals. However, after goal setting, what do you think happens to those goals? Most often they get filed, and no one looks at them until they are told it's time for performance reviews. Then everybody runs around, bumping into each other, trying to find the goals.

Of the three aspects of an effective performance management system, which one do people spend the least time on? The answer is performance coaching. Yet this is the most important aspect of managing people's performance, because it's during performance coaching that feedback—praising progress and redirecting inappropriate behaviour—happens on an ongoing basis.

In *Helping People Win at Work: A Business Philosophy Called "Don't Mark My Paper, Help Me Get an A,"* Ken Blanchard and WD-40 Company CEO Garry Ridge discuss in detail how an effective performance management system works.[1] The book was inspired by Ken's ten-year experience as a university professor. He sometimes got in trouble when he gave the students the final exam at the beginning of the course. When the faculty found out about that, they asked, "What are you doing?"

Ken said, "I thought we were supposed to teach these students."

The faculty said, "You are, but don't give them the final exam ahead of time!"

Ken said, "Not only will I give them the final exam ahead of time, what do you think I'll do throughout the year? I'll teach them the answers so that when they get to the final exam, they'll get As. You see, life is all about getting As—not some stupid normal distribution curve."

Do you employ losers? Do you go around saying, "We lost some of our best losers last year, so let's find some new ones to fill those low spots."? No! You employ either winners or potential winners. You don't employ people to fit a normal distribution curve. You want to find the best people possible, and you want them to perform at their highest level.

Giving people the final exam ahead of time is equivalent to performance planning. It lets people know exactly what's expected of them. Teaching direct reports the answers is what performance coaching is all about. If you see people doing something right, you give them an "attaboy" or "attagirl." If they do something wrong, you don't beat them up or save your feedback for the performance review. Instead, you say, "Wrong answer. What do you think would be the right answer?" In other words, you redirect them. Finally, giving people the same exam during the performance review that you gave them at the beginning of the year helps them win—get a good evaluation. There should be no surprises in an annual or half-yearly performance review. Everyone should know what the test will be and should get help throughout the year to achieve a high score on it. When you have a forced distribution curve—where a certain percentage of your people have to be average or less—you lose everyone's trust. Now all people are concerned about is looking out for number one.

After learning about this philosophy, Ridge implemented "Don't Mark My Paper, Help Me Get an A" as a major theme in his company. He is so emphatic about this concept that he would fire a poor performer's manager rather than the poor performer if he found out that the manager had done nothing to help that person get an A.

Not all managers are like Garry Ridge. Many still believe you need to use a normal distribution curve that grades a few people high, a few people low, and the rest average. The reason these managers and their organisations are often reluctant to discard the normal distribution curve is that they don't know how they will deal with career planning if some people don't get sorted out at a lower level. If they rated a high percentage of their people as top performers, they wonder how they can possibly reward them all. As people move up the hierarchy, aren't there fewer opportunities for promotion? We believe that question is quite naïve. If you treat people well and help them win in their present position, they often will use their creativity to come up with new business ideas that will expand your vision and grow the organisation. Protecting the hierarchy doesn't do your people or your organisation any good.

Ralph Stayer, coauthor with Jim Belasco of *Flight of the Buffalo*, tells a wonderful story that proves this point. Stayer was in the sausage manufacturing business. His secretary came to him one day with a great idea. She suggested that they start a catalogue business, because at the time they were direct-selling their sausages to only supermarkets and other distributors. He said, "What a great idea! Why don't you organise a business plan and run it?" Soon the woman who used to be his secretary was running a major new division of his company and creating all kinds of job opportunities for people, as well as revenue for the company.[2]

Leadership that emphasises judgement, criticism, and evaluation is a thing of the past. Leading at a higher level today is about helping people get As by providing the direction, support, and encouragement they need to be their best.

Partnering and the Performance Management System

To give you a better sense of how this works, we want to share with you a game plan that will help you understand how partnering for performance fits into the formal performance management system we just described. While you can put this game plan into action with no prior training, it is much more powerful when everyone involved—both leaders and direct reports—understands Situational Leadership® II or Situational Self-Leadership. That ensures that everyone is speaking the same language.

Performance Planning:
The First Part of a Performance Management System

As you can see in Figure 7.1, the first three steps in the Partnering for Performance Game Plan—goal setting, diagnosis, and matching—begin the performance process.

1. START
with

GOAL SETTING
(need agreement with employee)

1. Area of Responsibility/Goal

2. Performance Measure/Standard

ASK

1) What area of responsibility or goal do I want to influence?
2) How will I know the job is being done (measure)?
3) What constitutes good performance on this goal (standard)?

then
2. DIAGNOSE

DEVELOPMENT LEVEL
(need agreement with employee)

COMPETENCE

COMMITMENT

| Self-Reliant Achiever D4 | Capable but Cautious Performer D3 | Disillusioned Learner D2 | Enthusiastic Beginner D1 |

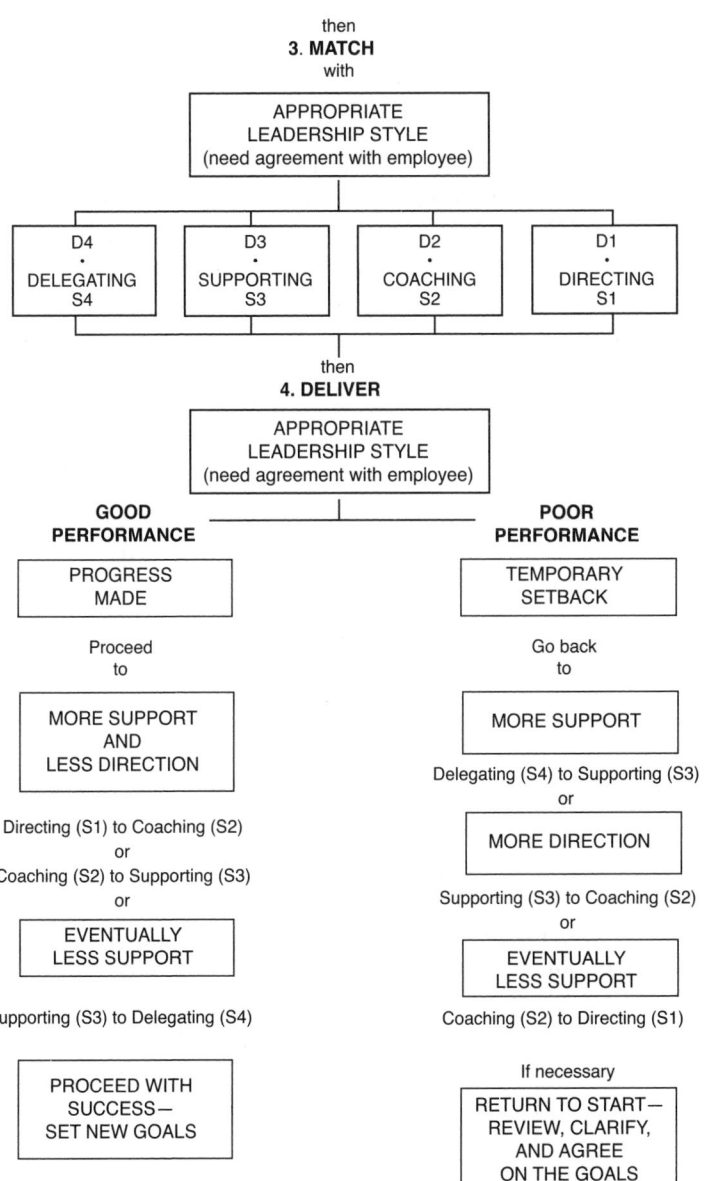

Figure 7.1   The Partnering for Performance Game Plan

The first key element of effective partnering for performance is *goal setting*. All good performance starts with clear goals. This is such an important concept that we discuss it in detail in Chapter 8, "Essential Skills for Partnering for Performance: The One Minute Manager." Clarifying goals involves making sure that people understand two things: first, what they are being asked to do—their areas of accountability—and second, what good performance looks like—the performance standards by which they will be evaluated.

Diagnosis is the second element of partnering for performance. It starts with the leader and direct report individually diagnosing the direct report's development level for each of the goals agreed on. When we say individually, we mean that both leader and direct report go to a quiet place and separately diagnose the development level for each goal area by asking two questions:

- To determine *competence, each should ask,* "Does this person/do I know how to do this task?"
- To determine *commitment*, each should ask, "How excited is my direct report/am I about taking this on?"

After both people in the partnering process have done their diagnostic homework, they should come back together and agree on who goes first. If the direct report goes first, the leader's job is to listen to that person's diagnosis. Then, before saying anything else, the leader has to tell the direct report what she heard him saying until he agrees that's what he said. When it's the leader's turn, she tells the direct report her diagnosis of his development level on each of his areas of responsibility. His job is now to listen and feed back what he heard until his manager agrees that's what she said. Why do we suggest this process? Because it guarantees that both people are heard. Without some structure like this, if one of the two people involved is more verbal than the other, that person will dominate the conversation.

After both people have been heard, they should discuss similarities and differences in their diagnoses and attempt to come to some agreement. If there is a disagreement between leader and direct report on development level that cannot be resolved, who should win? The direct report. It is not the manager's job to fight over development level. However, the manager should make the direct report accountable. This means asking him or her, "What will you be able to show me in this goal area in a week or two that will demonstrate that your development diagnosis was right and mine was wrong?" You want to help your people win, even if agreement has not been reached. We have found that people will work hard to prove they are right, which is exactly what you want them to do. If performance does not live up to agreed-on expectations, it will be clear to the direct report that the diagnosis should be reconsidered, and more direction and/or support should be given.

Once development level is clear, both parties, if they know Situational Leadership® II, should be ready to discuss which leadership style is needed. This leads to **matching**, the third step in the partnering for performance game plan. Matching ensures that the leader provides the kind of behaviours—a leadership style—that the direct report needs to perform the task well and, at the same time, enhances his commitment.

While the appropriate leadership style to use should be clear once development level is determined, that's just the beginning. When you're partnering for performance, you don't just leave it at saying you'll use a delegating or coaching style. You have to be more specific. For the leader, this provides an opportunity for what we call "getting permission to use a leadership style."

The purpose of getting permission to use a leadership style is twofold. First, checking to make sure that the style proposed is what the direct report agrees is needed creates clarity. Second, getting permission ensures the direct report's buy-in on the use of that style and increases commitment. For example, if a direct report is an **enthusiastic beginner** who does not have much in the way of task knowledge and skill, but is excited about taking on the task, this person obviously needs a **directing** leadership style. The leader might say, "How would it be if I set a task goal that I believe will stretch you but is attainable, and then develop an action plan for you that will enable you to reach the goal? Then I'd like to meet with you on a regular basis to discuss your progress and provide any help you need as you get started. Does this make sense as a way for you to get up to speed as quickly as possible?" If the direct report agrees, they are off and running.

On the other hand, suppose a direct report is a ***self-reliant achiever*** on a particular goal and therefore can handle a ***delegating*** leadership style. The leader might say, "Okay. The ball is in your court, but keep me in the loop. If you have any concerns, give me a call. Unless I hear from you, or the information I receive tells me otherwise, I'll assume everything is fine. If it isn't, call early. Don't wait until the monkey is a gorilla. Does that work for you?" If the direct report says yes, he is on his own until his performance or communication suggests differently. If in either of the two examples—the enthusiastic beginner or the self-reliant achiever—the direct report doesn't agree, what should happen? Further discussion should take place until a leadership approach is agreed on.

As you can tell from the examples, once an appropriate leadership style is agreed on, the leader still needs to provide work direction. ***Providing work direction*** might involve establishing clear performance expectations, creating an action plan, putting in place a process for checking progress, and expressing confidence that the person can deliver on the performance plan.

As part of that process, it's important to establish a monitoring process based on the agreed-on leadership style. This is where the leader and direct report commit to holding scheduled meetings—called progress-check meetings—to discuss how performance is going.

For example, if you agree that your direct report needs a ***directing*** style, you would meet quite frequently and maybe have the direct report attend some formal training. If a ***coaching*** style is chosen, you might say, "Let's schedule two meetings a week for at least two hours to work on the goal you need help with. How about Mondays and Wednesdays from 1 to 3 p.m.?" With a **supporting** leadership style, you might ask, "What's the best way for me to recognise and praise the progress you are making? At lunch every week or so?" If you agree to have lunch together, your role would be to listen and support his or her actions. With a **delegating** style, it would be up to the direct report to request help, since he or she's a self-reliant achiever.

Performance Coaching:
The Second Part of a Performance Management System

Once it's determined, the agreed-on leadership style establishes the number, frequency, and kind of progress-check meetings that leaders and their direct reports have with each other. The implementation of these meetings begins performance coaching. That's where leaders praise progress and/or redirect the efforts of their partners—their direct reports.

Leaders often assume that their work direction conversations are so clear there is no need for follow-up or they are so busy they can't take the time. If you want to save yourself time and misery, schedule and hold progress-check meetings. You will be able to catch problems before they become major and significantly increase the probability that your direct report's performance on the goal will meet your expectations. If they didn't schedule progress-check meetings, leaders could set up their people for failure. That's why one of our favourite sayings is

---

You can expect more if you inspect more.

While this might sound intrusive, it really isn't. As Ken Blanchard, Thad Lacinak, Chuck Tompkins, and Jim Ballard point out in *Whale Done!: The Power of Positive Relationships*, inspecting should emphasise catching people doing things right, not wrong. Praising progress and/or redirecting efforts begins with accentuating the positive. Redirection follows praising to keep progress going. If no progress is being made—in other words, if performance is not improving—leaders should move straight to redirection to stop any further decline in performance.

When they ***deliver*** the appropriate leadership style, managers are taking the fourth step in the partnering for performance game plan. Let's take a look at the model again and see what happens when performance is improving.

Improving Performance

As you examine Figure 7.2, you might be wondering what the curve running through the four styles means. We call it a performance curve, and for good reason.

The Situational Leadership® II Model

Figure 7.2   Situational Leadership® II Leadership Styles

Performance is what triggers a change in leadership style.

As development level moves from **enthusiastic beginner (D1)** to **self-reliant achiever (D4)**, the curve shows how a manager's leadership style moves from **directing (S1)** to **delegating (S4)**, with first an increase in **support (S2)**, and then a decrease in **direction (S3)**, until eventually there's also a decrease in **support (S4)**. At **self-reliant achiever (D4)**, the person can direct and support more and more of his or her own work. Your goal as a manager, then, should be to help your direct report improve performance by changing your leadership style over time.

To help yourself do that as a leader, *imagine the performance curve is a railroad track.* Each of the four leadership styles depicts a station along the performance curve. If you start with an **enthusiastic beginner (D1)** using a **directing style (S1)**, and you want to eventually get to **delegating (S4)**, appropriate for a **self-reliant achiever (D4)**, what two stations do you have to stop at along the way? **Coaching (S2)** and **supporting (S3)**.

You'll notice that no railway tracks go straight from **directing (S1)** to **delegating (S4)**. What happens to a fast-moving train if it goes off the tracks? People get hurt. It is important for managers not to skip a station as they manage people's journey to high-performance. By staying on track and stopping at all the stations, you will lead your direct reports to perform well on their own, with little or no supervision. Lao Tzu said it well:

When the best leader's work is done, the people say, "We did it ourselves!"

An experiment we did at the University of Massachusetts illustrates the power of Situational Leadership® II in partnering for performance. We worked with four instructors teaching an eight-week course in management. The first two instructors taught by either lecturing or leading discussions—in other words, they used **directing** and **coaching** styles. These two traditional instructors became our control group.

We taught the other two instructors Situational Leadership® II and showed them how to change their teaching style over the course of eight weeks. The first two weeks we asked them to use a *directing* style: lecturing. The next two weeks we asked the instructors to lead discussions, in essence using a *coaching* style. During the following two weeks we showed them how to move to a *supporting* style by restricting their involvement in the class; they sat back and made only process comments like "Has everybody had a chance to speak?" or supportive comments like "This is a really interesting class." During the last two weeks we showed them how to go to a *delegating* leadership style: they asked their students to run the class themselves, letting them know that they would be in the classroom next door writing an article for a business journal.

On the last day of class, a secretary came into all four classes and wrote a note on the whiteboard: "The instructor is sick tonight and won't be here. Carry on as usual."

What do you think happened to the students in the first two classes, where the control group instructors only lectured or led discussions? Within five minutes, those students were gone. Without the instructor there, they didn't know what to do.

In the classes with the changing leadership style, nobody left. Students made comments like "The instructor hasn't been here for the last two weeks. Big deal. What did you think about that case?" One of the two classes even stayed a half hour beyond the scheduled time.

At the end of the year, the experimental classes with the changing teaching style outperformed the other two classes. The students knew more, they liked the course better, and they weren't late or absent. How was that possible when their instructors weren't even there for the last two weeks? Because the instructors stayed on the railroad tracks and gradually changed their teaching style from directing to coaching to supporting to delegating, the students over time moved from dependence to independence, from enthusiastic beginners to self-reliant achievers.

Declining Performance

We rarely find decreases in performance resulting from a decline in competence. Unless you can cite cases of Alzheimer's at work, people generally don't lose their competency if they had it in the first place or were trained to have it. Changes in performance occur either because the job and the necessary skills to perform it have changed, or because people have lost their commitment.

> *Dealing with decommitment—a change in motivation or confidence—is one of the biggest challenges facing managers.*

For the most part, leaders avoid dealing with their decommitted people, largely because it is such an emotionally charged issue and they don't know how. When they do address it, they usually make matters worse: They turn the not-engaged into the actively disengaged. The core perception on the part of these decommitted people is that either their leader or the organisation has treated them unfairly.

We believe that the primary reason for loss of commitment is the behaviour of the leader and/or the organisation. More often than not, something the leader or organisation has done or failed to do is the primary cause of the eroded commitment.

Decommitted people are not provided with the kind of leadership that matches their needs—they are under- or oversupervised. Decommitment has numerous other potential causes: lack of feedback, lack of recognition, lack of clear performance expectations, unfair standards, being yelled at or blamed, reneging on commitments, being overworked and stressed out. The loss of commitment can affect most, if not all, of the person's job functioning.

People often assume that decommitment occurs mainly at the bottom of the organisation, with individual contributors. Not so. It occurs at every organisational level.

Current literature and training courses for addressing what is called "handling performance problems" are overwhelmingly focused on frontline leaders. This literature and these courses assume that the frontline employee is the problem. The language itself—"handling performance problems"—implies that the person with the problem *is* the problem. The literature and training courses emphasise issues such as employees' unacceptable performance or behaviour, documenting performance problems, developing organisational policies to deal with them, employee counselling, removing poor performers, corrective counselling, and discipline.[3]

In general, these are lose–lose strategies that intensify decommitment and that should be used only as a last resort. This approach is commonly called "blaming the victim." A process that does not address all the causes of the problem is guaranteed not to work, particularly if the person who is blaming the performer has a hand in causing it. If the leader and/or organisation have a role in causing the problem, their role has to be identified and resolved as part of the solution.

Placing Blame: Not a Good Strategy

First, let's assume that either the leader or the organisation has contributed to the cause of an individual's decommitment. This is not always the case, but the evidence suggests that it is in the substantial majority of instances where decommitment has occurred. Next, let's assume that the issue has been going on for some time. Again, evidence supports this assumption. When we ask leaders in organisations to identify the people they lead who have "performance problems" and to tell us how long this has been going on, the responses range from six months to ten years. These responses alone identify the leader as part of the problem: the issues are not being addressed.

Dealing with decommitment is a difficult and usually highly emotionally charged undertaking. If the situation has been going on for some time, a high level of emotional tension probably exists in the relationship between the leader and the direct report. The leader blames the direct report, and the direct report blames the leader and/or the organisation.

A sophisticated set of interpersonal skills *and* the ability not to let your ego get in the way are required to effectively address the problem. If you are unwilling to own up to any behaviour on your or the organisation's part that has contributed to the cause of the problem, resolution is unlikely.

Dealing with Decommitment

Decommitment occurs when a gap exists between the direct report's performance and/or behaviour and the leader's expectations. This gap occurs for two primary reasons. First, a gap occurs when the person has demonstrated the ability to perform or behave appropriately, and now his or her performance has declined or behaviour has changed in a negative way. Second, a gap occurs when the person is unwilling to gain knowledge and/or skills that would lead to improved performance or behaviour.

We see three possible strategies for addressing decommitment:

- Keep on doing what you've always done.
- Catch it early.
- Go to a supporting leadership style (high supporting/low directing leader behaviour).

The first alternative—keep on doing what you've always done—will get you what you've always gotten: escalating anger, frustration, and no resolution.

The most effective alternative is to catch decommitment early—the first time it is observed, before it gets out of control and festers. Early detection makes it easier for both you and your direct report to identify the causes and resolve them.

Just as improvements in performance prompt forward shifts in style along the curve, decreases in performance require a shift backwards in leadership style along the performance curve. If a person you are delegating to starts to decline in performance, you want to find out why. So, you would move from a delegating style to a supporting style, where you listen and gather data. If both of you agree that the direct report is still on top of the situation, can explain the decline in performance, and can get performance back in line, you can return to a delegating leadership style. However, if you both agree that this performance situation needs more attention from you, you now can go to a coaching style where you can provide closer supervision. Seldom, if ever, do you have to go all the way back to a directing style.

The third alternative for addressing decommitment when the problem has been going on for some time is to cautiously go to a supporting leadership style. That may seem inappropriate to impatient managers who would like to get off the railway tracks and head straight back to a directing leadership style. Let's explore why and how a supporting leadership style is a better choice.

Step 1: Prepare

Preparation should involve selecting a specific performance or behaviour that you believe you have a chance of jointly dealing with. Do not attempt to address everything at once.

After you have pinpointed the performance or behaviour you want to focus on, gather all the facts that support the existence of the performance or behaviour from your point of view. If it is a performance issue, quantify the decline in performance. If it is a behaviour issue, limit your observations to what you have seen. Don't make assumptions or bring in the perceptions of others. This is a sure way to generate defensiveness. And you probably won't be able to specifically identify these "others" anyway, because they usually don't want to be named. Also, use the most recent information possible. Next, identify anything you or the organisation might have done to contribute to the decommitment. Be honest. Owning up is the most important part of moving towards resolution.

Ask yourself questions to determine your role in the situation. Were performance expectations clear? Have you ever talked to the person about his or her performance or behaviour? Does the person know what a good job looks like? Is anything getting in the way of performance? Have you been using the right leadership style? Are you giving feedback on the performance or behaviour? Is the person getting rewarded for inappropriate performance or behaviour? (Often people in organisations are rewarded for poor behaviour—that is, nobody says anything.) Is the person getting punished for good performance or behaviour? (Often people get punished for good performance or behaviour—that is, they do well and someone else gets the credit.) Do policies support the desired performance? For example, is training or time made available to learn needed skills?

Once you have done a thorough job of preparing, you're ready for Step 2.

STEP 2: SCHEDULE A MEETING, STATE THE MEETING'S PURPOSE, AND SET GROUND RULES

Scheduling a meeting is vital. It is important to begin the meeting by stating the meeting's purpose and setting ground rules to ensure that both parties will be heard in a way that doesn't arouse defensiveness. Decommitted people with serious performance or behaviour issues are very likely to be argumentative and defensive when confronted. For example, you might open the meeting with something like this:

"Jim, I want to talk about what I see as a serious issue with your responsiveness to information enquiries. I would like to set some ground rules about how this discussion proceeds so that we can both fully share our perspectives on the issue. I want us to work together to identify and agree on the issue and its causes so that we can set a goal and develop an action plan to resolve it.

"First, I would like to share my perceptions of the issue and what I think may have caused it. I want you to listen, but not to respond to what I say, except to ask questions for clarification. Then, I want you to restate what I said, to make sure you understand my perspective and I *know* you understand it. When I am finished, I would like to hear your side of the story, with the same ground rules. I will restate what you said until you know I understand your point of view. Does this seem like a reasonable way to get started?"

Using the ground rules you have set, you should begin to understand each other's point of view on the performance issue at hand. Making sure that both of you have been heard is a wonderful way to reduce defensiveness and move towards resolution.

Once you have set ground rules for your meeting, you are ready for Step 3.

STEP 3: WORK TOWARDS MUTUAL AGREEMENT ON THE PERFORMANCE ISSUE AND ITS CAUSES

The next step is to identify where there is agreement and disagreement on both the issue and its causes. Your job is to see if enough of a mutual understanding can be reached so that joint problem solving can go forward. In most conflict situations, it is unlikely that both parties will agree on everything. Discover if there is sufficient common ground to work towards a resolution. If not, revisit those things that are getting in the way, and restate your positions to see if understanding and agreement can be reached.

When you think it is possible to go forward, ask, "Are you willing to work with me to get this resolved?"

If you still can't get a commitment to go forward, you need to use a directing leadership style. Set clear performance expectations and a time frame for achieving them; set clear, specific performance standards and a schedule for tracking performance progress; and state consequences for non-performance. Understand that this is a last-resort strategy that may resolve the performance issue but not the commitment issue.

When you get a commitment to work together to resolve the issue, it is normal to feel great relief and assume that the issue is resolved. Not so fast.

If you or the organisation has contributed to the cause of the problem, you need to take steps to correct what has been done.

Anything you have done to cause or add to the problem needs to be addressed and resolved. Sometimes, you have no control over what the organisation has done, but just acknowledging the organisation's impact often releases the negative energy and regains the other party's commitment.

If you finally get a commitment to work together to resolve the issue, you can go to Step 4 and partner for performance.

STEP 4: PARTNER FOR PERFORMANCE

Now you and the direct report need to have a partnering for performance discussion in which you jointly decide the leadership style you will use to provide work direction or coaching. You should set a goal, establish an action plan, and schedule a progress-check meeting. This step is crucial.

Resolving decommitment issues requires sophisticated interpersonal and performance management skills. Your first try at one of these conversations is not likely to be as productive as you would like. However, if you conduct the conversation in honest good faith, it will reduce the impact of less-than-perfect interpersonal skills and set the foundation for a productive relationship built on commitment and trust.

Performance Review:
The Third Part of a Performance Management System

The third part of an effective performance management system is **performance review**. This is where a person's performance over the course of a year is summed up. We have not included performance review in the traditional sense in our partnering for performance game plan. Why? Because we think effective performance review is not an annual event, but an ongoing process that takes place throughout the performance period. When progress-check meetings are scheduled according to development level, open, honest discussions about the direct report's performance take place on an ongoing basis, creating mutual understanding and agreement. If these meetings are done well, the year-end performance review will just be a review of what has already been discussed. There will be no surprises.

Partnering as an Informal Performance Management System

What we have been talking about so far is how partnering for performance could fit in with a formal performance management system. Unfortunately, most organisations don't have a formal performance management system. Organisational goals are usually set, but often no system is established to accomplish them. As a result, the management of people's performance is left to the discretion and initiative of individual managers. While annual performance reviews are usually done, they tend to be haphazard at best in most organisations. Managers working in that kind of environment can implement partnering for performance on an informal basis in their own areas, even when it comes to performance review. As we stated earlier, we believe that effective performance review is an ongoing process that should take place throughout the performance period, not just once a year. If managers do a good job with an informal performance review system, perhaps through their good example, a formal performance management system will emerge organisation-wide, with partnering for performance as a core element.

One-on-Ones: An Insurance Policy for Making Partnering for Performance Work

How can people close the gap between *learning* about partnering for performance and really *doing* it?

Margie Blanchard and Garry Demarest developed a one-on-one process that requires managers to hold 15- to 30-minute meetings a minimum of once every two weeks with each of their direct reports.[4] Since managers have more people to worry about than an individual contributor, the onus is on the direct report to schedule these meetings as well as set the agenda. This is when people can talk to their managers about anything on their hearts and minds—it's their meeting. The purpose of one-on-ones is for managers and direct reports to get to know each other as human beings.

In the old days, most businesspeople had a traditional military attitude that said, "Don't get close to your direct reports. You can't make hard decisions if you have an emotional attachment to your people." Yet rival organisations will come after your best people, so knowing and caring for them is a competitive edge.

Too often, talented people report that their executive recruiter knows and cares more about their hopes and dreams than their manager does.

Don't let this be said about you. One-on-one meetings not only deepen the power of partnering for performance, they also create genuine relationships and job satisfaction. In the next chapter, we'll reveal the final secrets of leading people one-on-one.

Chapter 8

ESSENTIAL SKILLS FOR PARTNERING FOR PERFORMANCE: THE ONE MINUTE MANAGER®

Ken Blanchard
and Fred Finch

W e are firm believers in the 80/20 rule: 80 per cent of the results that leaders need to get in working with their people come from about 20 per cent of the leadership activities they could do. The three secrets of *The One Minute Manager*[1] are a perfect example. In this book, Ken Blanchard and Spencer Johnson focus on three basic concepts: one minute goals, one minute praisings, and one minute reprimands or redirection. While these three skills probably represent only 20 per cent of the activities that managers engage in, they could provide them with the outcome they desire (the 80 per cent). These three skills are core to effective partnering for performance.

One Minute Goal Setting

Without clear goals, Situational Leadership® II doesn't work. Why not? Because development level is task-specific. As we've indicated, people are not globally enthusiastic beginners, disillusioned learners, capable but cautious performers, or self-reliant achievers. It all depends on which goal area of their job you're talking about.

According to research, goal setting is the single most powerful motivational tool in a leader's toolkit.[2] Why? Because goal setting provides purpose, challenge, and meaning. Goals are the guideposts along the road that make a compelling vision come alive. Goals energise people. Specific, clear, challenging goals lead to greater effort and achievement than easy or vague goals do.

Of course, people must have the knowledge, skills, and commitment necessary for goal achievement. That's what Situational Leadership® II focuses on. When dealing with enthusiastic beginners and disillusioned learners, it's probably better to set learning goals than outcome goals. For example, it is better for beginning golfers to hit balls into a net than on a driving range, because if the outcome of their efforts is evident, they could get discouraged after every shot. When they hit into a net, all they are focused on is if they are learning how to swing properly. When these golfers begin to demonstrate a competent swing, they can go out on to the driving range.

If all good performance starts with a clear goal, how do you know a clear goal when you have one? For a goal to be clear, people need to know what they are being asked to do (their areas of accountability) and what good performance looks like (the performance standards by which they will be evaluated).

Areas of Accountability

One of the biggest obstacles to productivity improvement is the problem of unclear organisational expectations and accountability. For example, when people are asked what they do and their managers are asked what their people do, they both typically give widely divergent answers, particularly if the group is asked to prioritise its list of responsibilities. As a consequence, individuals in organisations often get punished for not doing what they didn't know they were supposed to do.

At times, the people management deems most responsible for a specific activity may be completely unaware of their role. For example, a group of restaurant managers concerned about sales were asked, "Who is responsible for generating sales in your organisation?" They said the waiters and waitresses were. But when the waiters and waitresses were asked what their primary responsibilities were, their reply was consistently "Serving food and taking orders." They made no reference to selling. So, although it may seem very basic, managers need to make sure their people know what is expected of them.

Performance Standards

People must also know what good performance looks like. Performance standards help managers and direct reports more easily monitor performance, and they serve as a basis for evaluation. Whether an organisation has clear performance standards can be determined by asking people, "Are you doing a good job?" Most people will respond by saying either "I don't know" or "I think so." If they answer "Yes, I think so," a revealing follow-up question would be "How do you know?" Typical responses are "I haven't been chewed out by my boss lately" or "No news is good news." Such answers imply that people receive little feedback on their performance until they make a mistake. This is a sad state of affairs. That habitual practice by managers leads to the most commonly used management style in the West: leave-alone-then-zap. This style of management can also be called "seagull management." When someone makes a mistake, seagull managers fly in, make a lot of noise, dump on everyone, and fly out. Since this is the predominant style of management in organisations, it is no wonder that motivating people is a major organisational problem today.

Scott Meyers, a longtime consultant in the field of motivation, made the same point using a novel analogy.[3] Meyers was struck by the number of unmotivated people in organisations. Yet he had never seen an unmotivated person after work. Everyone seemed to be motivated to do something.

One night when Meyers was bowling, he saw some of the "problem" employees from the last organisation where he worked. One of the least motivated people—someone he remembered all too well—took the bowling ball, approached the line, and rolled the ball. The employee started to yell and jump around. Why do you think he was so happy? The answer was obvious to Meyers: The employee got a strike. He knew he had performed well—he had knocked down all the pins.

Goals Need to Be Clear

The reason people are not jumping for joy in organisations, Meyers contended, is that, in part, it is not clear what is expected of them. To continue his bowling analogy, when people approach the alley, they notice there are no pins at the end; that is, they don't know what their goals are. How long would you want to bowl without pins? Yet, every day in the world of work, people are bowling without any pins, and, as a result, they cannot tell how well they are doing. Managers know what they want their people to do; they just don't bother to tell them. They assume people know. Never assume anything when it comes to goal setting.

Reaching Goals Requires Feedback

When managers assume that their people know what's expected of them, they are creating a second ineffective form of bowling. They put up the pins, but when bowlers go to roll the ball, they notice there is a sheet across the alley. When they roll the ball and it slips under the sheet, they hear a crack, but they don't know how many pins they knocked down. When asked how they did, they say, "I don't know, but it felt good."

It's like playing golf at night. A lot of our friends have given up golf. When we ask them why, they say, "The courses are too crowded." When we suggest they play at night, they laugh, because who would ever play golf without being able to see the flags? To move towards goals, people need feedback on their performance.

The number one motivator of people is feedback on results.

As former colleague Rick Tate often said, "Feedback is the breakfast of champions." Can you imagine training for the Olympics with no one telling you how fast you ran or how high you jumped? The idea seems ludicrous, yet many people operate in a vacuum in organisations, not knowing how well they are doing on their jobs.

Money motivates people only if it is feedback on results. Have you ever gotten a pay rise that you were pleased with, only to find out that somebody else who you don't think works as hard as you got the same or even better? Not only was that increase in money not *motivating*, it became *demotivating* once you knew it had nothing to do with results. Suddenly, it didn't matter how hard you worked.

Once managers are convinced that the number one motivator of people is feedback on results, they usually set up a third form of bowling. When the bowler goes to the line to roll the ball, the pins are up and the sheet is still in place, but now the game has another ingredient: a superviser standing behind the sheet. When bowlers roll the ball, they hear the crash of the falling pins. The superviser holds up two fingers and says, "You knocked down two." In fact, most bosses would not phrase the feedback so positively, but would say, "You missed eight."

Performance Reviews Can Undermine Performance

Why don't managers lift the sheet so that everyone can see the pins? Because organisations have a strong tradition known as *the performance review*. We call it NIHYYSOB ("Now I have you, you

SOB."). Sadly, many managers use the performance review as a once-a-year opportunity to get even with their people.

As we indicated in the last chapter, the performance review process is often used to spread people over a normal distribution curve, thereby categorising them and distorting their performance. Having a set budget or per centage for a group's salary increases often encourages this practice. In most organisations, if six or seven people report to you, the practice of rating them all high—even if they all deserve it—is discouraged. It doesn't take managers very long to realise that if they rate all their people high, they subsequently get rated low by *their* managers. The only way they can get rated high is if they rate some of their people low.

One of a manager's toughest jobs is deciding who gets the low ratings. Most of us grow up with this win–lose mentality, in which some people in every group must lose. It pervades our educational system. For example, a teacher giving 10- to 11-year-olds a test on capitals would never consider making atlases available during the test to allow the students to look up the answers. Why? Because all the children would get 100 per cent. Can you imagine what would happen to education if kids who had to take vocabulary tests were allowed to keep dictionaries on their desks? There would be an uproar!

Limit the Number of Goals

Three to five goals are the ideal number on which peak performers can concentrate, according to most research.[4] Once these goals are established, they should be written down so that they can be frequently used to compare actual behaviour to targeted behaviour.

Often, goal setting is considered a paperwork activity—a necessary evil in getting the job done. When this is the case, goals are filed and people go off and do whatever they want until a performance review draws near. With one minute goal setting, the philosophy is that you should keep your goals close at hand and be able to read each in a minute or less.

Good Goals Are SMART Goals

Although most managers agree with the importance of setting goals, many do not take the time to clearly develop goals with their people and write them down. As a result, people tend to get caught in the "activity trap," where they become busy doing things, but not necessarily the right things. To focus on what *is* important, you should set SMART goals with your people. SMART is an acronym for the most important factors in setting quality goals:

Specific and measurable. You have to be specific about the area that needs improvement and what good performance looks like. Being specific reinforces the old saying "If you can't measure it, you can't manage it." Therefore, goals have to be specific, observable, and measurable. If somebody says, "But my job can't be measured," offer to eliminate it to see if anything will be missed.

Motivating. Not every job people are asked to do will be super-exciting, but having motivating goals helps. Sometimes all people need to know is why the task is important. People want to know that what they do makes a difference. That's motivating.

Attainable. What really motivates people is to have moderately difficult but achievable goals. This has been proven time and again by setting up a version of the old ring toss game. People are asked to throw rings at a stake from any distance they choose. Unmotivated people, it has been found, stand either very close to the stake, where the goal is easily accomplished, or far away, where their chances of success are minimal. High achievers, based on classic research on achievement motivation conducted by David McClelland, find the appropriate distance from the stake through experimentation.[5] If they throw the rings from a certain spot and make most of their tosses, they move back. Why? It's too easy a goal. If they miss most of their tosses, they move forward. Why? It's too difficult a task. McClelland found that high achievers like to set moderately difficult but attainable goals—that is, goals that stretch them but are not impossible. That's what we mean by attainable.

Relevant. As we stated earlier, we believe in the 80/20 rule. Eighty per cent of the performance you want from people comes from the 20 per cent of the activities they could get involved in. Therefore, a goal is relevant if it addresses one of the 20 per cent activities that make a difference in overall performance.

Trackable and time-bound. To praise progress or redirect inappropriate behaviour, managers must be able to measure performance frequently. This means using a record-keeping system and timeline to track performance. If a goal consists of completing a report by 1 June, the chances of receiving an acceptable, even outstanding, report will increase if interim reports are required and progress is praised along the way.

One Minute Praisings

Once your people understand what they are being asked to do and what good behaviour looks like, you are ready for the second key to obtaining desired performance: the one minute praising. Praising is the most powerful activity a manager can do. In fact, it is the key to training people and making winners of everyone working for you. A praising focuses on reinforcing behaviour that moves people closer to their goals.

Of all the keys of the One Minute Manager,
one minute praisings are the most powerful.

Look around your organisation and see if you can "catch people doing something right." When you do, give them a one minute praising that is immediate and specific and that states your feelings.

Be Immediate and Specific

For a praising to be effective, it must be *immediate* and *specific*. Tell people exactly what they did right as soon as possible. For example, "You submitted your report on time Friday, and it was well written. In fact, I used it in a meeting today, and that report made you and me and our whole department look good." Comments that are too general, such as "I appreciate your efforts" and "Thank you very much," are less likely to seem sincere and thus are unlikely to be effective.

State Your Feelings

After you praise people, tell them how you feel about what they did. Don't intellectualise. State your gut feelings: "I felt so happy and proud after hearing your financial report presentation at the Board of Directors meeting. I'm delighted you're on our team. Thanks so much." Although praisings do not take very long, they can have lasting effects.

Praisings Are Universally Powerful

Praisings drive all effective human interaction. These same concepts apply to any relationship, not only making people better managers, but also making them better parents, spouses, friends, and customers. Consider marriage, for example.

When you first fall in love, everything is right. You seldom see the faults or limitations of your loved one. Love is blind—you see only the positive. When you decide to get married or commit to some permanency in your relationship, you often start to see things wrong with each other. You begin to say such things as "I didn't know you thought that" or "I can't believe you would do something like that." Your emphasis shifts to what's wrong with the other person, rather than what's right. The ultimate demise of a loving relationship is when you do something right and you get yelled at anyway because you didn't do it right enough. You hear things like "I shouldn't have to ask" or "You should have done it earlier."

How do two people go from being excited about each other to squabbling? It's really quite simple. Good relationships are all about the frequency with which you catch each other doing something right.

Being Close Counts

This discussion brings up one of the important points to remember about praising: Don't wait for exactly the right behaviour before praising someone. Catch people doing things approximately right. We want exactly right behaviour, but if we wait for exactly right behaviour before we recognise it, we'll probably never get it. We have to remember that exactly right behaviour is made up of a whole series of approximately right behaviours. We all know that with animals and little people—we just forget it with big people.

For example, suppose you want to teach a child who is learning to speak to say, "Give me a glass of water, please." If you wait until the child says the whole sentence before you give her any water, the child will die of thirst. So you start off by saying, "Water! Water!" All of a sudden one day the child says "waller." You jump all over the place, hug and kiss the child, and get Grandmother on the phone so the child can say, "Waller, waller." It isn't "water," but it's close.

You don't want a kid going into a restaurant at the age of 21 asking for a glass of waller, so after a while you only accept the word "water," and then you start on "please." So in training someone, you should emphasise catching that person doing something right—in the beginning, approximately right—and then gradually moving them towards the desired behaviour.

Bob Davis, former president of Chevron Chemical, has as one of his favourite mottos "Praise progress—at least it's a moving target." What we need to do in all our interactions at work and at home is accentuate the positive and catch people doing things right, even if it's only approximately right.

If you are having difficulty with a spouse, child, team member, boss, or friend, you have to first ask yourself, "Do I want this relationship to work?" Examine your gut feelings. If deep down you don't want to make the relationship work, you won't. Why? Because you have control of the qualifier—the "Yes, but..." If you want to make the relationship work, you will catch the other person doing things right or approximately right. But if you don't want to make it work for whatever reason, you can easily undermine another person's best efforts to please you. No matter what that person does right, you will say, "Yes, but you didn't do this or that right."

Make Time for Praisings

We ask people all the time, "How many of you are sick and tired of all the praisings you get at work or at home?" Everybody laughs, because most of us do not naturally think of cheering each other on. Yet we all know people who carry around in their wallet or pocketbook a praising note they got years ago. It seems "gotcha" comes more easily to most of us than "well done." How do we break this pattern? Maybe we need to be more intentional about it.

You should set aside at least two hours a week for cheering people on. Write it on your calendar, just as you would any other appointment. Then, use the Hewlett-Packard philosophy of Management by Wandering Around.[6] Wander around your operation, catch people doing things right or approximately right, and tell them about it. Do the same with your spouse, children, and friends. At home, you may not need two hours a week, but ten minutes surely wouldn't hurt.

Reprimanding Versus Redirection

If one minute praisings are focused on catching people doing things right and accentuating the positive, the question that inevitably arises is, "That's all well and good. What do you do if somebody's performance is not up to snuff?"

Although the label for the third secret of the One Minute Manager is the one minute reprimand, there are actually two strategies for dealing with poor performance: one minute reprimands and redirection. A reprimand works best with people who have "won't do" or attitudinal problems. These people are winners, and they know how to do what they are being asked to do, but for some reason they're not doing it. Redirection is appropriate for people with "can't do" or experience problems. These people are learners and therefore do not yet know how to do what they are being asked to do.

If there are two different strategies for dealing with poor performance, why is the one minute reprimand highlighted in *The One Minute Manager*? Because people generally are not very good at giving negative feedback to normally good performers. While that is still true, Ken is quick to admit that today he would probably highlight redirection. Why? Because things are changing so fast now in most fields that people's competency to do a job is often short-lived.

Ongoing learning is necessary for all of us to keep up today. As a result, there are far fewer situations where a one minute reprimand is more appropriate than redirection. That's one of the main reasons why Ken got excited about writing *Whale Done!: The Power of Positive Relationships* with one of his old writing buddies, Jim Ballard, and with Thad Lacinak and Chuck Tompkins, who've been training killer whales for more than 30 years.[7] It doesn't take much intelligence to realise that it wouldn't make sense to punish a killer whale and then tell its trainers to get in the water with it. Thad and Chuck point out that there is no negative interaction between killer whales and trainers. When a whale does something right or approximately right, a praising follows. That's why, when a whale successfully performs a trick and returns to the stage, it is greeted with a bucket of fish, a rub on its tongue, or a big hug. If the trick wasn't up to standard, when the whale returns to the stage, the trainers don't yell at it or punish it in any way. They simply give a hand signal that says to the whale,

"Let me see that again." If trainers can't be positive with a whale, redirection comes into play.

Because there is a distinct difference between redirection and a reprimand, let's take a look at each separately.

One Minute Reprimands

As we said earlier, a reprimand is appropriate only for someone who has the skills to do the job but for some reason lacks the commitment. Keeping that in mind, consider the four keys to giving a reprimand:

- First, as with one minute praising, **reprimand as soon as possible** after an incident. Do not save up your feelings. If you suppress and store up your feelings, when you finally let go of them, they are apt to be out of proportion to the event that triggered your emotional release. The longer you wait to give someone negative feedback, the more emotional it becomes, so give negative feedback as soon as possible. Doing so causes fewer problems.

- Second, **be specific**. Tell people specifically what they did wrong—for example, "John, you didn't get your report in on time Friday" or "I notice your sales were down 20 per cent this quarter."

- Third, **share your feelings** about what was done. "Let me tell you how I feel about the late report, John. I'm angry because everyone else got their reports in on time, and not having your report delayed my analysis of our market position. It really frustrated me." Don't intellectualise about what the person did wrong. Focus on your feelings, and describe them sincerely and honestly.

- Fourth—and this is probably the most important step— **reaffirm the person**. In the case of the late report, you might say: "Let me tell you one other thing. You're good.

You're one of my best people. That's why I was angry about your late report. It's so unlike you. I count on you to set an example for others. That's why I won't let you get away with that late report behaviour. You're better than that."

Reprimand the Behaviour, Not the Person

Many people can't understand why you would praise people after you have reprimanded them. You do it for two very important reasons. First, you want to separate people's behaviour from them as individuals. That is, you want to keep the people but get rid of their poor behaviour.

By reaffirming people after you have reprimanded them, you focus on their behaviour without attacking them personally.

Second, when you walk away after reprimanding, you want people to think about what they did wrong, not about how you treated them. If no reaffirmation is done, people who are reprimanded tend to redirect their energy to you, the reprimander. Why? Because of how they were treated. For example, many reprimands not only don't end with a praising, but end with a comment such as "And let me tell you one other thing..." and then the individual is given a parting shot: "If you think you'll get that promotion, you have another thing coming."

Then, when you walk away, the one who has been reprimanded often turns to a coworker and, instead of discussing his poor performance, talks about the incident and the manager's poor behaviour. That person is psychologically off the hook with his or her poor performance, and the manager becomes the villain.

However, if you end a reprimand with a praising, you just told the person how good he or she is. Now that person has to think about what he or she did wrong, not about your leadership style.

Many problems in life stem not from making mistakes,
but from not learning from them.

Whenever we do not learn from our mistakes, it is often because we are attacked for those mistakes. We are called names and generally downgraded by other people who discover our mistakes—good old seagull managers.

When our self-concept is under attack, we feel the need to defend ourselves and our actions, even to the extent of distorting the facts. When people become defensive, they never hear the feedback they are getting. As a result, little learning takes place. The effective use of the one minute reprimand with someone who makes a mistake should eliminate this defensive behaviour.

Remember, people are okay.
It is just their behaviour that is
sometimes a problem.

The proper use of the one minute reprimand helps communicate important information necessary to get poor performance back on track.

Redirection

When people's performance isn't up to standard and they are still learning, redirection is more appropriate than a reprimand.

An effective redirection response has several key aspects:

- When people who are still learning do something wrong, the first thing you have to do is **make sure they know that they have made a mistake** or that a problem exists. **Be specific**. Share what happened clearly and without blame. For example, if a customer did not receive the correct order, the person responsible in the shipping department needs to know that.

- Second, ***the person being redirected needs to know the negative impact*** that the error caused. You might say, "One of our best customers was really upset. She needed that order for a sales presentation, and the fact that it didn't arrive on time resulted in a less-than-stellar presentation."

- Third, ***the manager*** in this situation, if appropriate, ***should take the blame for not making the task clear***. Maybe the order was unclear. "It's my responsibility that you get the best information possible so that you can do your job right."

- Fourth, ***go over the task in detail, and make sure it is clearly understood***. "To rally from this mistake, we need to overnight exactly what the customer ordered. If necessary, we might have to get someone to hand-deliver the order. We must do everything we can to make this situation right. Let's double-check the order so that we're all on the same page."

- The final aspect of a redirection response is to ***express your continuing trust and confidence in the person***. "I appreciate your enthusiasm and desire to learn. I still have confidence that you can be excellent in this role."

As is evident, these steps are similar to the one minute reprimand. The big difference is that redirection focuses on teaching as the person is still learning, while the reprimand is focused on getting people back using the skills they already have. In both cases, the goal is not to tear people down, but to build them up in a way that they will return to top performance with a reprimand or continue to learn with redirection.

Praisings and Redirection Are Key to Partnering for Performance

The fourth step in partnering for performance is delivering the appropriate leadership style. Again, as a leader you are constantly looking for opportunities to move your leadership style forward so that you can eventually get to delegating. As people's performance increases, praising their progress is key to supporting their efforts. If at any time their performance stalls or moves backwards, rather than reprimanding or punishing them, the best strategy is to redirect and get them back on course. As managers manage by wandering around, it behooves them to praise progress and/or redirect. That is how you teach your people the right answers, so that when they get to the final exam—the performance review— they have the best opportunity to get an A.

Where does that leave reprimands? Again, reprimands can be helpful when performance is declining because of an attitude problem, not a skill problem. As we discussed in the last chapter, a reprimand can play a key role when decommitment is detected early.

The follow-up book to *The One Minute Manager*, *Putting the One Minute Manager to Work*, by Ken Blanchard and Robert Lorber, shows practising managers how to apply the three secrets—one minute goals, one minute praisings, and one minute reprimands or redirection—to improve performance on an ongoing basis.[8]

The Fourth Secret of the One Minute Manager

Shortly after Ken Blanchard and Spencer Johnson's *The One Minute Manager* came out, a top manager wrote to Ken and expressed how much he enjoyed the three secrets of the one minute manager. But he suggested that managers aren't always right. He insisted that managers make mistakes all the time. "I think the fourth secret of the one minute manager should be the one minute apology," he said.

That resonated with Ken, because his mother always said, "Two phrases that are not used enough in the world that could make it a better place are 'Thank you' and 'I'm sorry.'" One minute praising covered thank you, but the three secrets didn't cover I'm sorry. That's when Ken and Margret McBride decided to write *The Fourth Secret of the One Minute Manager: A Powerful Way to Make Things Better*.[9]

The One Minute Apology

As with praisings, reprimands, and redirection, the one minute apology has several key aspects:

- A one minute apology *begins with honesty*. That starts with your being truthful and admitting to yourself that you've done something wrong and need to make up for it. The key here is a willingness to take full responsibility for your actions and any harm done to anyone else.

- A one minute apology *ends with integrity*. This involves recognising that what you did or failed to do is wrong and inconsistent with who you want to be. It is important that you reaffirm that you are better than your poor behaviour and forgive yourself.

- Once these two things are done, your focus has to be on making amends to that person for the harm you caused.

- Finally, commit to yourself and others not to repeat what you did wrong, and keep this commitment by changing your behaviour.

What would an apology look like? Suppose at a meeting you kept interrupting a colleague, not permitting her to finish a thought. When another of your associates points this out after the meeting, you have a big aha, realising that what you did was wrong and not beneficial to your team.

As soon as possible, go to the offended person and say something like, "I got some feedback about how I kept interrupting you at the meeting today and not letting you finish. I want to apologise, because I recognise the truth in that feedback, and I feel bad. That's not who I want to be. In fact, I think I'm better than that. I promise I will never do that again. How can I make amends for what I did today?"

History would have been rewritten if President Nixon had quickly apologised for Watergate when what happened became clear. The same holds true for President Clinton and the Monica

Lewinsky incident. When President Kennedy took full responsibility for the Bay of Pigs debacle, even the press didn't have much more to talk about.

A one minute apology can be an effective way to correct a mistake you have made and restore the trust needed for a good relationship. Adding the one minute apology to goal setting, praising, reprimanding, and redirection makes partnering for performance a real give-and-take process where admitting your vulnerability can be more of a rule than an exception. Effective one-on-one leadership relationships depend on trust, and trust can occur only when we can get out of our own way and be authentic as we work with our people.

Are there other tools that can be applied to one-on-one relationships? Absolutely. In the next chapter, you'll see how coaching can be used to develop people's leadership skills.

Chapter 9

COACHING: A KEY COMPETENCY FOR LEADERSHIP DEVELOPMENT

Linda Miller
and Madeleine Homan Blanchard

In companies all over the world, surveys are showing that a leadership shortage is coming soon. Future leaders are needed in all industry sectors and functional areas and at all levels within organisations. The development of new leaders is becoming an important focus for executives and senior managers. More and more, coaching is being recognised as one of the key competencies that effectively develops future leaders.

A 2008 American Management Association study found that coaching is associated with higher performance in organisations, yet it is used by only about half of today's companies. Coaching continues to gain in popularity, and the field offers great growth opportunities.[1] The AMA concluded its report by stating: "We expect that coaching will become one of the keys to developing and retaining scarce talent in the future, and we think companies that learn to leverage it well will have a significant competitive advantage in the global marketplace."

Definition of Coaching

When we talk about coaching in this context, we are expanding our definition far beyond the **coaching** leadership style described in Situational Leadership® II. In the narrow definition, a coaching leadership style involves providing the appropriate direction and support needed when disillusionment sets in, either because a task is more complicated than anticipated or circumstances have caused a change in attitude. Coaching as we describe it in this chapter is a broader term that encompasses several applications. We define this broader term as follows:

> Coaching is a deliberate process using focused conversations to create an environment that results in individual growth, purposeful action, and sustained improvement.

Regardless of people's function or position, successful coaching encourages them to be deliberate, purposeful, and fully aligned with team and organisational objectives as they make decisions and take action. Central to coaching is a focus on self responsibility, forward movement, and taking intentional action.

Five Applications of Coaching

Coaching can be provided for leaders in organisations by the use of external coaches or managers and HR professionals trained to provide coaching as one of their job responsibilities. In our discussion, all the examples used focus on internal coaches. Regardless of who performs the coaching, it has five common applications:

- **Performance coaching** is used when individuals need help returning their performance to acceptable standards.
- **Development coaching** is used when high-performing individuals are ready to become more fully rounded in their current role.

- **Career coaching** is employed when individuals are ready to plan their next career moves.
- **Coaching to support learning** occurs when managers or direct reports need support, encouragement, and accountability to sustain recent training and turn insights into action.
- **Creating an internal coaching culture** is what happens when leaders recognise the value of coaching and use it to develop others.

After working with thousands of people in organisations, we have found that many managers and leaders spend the majority of their time dealing with performance challenges. With the leadership shortage ahead, it is important to shift from managing performance to focusing on development. As shown in Figure 9.1, while coaching sometimes involves discussions or conversations about performance and career, the coaching sweet spot centres on development.

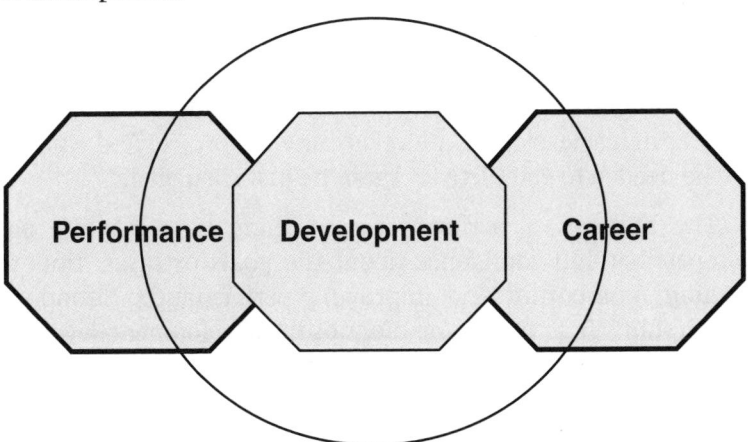

Figure 9.1   The Coaching Sweet Spot

Let's take a deeper look at the five applications of coaching.

Application One: Performance Coaching

Performance coaching is needed when individuals have been capable and confident about goals or tasks in the past, but their present performance no longer reflects that. Often they seem to be regressing. This usually results from a change in attitude, not skills.

Let's take the example of Erin and Max:

> For the past two years, Erin knew that Max could deliver on his key responsibility areas without much direction. However, over the past three months Erin has noticed that Max isn't completing projects the way he used to. Being extremely busy, Erin hadn't scheduled regular one-on-ones to check in with Max. Finally, she called him into her office.

> "You missed that last deadline," Erin said to Max. "What's going on?"

> With a shrug he said, "What's the big deal with missing one deadline? We have lots of time to take care of it. I'll get it by next week."

> Surprised by his comment, Erin asked Max where he was in his development level around the project and what he needed to complete it. Again he just shrugged.

The purpose of performance coaching is to reignite past competence and confidence about the goals or tasks, thus regaining momentum and improving performance. Situational Leadership® II is useful for diagnosing development level and matching the leadership style that's needed.

> Erin was concerned about Max's response. After observing him for several months, she decided it was time to give him feedback.

"Max, I want to share with you what I've noticed the past few months. Prior to January, you seemed to enjoy the team and the work we were doing. On most of the projects and goals, you have been either a capable but cautious performer or a self-reliant achiever. You certainly haven't needed much direction from me. You've been a major contributor to this team's work for years, but lately you've been missing deadlines and keeping your door closed." Erin paused to look him in the eye. "What's going on?" she asked.

Max did not respond.

Erin continued, "We have a lot at stake with this project. I'm happy to give you more direction if that's what you need to continue moving forward. If we don't get the project done this week, our unit will hold up others who are relying on us for the next step. I need you to step back in, or I will have to get someone else involved."

Max raised his eyes and looked at Erin. "You don't have to do that. I admit I've gotten a little disillusioned about the project, but now that I hear from you how important it is, I'm ready to roll up my sleeves and tackle it."

Erin said, "Wonderful. You've been a great contributor to our team in the past, and I value your work. Let's keep in touch with the steps you're taking this week, because I want both of us to be successful with the deadline. When would be a good time for our next meeting?"

Tips for Performance Coaching

Managers and HR professionals who use coaching when performance is dropping need to be comfortable giving accurate and objective feedback. They need to be clear about what is at stake and who is accountable for what.

It's important to remain neutral when giving feedback and talking about consequences. It's also important to be clear that the person has a choice whether to make the changes. Come to an agreement about the changes that are needed. This step may take time and is not always as easy as it sounds.

Beware of being pulled off focus. Stay on track with the points you want to make. Take care not to come across as punishing. As much as possible, be positive and encouraging. Also be certain to clearly state the consequences if the agreed-upon goals are not met. To avoid confusion and misunderstandings, it's important to be clear in your mind about the consequences before you begin performance coaching conversations.

Application Two: Development Coaching

Most managers are so busy putting out fires that they overlook development conversations. They may forget that team members, like themselves, are energised and encouraged when their development is kept in mind.

Development coaching is useful when direct reports are doing well and are ready for the next steps. They may be functioning at a **self-reliant achiever** level (D4) on most of their projects and goals. They are ready to be more fully rounded in their current role. The responsibility remains primarily on the direct report for keeping development top of mind. Yet when the manager focuses on it too, it conveys an underlying message of trust and support to the team member.

Becca loved her job. She had been in it for four years, often taking on new responsibilities and projects. She also knew that she needed to be challenged more often so that she wouldn't get bored. One day she noticed that Aidan, her manager, had requested a meeting on her calendar. Because their company had many locations, she called Aidan at the meeting time.

"Hi, Becca. Thanks for calling and for being so prompt. I've always liked that about you. I've been thinking of you recently and realised we haven't talked about your development lately. You consistently are such a self-reliant achiever with your responsibilities and projects that I sometimes forget to talk with you about what's next for you in this role. Can we talk about that for a few minutes?"

Becca felt a rush of excitement. "That would be great," she said.

Development coaching is focused on encouraging and increasing opportunities that lead to further development in the same role. To keep people engaged and growing, it's important for managers to keep expanding people's capability whenever possible. This helps develop them as future managers or leaders.

When using coaching for development, a **supporting** style (S3) is useful. Be sure to listen for what's most important to the person and to ask probing questions. Be sure to ask what the team member thinks is a developmental opportunity and what ideas he or she has. Think about the conversation as a way of challenging and inspiring the person to think more broadly.

When Aidan heard the enthusiasm in Becca's voice, he continued. "Becca, what do you see as some development opportunities ahead?"

Becca replied, "You know, I would love to know more about the budgeting process for our team. I've always been fascinated by that area."

Aidan was pleased to hear that Becca had been thinking about her development, even though she hadn't brought it up before. "Becca, I think it's very timely that you're interested in budgeting, especially since we're about to start our budgeting process for next year. I've got a couple of people who might be good for you to connect with."

Tips for Development Coaching

When thinking about coaching to develop others, remember that either the team member or the manager can begin these conversations. When identifying a person's strengths and weaknesses, keep the emphasis on maximising strengths. Focus broadly on developmental opportunities for the person, but beware of making specific promises. Don't forget that introducing your direct reports to your network of professionals may be as important as finding a new project for them.

Application Three: Career Coaching

Career coaching is taking off in organisations as the need for leaders continues to increase. It's a strategy that retains talent and increases reserve strength over time. Even in flat organisations that don't have a lot of upward mobility, it's energising for people to talk about their future.

When should a manager broach these discussions? When a direct report is consistently functioning at a *self-reliant achiever* level, it's time to begin conversations about that person's career. Coaching at this time can help the direct report look ahead to where he or she wants to be in the next few years, and the leader, as coach, can assist in planning the next career moves.

Several signals can indicate that it's time to have a career discussion. When direct reports continually exceed expectations, they might be ready to grow. Has one of your direct reports told you he or she wants more responsibility? That can also be a sign. An obvious signal is when a direct report brings up the topic. But just because high-performers haven't asked to talk about their careers doesn't mean they don't want to. In the majority of cases, they do.

Leaders and managers might find career coaching conversations threatening, since they could lead to losing an important team member. Be sure to curb your anxiety about losing the person and move bravely into the discussion. Marshall Goldsmith's research shows that one of the reasons top performers leave a company is because nobody asked them to stay.[2] Conversations about career are opportunities to show your direct reports how valued they are. In the end, it's important to think about what's best for the direct report as well as for the organisation.

Don't avoid career coaching conversations because you think they take too much time. These are exactly the conversations that high-performers want to have to stay in the organisation. A gentle transition generally is less time-consuming than having to fill a position that's been vacated without discussion.

Career conversations are a time to challenge and encourage high-potential employees to keep developing as they look ahead. Focusing on the future creates a win for the organisation as well as the direct report. When part of the career strategy includes bringing people into the role that may be vacated, it creates a win for the manager, too.

As the following example shows, most employees look to their leaders for guidance and support in the career area:

> Hannah had been with her company for eight years when she started wondering what might be ahead. She knew it was time to talk with Niki, her manager. Niki had also been thinking about Hannah's development, but she hadn't said anything yet, except in conversations with colleagues.
>
> Hannah brought it up at their next one-on-one meeting. "Niki, I'd really like to talk with you about what's next for me. I've worked with you for several years, and most of the time I feel like I'm a self-reliant achiever in my tasks and goals. What's next?"
>
> Niki knew this conversation had been coming. She also knew that she didn't want to lose Hannah. Yet she knew that keeping her would stunt Hannah's growth, which ultimately wouldn't be good for their company.

"Hannah," Niki said, "I'm glad you're thinking about this. I've thought about it, too, and I apologise for not talking with you sooner. I'd love to hear your thoughts about your goals and how they support our corporate goals. Thanks for starting the conversation."

Hannah began by telling Niki about the things she was doing, being sure to mention that she was ready for new challenges and opportunities.

Niki listened carefully, thinking about where Hannah's skills and passion aligned with their organisation's needs. "Hannah, I'm thinking that a cross-functional project would be perfect for you and will expand your skills and network." Niki went on to describe the project.

"I'd love to get involved in that," said Hannah.

"Who could you be training to take over your job if this leads to a career change for you?" Niki asked.

Hannah thought for a moment. "I have a couple of people in mind."

Niki said, "Great. You'll have to reach out to them and see if they are ready and willing to take on your old role. Let's keep talking about this, okay?"

"Absolutely," said Hannah. Both she and Niki were pleased when the meeting ended.

Tips for Career Coaching

Hold career coaching conversations on a regular basis with your high-performing direct reports. Again, when a manager brings up the subject of careers, it's a proactive move that makes direct reports feel cared about. During these conversations, it's important to explore what the employee is thinking and how his or her ideas align with organisational objectives. Familiarise yourself with the career services your HR department offers and what information is available about job roles and their corresponding competencies. Share this information with your direct report as you talk about all aspects of the next steps: when, where, and how the person's career will move forward. Finally, be sure to offer resources and make introductions when needed.

Application Four: Coaching to Support Learning

People learn through training, and training is one of the best ways to develop people in your organisation. Training can enhance any number of areas: management, leadership, skills, processes, communication, and a host of other job-related areas. A major challenge with training, though, is narrowing the learning–doing gap—getting people to use what they've learned after the training. One of the best ways to maximise an organisation's investment in training is to do follow-up coaching.

We have found that coaching to support learning is most effective when the learning process is followed by at least three follow-up coaching conversations. These are conversations that managers, HR professionals, and internal or external coaches can have immediately after the training.

With as few as three coaching sessions during the eight-week period following a training event, participants consistently apply what they've learned. Having the first follow-up coaching session within two weeks of the training and continuing with a coaching session once every two to three weeks generates the best results. Each coaching conversation should be focused on how to apply information from the training to the workplace.

Here's an example of what it might look like to follow up training with coaching:

> Morgan loved to learn as part of her new manager training. Her company offered excellent training. She was pleased when her manager told her she could attend an advanced management course that focused on Situational Leadership® II. What she didn't know was that this course would be different, in that it included six months of follow-up coaching with an external professional coach.

During their first call, her coach, Kyle, asked Morgan what she had learned that would be helpful to implement on the job. This caused her to think about the material and revisit her notes. She realised that some of her interactions with her team members had not been going well. Kyle asked her what she could immediately apply from the training that would help with those conversations. First, Morgan realised that she tended to use the same leadership style with all her people. Diagnosing the specific development levels of her team members and determining the appropriate leadership style for each was eye-opening for her. She learned that having one-on-one meetings with her people would not only help their relationships, but also would help her apply what she had learned.

Kyle asked Morgan what actions she was willing to take between this call and the next to move forward in these areas. Morgan agreed to schedule one-on-one meetings with each of her people before her next call with Kyle.

Tips for Coaching to Support Learning

It's important to get started with the coaching as soon as possible after the training event. Have a system in place to get people scheduled with their first and subsequent sessions. Focus on how your direct reports can apply their new learning to their jobs. Help them identify action items and obstacles to action.

Don't fall into the trap of debating the point of the training. The purpose of the coaching is to help your people apply the learning, not to debate the learning itself. Stay focused on action. Coaching to support learning is a time to talk about how to use the material in the real world.

Finally, don't use the excuse that you don't have time for coaching to support learning. Remember that time spent coaching maximises the investment in training, empowers you and your direct reports, and saves time down the road.

Application Five: Creating an Internal Coaching Culture

The best way for coaching to positively impact an organisation is to create your own internal coaching culture. This can happen only when leaders and managers recognise the value of coaching and use it to develop people for much-needed future leadership roles.

In *Coaching in Organisations*, Madeleine Homan and Linda Miller contend that creating an internal coaching climate has a number of benefits.[3] Not only does coaching emphasise leadership development, but it also fosters a mentality of taking ownership for work that is done. A coaching culture is a culture of self-responsibility rather than blaming or pointing to others when things go awry. Even though it takes a while to cultivate, this type of culture creates a wonderful work environment that supports productivity and boosts morale.

It can take 12 to 18 months to roll out an internal coaching culture. The ramp-up and rollout process may include coach training for managers and leaders, mentor coaching for those who are learning how to coach others, and time to develop the support systems and measurement strategies that ensure success.

The following example shows the extent of thinking that must be done prior to establishing an internal coaching culture:

> When Rob realised how much he loved coaching and how important it could be for his manufacturing company, he wasted no time in interviewing coaching companies with which he could partner. The company he hired assigned a team lead, Alec, to work with Rob because Alec knew coaching and had experience setting up coaching systems in other companies. When Rob and Alec first met face to face, Alec began asking questions.
>
> "Rob, we need to address several areas before we go any further with this project. First, what does coaching mean to you, and what do you expect coaching to do for your company?"

Rob responded, "Since I've been working with my coach over the past year, I've experienced such great growth. My team has become much more productive than it was, and this has gained the attention of senior leadership. They're asking me what I'm doing differently. The only thing I'm doing differently is coaching my team. I think it's time for others to get the same experience, and I want to lead the way here in our company."

"How will you get senior-level sponsorship and clarity on the objectives for the coaching?" Alec asked.

Rob replied, "Our CEO and COO have already bought in. Your question about the objectives is interesting. I think I need to do a bit more work on that. I'm not sure we're clear enough on the objectives."

Alec nodded. "While you're talking about the objectives, be sure to ask how your top managers want the outcomes measured. Many organisations are measuring the success of coaching by thinking about ROE, return on expectations, rather than ROI, return on investment."

Rob agreed. "Yes, it would be good to figure that out now. We're a company that's big on ROI, so I'll start talking about the difference. I know that measuring this type of thing can be challenging, and we'll need to talk more about it down the road."

"That's for sure," said Alec. "The clearer you can be on what you want to measure and how you'll go about measuring it, the better. You'll also want to agree with senior leaders on what information is shared and what is kept confidential. Keeping confidential the content of the coaching conversations is a critical part of coaching."

Rob nodded. From his own coaching experience, he knew immediately what Alec was talking about.

Tips for Creating an Internal Coaching Culture

First, define the purpose and objectives of the coaching culture, and make sure they fit with the organisation's purpose and values. Next, find senior leadership advocates who can role-model the coaching culture, and be sure to get administrative help to roll out the initiative. Reward coaching behaviours and activities, and set up an internal communication about the coaching to help cascade it throughout the organisation. Depending on who is available, it may be appropriate to provide professional coaches from outside the organisation.

As you take steps to create an internal coaching culture, you should watch for several things. First, be sure to define and honour confidentiality. One breach of confidentiality from coaching conversations can severely damage the entire coaching initiative. Second, remember that a coaching culture isn't established overnight. Allocate plenty of time to get started. Third, remember to stay flexible. If something isn't working, you can always change it.

The examples of Situational Leadership® II, partnering for performance, and now coaching have focused on one-on-one relationships. The next step in the transformation leadership journey is towards groups. The following chapter focuses on creating high-performing teams.

Chapter 10

SITUATIONAL
TEAM LEADERSHIP

Don Carew, Eunice Parisi-Carew,
Lael Good, and Ken Blanchard

Teams have become a major strategy for getting work done. We live in teams. Our organisations are made up of teams. We move from one team to another without giving it a thought. The percentage of time we spend in team settings—project teams, work groups, cross-functional teams, virtual teams, and management teams—is ever-increasing. Managers typically spend between 30 and 99 per cent of their time in a meeting or team setting. In *High Five!: The Magic of Working Together*, Ken Blanchard, Sheldon Bowles, Don Carew, and Eunice Parisi-Carew show that being effective in today's organisations is a team game, and without collaboration and teamwork skills, a leader is unlikely to be successful.[1]

Why Teams?

Teams can execute better and faster than traditional hierarchies. They have the power to increase productivity and morale or destroy it. Working effectively, a team can make better decisions, solve more complex problems, and do more to enhance creativity and build skills than individuals working alone. The team is the only unit that has the flexibility and resources to respond quickly to changes that have become commonplace in today's world.

The business environment has become more competitive, and the issues it faces are increasingly complex. As we emphasised in Chapter 4, "Empowerment Is the Key," this challenging environment has caused organisations to realise that they can no longer depend on hierarchical structures and a few peak performers to maintain a competitive advantage. The demand is for collaboration and teamwork in all parts of the organisation. Success today comes from using the collective knowledge and richness of diverse perspectives. There is a conscious movement towards teams as the strategic vehicle for getting work accomplished and moving organisations into the future.

Fast-paced work environments require teams to operate virtually around the world. These geographically dispersed teams face special challenges in building trust, developing effective communication, and managing attentiveness.[2] However, with the proper leadership and technology, virtual teams are every bit as productive and rewarding as face-to-face teams.

Teams are not just nice to have. They are hard-core units of production.

It's a fact that people's health and well-being are directly affected by the amount of involvement they have in the workplace. Twelve thousand male Swedish workers were studied over a 14-year period. Workers who felt isolated and had little influence over their jobs were 162 per cent more likely to have a fatal heart attack than were those who had greater influence in decisions at work and who worked in teams.[3] Data like this—combined with the fact that teams can be far more productive than individuals functioning alone—provides a compelling argument for creating high-involvement workplaces and using teams as the central vehicle for getting work done.

Why Teams Fail

Teams are a major investment of time, money, and resources. The cost of allowing them to falter or underproduce is staggering. Even worse, a team meeting that is considered a waste of time has wide-ranging effects. The energy does not dissipate as you leave, but spills into every aspect of organisational life. If people leave a meeting feeling unheard, or if they disagree with a decision made in the team, they leave angry and frustrated. This impacts the next event. The opposite happens when meetings feel productive and empowering—the positive energy spreads.

Teams fail for a number of reasons, from lack of a clear purpose to lack of training. Following are the top ten reasons why a team fails to reach its potential. An awareness of the obstacles to optimal team performance can prepare team members and leaders to proactively address these issues.

Top 10 Reasons Why Teams Fail

1. Not taking time to clarify purpose and goals
2. Uncertainty about what requires team effort
3. Lack of mutual accountability
4. Lack of resources
5. Lack of effective leadership and/or shared leadership
6. Lack of focus on creativity and excellence
7. Lack of planning
8. Lack of support for a team culture
9. Inability to deal with conflict
10. Lack of training

Five Steps to High-Performing Teams

Working in a team is both an art and a science, and understanding the dynamics of teamwork has never been easy. However, after decades of research, we have identified five key processes that leaders can use to create high-performing teams (see Figure 10.1):

1. Benchmark your team with PERFORM.
2. Create a team charter.
3. Diagnose your team's development level.
4. Match leadership style to your team's development level.
5. Develop strategies for higher team performance.

This five-step method for increasing team effectiveness can be adapted to any team, regardless of its purpose, pursuit, type, or size.

Figure 10.1   Team Performance Process

To help you fully understand how the models interact and become a systematic process, the following overview of each step illustrates our approach.

Step One: Benchmark Your Team with PERFORM

We define a team as *two or more persons who come together for a common purpose and who are mutually accountable for results.* This is the difference between a team and a group. Often, work groups are called teams without developing a common purpose and shared accountability. This can lead to disappointing results and a belief that teams do not work well. A collection of individuals working on the same task are not necessarily a team. They have the potential to become a high-performing team once they clarify their purpose and values, strategies, and accountabilities.

Some teams achieve outstanding results no matter how difficult the objective. They are at the top of their class. What makes these teams different? What sets them apart and makes them capable of outperforming their peers? Although each team is unique, they all have characteristics that are shared by all outstanding teams regardless of their purpose or goals.

Building highly effective teams, like building a great organisation, begins with a picture of what you are aiming for—a target. It is imperative to know what a high-performing team is. That is why the Team Performance Process begins with PERFORM, an acronym that represents seven key characteristics found in all high-performing teams. These represent the gold standard for teams committed to excellence. By benchmarking your team in each of these areas, you can identify the areas where you need to focus team development.

Purpose and values are the glue that holds the team together and form the foundation of a high-performing team. Identifying a clear purpose is the first step in getting a team off to a good start. In high-performing teams, the team is dedicated to a common purpose and shared values. Team members understand the team's work and its importance, and strategies for achieving clear goals are agreed on.

Empowerment is what happens when the organisation supports the team in doing its work effectively. An empowered team has access to business information and resources. Team members have the authority to act and make decisions with clear boundaries, and they have a clear understanding of who is accountable for what.

Relationships and communication, both internal and external, are the team's lifeblood. Team members must respect and appreciate each other's differences and be willing to work towards the common good rather than individual agendas. When relationships and communication are running smoothly, trust, mutual respect, and team unity are high. Team members actively listen to one another for understanding. The team uses effective methods to find common ground and manage conflict.

Flexibility is the ability to adapt to constantly changing conditions and demands, with team members backing up and supporting one another as needed. In a flexible team, roles are shared as team members work together. Team members share in team development and leadership. Team members identify and use their individual strengths. The team anticipates change and readily adapts to it.

Optimal productivity is what's generated by a high-performing team. When operating at optimal productivity, the team consistently produces significant results. Its members are committed to high standards and measures for goal accomplishment. The team uses effective problem solving and decision making to achieve goals.

Recognition and appreciation are ongoing dynamics that build and reinforce productivity and morale by focusing on progress and the accomplishment of major milestones throughout the team's life. Everyone—including the team members, the team leader, and the larger organisation—is responsible for recognition and appreciation. When recognition and appreciation flourish, the team leader and members acknowledge individual and team accomplishments. The organisation values and recognises team contributions. Finally, team members feel highly regarded within the team.

Morale is the sense of pride and satisfaction that comes from belonging to the team and accomplishing its work. High morale is essential for sustaining performance over the long term. When morale is high, team members are confident and enthusiastic about their work. Everyone feels pride and satisfaction in being a part of the team. Team members trust one another.

After reviewing the characteristics of high-performing teams through the PERFORM model, most people's reaction is "Duh." If a team really had those characteristics, you'd better believe it would be effective.

For example, Ken was invited to a Boston Celtics practice during the heyday of Larry Bird, Robert Parish, and Kevin McHale. Standing on the sidelines with Coach KC Jones, Ken asked, "How do you lead a group of superstars like this?" KC smiled and said, "I throw the ball out and every once in a while shout 'Shoot!'" In observing Jones as a leader, Ken noticed he didn't follow any of the stereotypes of a strong leader. During time-outs, the players talked more than KC did. He didn't run up and down the sidelines yelling things at the players during the game; most of the coaching was done by the team members. They encouraged, supported, and directed each other.

This team really knew how to PERFORM. Everyone knew the team's *purpose and values*. They were *empowered* to get the job done. They had great *relationships* and *communicated* well with each other. They were *flexible* and changed plans as the need arose. They certainly got *optimum* performance. *Recognition* and support for each other was a way of life, and high *morale* was evident to everyone who watched them play.

When this low-key leader, KC Jones, retired, all the players essentially said he was the best coach they'd ever had. Why? Because he permitted everyone to lead, and that's what a team is all about.

Don Carew observed an extraordinary example of team leadership while working with Caterpillar's Track Type Tractors (TTT) division in Illinois.[4] The TTT division was in deep trouble. The lowest-performing division of the company, it was losing millions of dollars a year and had been involved in a bitter strike. The Blanchard team worked with TTT to implement a new set of values and behaviours based on trust, mutual respect, teamwork, empowerment, risk taking, and a sense of urgency. In less than three years, the company realised a $250 million turnaround. Quality as measured by customers improved by 16 times. Employee satisfaction moved from being the lowest in Caterpillar to being the highest. All of this was achieved by people at all levels working together in teams and by the organisation creating the conditions that supported teamwork, mutual respect, and trust.

Step Two: Create a Team Charter

Knowing where you are headed is the first step on the journey to high team performance. But just calling together a team and giving it a clear charge does not mean the team will become high-performing. As we've said, team leadership is much more complicated than one-on-one leadership. Yet managers typically spend more time preparing for a meeting with one of their people than they do with their team. Often people just don't get it: Managing a high-performing team takes considerable effort. One of the single most important things a team leader can do is set up the environment for and support the team in creating a team charter.

To create a solid foundation for the team's work, it's important to complete a team charter at this early point in the team's life cycle. A charter is a set of agreements that clearly states what the team is to accomplish, why it is important, and how the team will work together to achieve results. The charter documents common agreements, but it is also a dynamic document that can be modified as team needs change. Figure 10.2 shows a model for developing a charter.

Figure 10.2   The Team Charter

The team charter agreements directly link the team's purpose to the organisational vision and purpose. Team values and norms should reflect the organisation's values, as well as provide guidelines for appropriate behaviour within the team. Identifying team initiatives sets the foundation for determining goals and roles. This is when the team establishes strategies for communication, decision making, and accountability. If the team will need resources, they are identified at this time. Once completed, the charter provides a touchstone for making sure the team is on track. The team is now ready to move from planning to doing, and it will keep the charter visible and available to navigate the stages ahead.

Step Three: Diagnose Your Team's Development Level

Building a high-performing team is a journey—a predictable progression from a collection of individuals to a well-oiled system where all the PERFORM characteristics are evident.

All teams are unique and complex living systems. The whole of a team is different from the sum of its members. Knowing the characteristics and needs of a high-performing team is critical. It gives you a target to shoot for. Obviously, teams don't start with all the PERFORM characteristics in place. Research over the past 60 years has consistently demonstrated that, regardless of their purpose, teams, like individuals, go through a series of developmental stages as they grow.

All these comprehensive research efforts were surprisingly consistent in their conclusions.[5] They all identified either four or five stages of development and were very similar in their descriptions of the characteristics of each stage. After a comprehensive review of more than 200 studies on group development, Roy Lacoursiere identified five stages of team development (see Figure 10.3), which we will examine in detail in a moment:

1. Orientation
2. Dissatisfaction
3. Integration
4. Production
5. Termination

Understanding these development stages and a team's characteristics and needs at each stage is essential for team leaders and team members if they will be effective in building successful, productive teams.

That's what **diagnosis** is all about. The ability to determine a team's stage of development and assess its needs requires stepping back and looking at the team as a whole, rather than focusing on individual behaviours and needs.

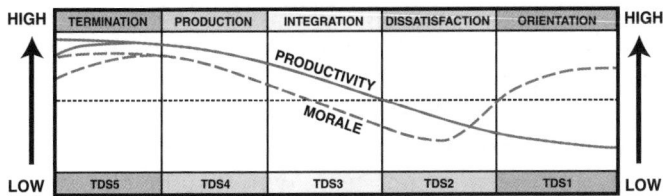

Figure 10.3   The Stages of Team Development Model[6]

Productivity and Morale

Two variables determine the team development stage: productivity and morale.

Productivity is the amount and quality of the work accomplished in relation to the team's purpose and goals. Productivity is dependent on members' ability to collaborate, their knowledge and skills, clear goals, and access to needed resources. **Morale** is the sense of pride and satisfaction that comes from belonging to the team and accomplishing its work.

Productivity often starts out low. When a group first comes together, they can't accomplish very much. They don't even know each other. Over time, as they learn to work together, their performance should gradually increase. If that is not the case, something is seriously wrong. Either they have a leadership problem, or the skills necessary to perform well are not present in the group.

Morale, on the other hand, starts out high and takes a sudden dip. People are usually enthusiastic about being on a new team, unless they've been forced to join. The initial euphoria dissipates quickly when the reality of the difficulty of working on a team comes into play. Now you might hear people say, "Why did I agree to be on that team?" As differences are explored and people begin to break through initial frustrations and working together becomes easier, the team begins to achieve results, and morale begins to rise again. Ultimately, both morale and productivity are high as a group becomes a high-performing team.

Why are high morale and high productivity the ultimate goals? High morale with no performance is a party, not a team. On the other hand, a team that is achieving good results yet has low morale will eventually stumble, and its performance will fade. The bottom line is that both productivity and morale are required to produce a high-performing team with sustainable results.

Diagnosing the level of productivity and morale is a clear way to determine a team's development stage and understand team needs at any point in time.

Team Development Stage 1 (TDS1): Orientation

Most team members, unless coerced, are fairly eager to be on the team. However, they often come with high, unrealistic expectations. These expectations are accompanied by some anxiety about how they will fit in, how much they can trust others, and what demands will be placed on them. Team members are also unclear about norms, roles, goals, and timelines.

In this stage, team members depend strongly on the leader for purpose and direction. Some testing of boundaries occurs, and the central leader's behaviour is usually tentative and polite. Morale is moderately high and productivity is low during this stage.

Two of us were asked to serve on a project team to study and modify the compensation system for our consulting partners. At the first meeting, we were excited and eager to see who else was a part of the project team. Many complaints about the system had been registered, and we were eager to make positive changes. We were apprehensive about if "they" would really listen. We also wondered how much time this would take, who would be in charge of the team, and how we would fit in with the other members. We had no idea how to proceed or even what our goals should be. We looked to the team leader to steer us in the right direction. These feelings of excitement, anxiety, and dependence on the leader are normal for team members at Stage 1.

The challenge at the orientation stage is to get the team off to a good start by developing purpose and structure for the team, as well as building relationships and trust.

The duration of this stage depends on the clarity and difficulty of the task, as well as clarity about how the team will work together. With simple, easily defined tasks, the orientation stage may be relatively short—5 to 10 per cent of the team's life. On the other hand, with complex goals and tasks, the team may spend 30 to 60 per cent of its time in this stage.

Team Development Stage 2 (TDS2): Dissatisfaction

As the team gets some experience under its belt, morale dips as team members experience a discrepancy between their initial expectations and reality. Reluctant team members start out in Stage 2. The difficulties in accomplishing the task and in working together lead to confusion and frustration, as well as a growing dissatisfaction with dependence on the leader. Negative reactions to each other develop, and subgroups form that can polarise the team. The breakdown of communication and the inability to solve problems result in lowered trust. Productivity increases somewhat but may be hampered by low morale.

Back to that compensation project team we just mentioned: While we started off with enthusiasm, we quickly realised how much hard work would be involved, the goal's controversial nature, and the possibility that recommendations we would make might not be accepted. We began to experience some strong negative feelings among members, and subgroups began to form. Frustration with the team leader began to develop. We started to wonder if this was worth our time. These feelings of questioning, doubt, and frustration are typical of team members during Stage 2.

The challenge in the dissatisfaction stage is helping the team manage issues of power, control, and conflict and to begin to work together effectively.

The amount of time spent in this stage depends on how quickly issues can be resolved. It is possible for the team to get stuck at the dissatisfaction stage and to continue being both demoralised and relatively unproductive.

Team Development Stage 3 (TDS3): Integration

Moderate to high productivity and variable or improving morale characterise a team at the integration stage. As issues encountered in the dissatisfaction stage are addressed and resolved, morale begins to rise. The team develops practices that allow members to work together more easily. Task accomplishment and technical skills increase, which contributes to positive feelings. Increased clarity and commitment to purpose, values, norms, roles, and goals occur. Trust and cohesion grow as communication becomes more open and task-orientated. Team members are willing to share leadership and control.

You will never, never, never have a high-performing team unless leadership and control are shared.

Team members learn to appreciate the differences among themselves. The team starts thinking in terms of "we" rather than "I." Because the newly developed feelings of trust and cohesion are fragile, team members tend to avoid conflict for fear of losing the positive climate. This reluctance to deal with conflict can slow progress and lead to less effective decisions.

Back to our project team: As we began resolving the frustrations we experienced in Stage 2, we began listening more carefully and came to appreciate different points of view. We developed some initial strategies for accomplishing our team purpose and clarified our goal and roles. In spite of the difficulty of achieving our goal, working with the team now became more fun. People were getting along, and at every meeting we were more clearly seeing what needed to be done. We even began to see the possibility of some success down the road. These feelings of increasing satisfaction and commitment and the development of skills and practices to make working together easier are typical of Stage 3.

Learning to share leadership and getting past the tendency to agree in order to avoid conflict are the challenges at the integration stage.

The integration stage can be quite short, depending on the ease of resolving feelings of dissatisfaction and integrating new skills. If members prolong conflict avoidance, there is a possibility that the team could return to the dissatisfaction stage.

Team Development Stage 4 (TDS4): Production

At this stage, both productivity and morale are high and reinforce one another. This is PERFORM in action. There is a sense of pride and excitement in being part of a high-performing team. The primary focus is on performance. Purpose, roles, and goals are clear. Standards are high, and team members are committed not only to meeting standards, but also to continuous improvement. Team members are confident in their ability to perform and overcome obstacles. They are proud of their work and enjoy working together. Communication is open, and leadership is shared. Mutual respect and trust are the norm. The team is flexible and handles new challenges as it continues to grow.

Our project team really started to hum, and the completion of the job became a reality in our minds after many meetings and a careful study of alternatives. It finally began to feel as if the effort was worth it, and we were optimistic that the outcomes would be positive for both the company and the consulting partners. We all shared the responsibility for team leadership. We felt this had become a really great team to be on, and we were proud to be part of it. These feelings of accomplishment, pride, confidence, and a sense of unity are typical of teams who have reached Stage 4.

The challenge in the production stage is sustaining the team's performance through new challenges and continued growth. This stage is likely to continue—with moderate fluctuations in feelings of satisfaction—throughout the team's life.

Team Development Stage 5 (TDS5): Termination

With ongoing teams, this stage is more often a "mini termination" at different points, such as when a goal is achieved or a milestone is reached. Termination occurs in any team that is time-limited, such as project teams, ad hoc teams, or temporary task forces, so team members need to be prepared for its outcomes. Productivity and morale may increase or decrease as the end of the experience draws near. Team members feel sadness or loss—or, on the other hand, a rush to meet deadlines.

After presenting the findings of our project team, we realised we had some regrets that it was all over. We had shared some tension-filled times and had developed a real appreciation for each other, as well as a sense of bonding. This great group of people we had been meeting with for the last several months would probably never be together in the same way again. So, although we felt proud of what we had accomplished, we also felt a sense of loss as it was coming to an end. The praise and acknowledgement from the company and the consulting partners helped.

The challenge at the termination stage is to maintain necessary productivity and morale while managing closure, recognition, and celebration. This stage may vary in duration from a small part of the last meeting to a significant portion of the last several meetings, depending on the length and quality of the team experience.

* * *

While the five stages are described as separate and distinct, they share considerable overlap. Some elements of each stage can be found in every other stage. For example, just because a team is getting started (orientation stage) and needs to focus on developing a clear purpose and building a strong team charter doesn't mean that it won't need to revisit and refine the charter in Stage 2 or 3. The team's dominant characteristics and needs, however, determine its development stage at any given time. A change in these characteristics and needs signals a change in the team's development level.

Why is understanding your team's stage of development and corresponding needs such an important step in the process? Because it allows team leaders or members to accomplish the next key step: providing leadership that responds to those needs.

Step Four: Match Leadership Style to Your Team's Development Level

As it moves through the different development stages, a team requires leadership that is responsive to its needs at each stage. Situational Leadership® II, used extensively to develop individual performance, works equally well when applied to a team or collabourative group.

As we discussed in Chapter 5, Situational Leadership® II consists of two variables—directing behaviour and supporting behaviour, which combine to form four leadership styles. This same framework applies to leading teams.

Directing behaviour structures and guides team outcomes. Behaviours that provide direction include organising, structuring, educating, and focusing the team. For example, when you first join the team, you want to know how it will be organised. What do you need to learn to be a good team member? Where will the team focus its efforts? What's the structure? Does anybody report to anybody? Who does what? When? And how?

Supporting behaviour develops mutual trust and respect within the team. Behaviours that provide support include involving, encouraging, listening to, and collaborating with team members. For example, in developing team harmony and cohesion, people want to be involved in decision making, encouraged to participate, acknowledged and praised for their efforts, valued for their differences, and able to share leadership when appropriate.

Without team leadership training, people who are called to lead a team are usually clueless about what to do. They often operate on instinct. For example, suppose an inexperienced team leader thinks that the only way to lead a team is to use a participative leadership style. From Day 1, she asks everybody for suggestions about how the team should operate. The team members think the leader should answer that question. "After all," they say, "she's the one who called the meeting." They begin to question why they joined this team. The leader, getting little response from her team, gets frustrated and wonders why she agreed to lead the team in the first place. Everyone is confused.

Without understanding the framework of team stages of development, it is only by chance that a leader's behaviour matches the team's needs. Combining the Stages of Team Development Model with the Situational Leadership® II Model will help everything begin to make sense (see Figure 10.4).

The directing and supporting behaviours of the Situational Leadership® II model provide a framework for meeting team needs. They can be used by any member of the team.

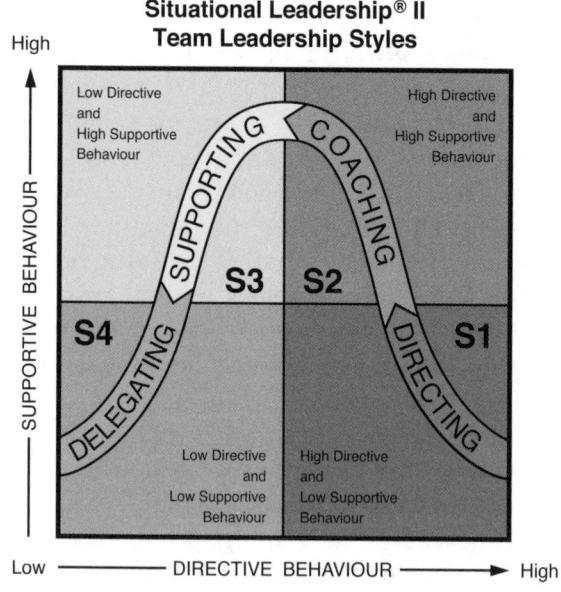

Figure 10.4   Situational Leadership® II Team Leadership Styles

Match Leadership Style to Team Development Stage

When we combine the four leadership styles with the first four stages of team development, as illustrated in Figure 10.5, we have a framework for matching each stage with an appropriate leadership style.

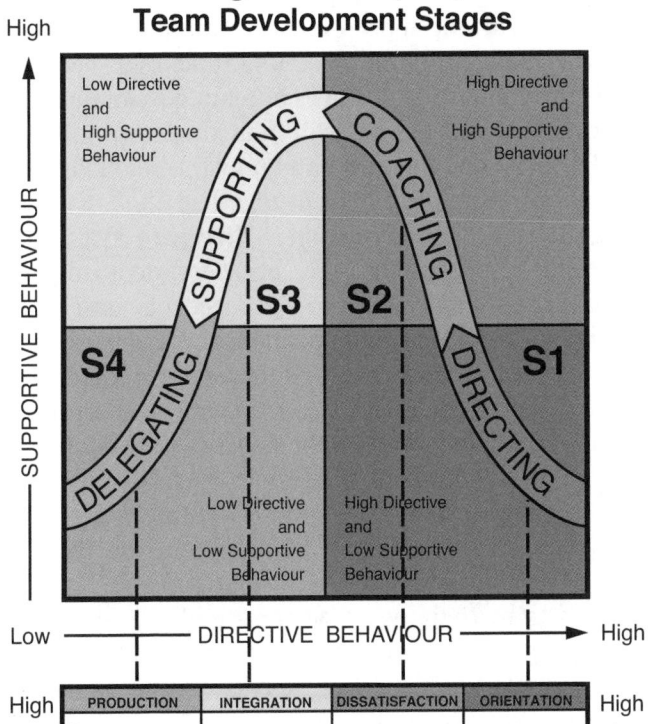

Figure 10.5 Situational Leadership® II: Matching Leadership Style to the First Four Team Development Stages

For team leaders and members to determine the appropriate leadership style, first diagnose the team's stage of development in relation to its goal, considering both productivity and morale. Then locate the team's present stage of development on the Stages of Team Development Model, and follow a vertical line up to the curve on the Situational Leadership® II Model. The point of intersection indicates the appropriate leadership style for the team.

Intervening with the appropriate leadership style at each stage will help the team progress to or maintain high-performance. Matching leadership style to stages of team development, similar to partnering for performance with individuals, works best when the team leader(s) and members all know the Team Performance Process and are doing the diagnosis together.

At Stage 1, the **orientation stage**, a **directing** style is appropriate. The team is moderately eager but dependent on authority. Leaders need to get the team off to a good start by developing purpose and structure while building relationships and trust. This is the time to create a team charter and link the team's work to the organisation's purpose and goals. Team leaders should assess training and resource needs and orientate team members to one another.

At the beginning of any team, people are relatively eager to be there, and they have high expectations. Morale is high, but productivity is low due to a lack of knowledge about the task and each other. The team members need some support, but this need is much less than their need for goal- and purpose-orientated behaviour. People need to clearly understand what kind of participation is expected from them. Norms should be established around communication and accountability. There should be consensus on structure and boundaries: what work will get done and by whom, what the timelines are, what tasks are to be completed, and what skills are needed to complete them.

At Stage 2, the **dissatisfaction stage**, a **coaching** leadership style is appropriate. At this point the team is probably experiencing confusion and frustration and needs to learn how to manage conflict and work together more effectively. Now is when the leader should reconfirm or clarify the team's purpose, norms, goals, and roles; develop both task and team skills; confront difficult issues; and recognise helpful behaviours and small accomplishments.

The dissatisfaction stage is characterised by a gradual increase in task performance and a decrease in morale. Anger, frustration, confusion, and discouragement can arise due to the discrepancy between initial expectations and reality.

The dissatisfaction stage calls for continued high direction and an increase in support. Team members need encouragement and reassurance as well as skill development and strategies for working together and task achievement. At this stage, it is important to clarify the big picture and reconfirm the team's purpose, values, and goals. It is also important to give the team more input into decision making. Recognising team members' accomplishments and giving feedback on progress reassures people, encourages progress, and boosts morale. This is a good time to encourage active listening and reaffirm that the team values differences of opinion. It is also helpful at this stage to have open and honest discussions about issues such as emotional blocks and coalitions, and to resolve any personality conflicts.

At Stage 3, the **integration stage**, a **supporting** leadership style is appropriate. The team, now working together more effectively but cautiously, must learn to share leadership and address conflict.

Goals and strategies are becoming clearer or have been redefined. Negative feelings are being resolved. Confidence, cohesion, and trust are increasing but still fragile. People tend to avoid conflict for fear of slipping back into the dissatisfaction of Stage 2. Team members are more willing and able to assume leadership functions.

Support and collaboration are needed in the integration stage to help team members develop confidence in their ability to work together. The team needs less direction around the task and more support focused on building confidence, cohesion, involvement, and shared leadership. This is a time to encourage people to voice different perspectives, share responsibility for leadership, and examine team functioning. Now the focus should be on increasing productivity and developing problem-solving and decision-making skills.

At Stage 4, the ***production stage***, a ***delegating*** leadership style is appropriate. Now operating with high productivity and high morale, the team is challenged by the need to sustain its high-performance.

At this stage, the team members have positive feelings about each other and their accomplishments. The quality and amount of work produced are high. Teams at this stage often need new challenges to keep morale and task focus high.

The team generally provides its own direction and support at this point and needs to be validated for that accomplishment. People are sharing leadership responsibilities, and team members are fully participating in achieving the team's goals. Continued recognition and celebration of the team's accomplishments are needed at this time, as well as the creation of new challenges and higher standards. Because the team is functioning at a high level, at this stage it is appropriate to foster decision-making autonomy within established boundaries.

At Stage 5, the ***termination stage***, a ***supporting*** leadership style is appropriate. For teams with a distinct ending point, productivity can continue to increase, or it may go down because of a rush to complete the task. The approaching end of an important experience may also cause morale to increase or to drop from previous high levels.

Accepting and acknowledging the feelings that are present during this stage may be helpful. If a significant downturn in productivity and morale occurs, an increase in support, as well as some direction, is needed to maintain high-performance.

Stay on the Railway Tracks

As we talked about with one-on-one leadership, it is important in developing a team to stay on the railway tracks—to follow the leadership style curve as the team progresses through the stages of development. After developing a team charter, a team leader can't go to a delegating leadership style. He or she will go off the tracks, and the team may crash and burn. Building a high-performing team requires a leader who can manage the journey from dependence to interdependence. When a great team leader's job is done, team members will say, "We did it ourselves."

Step Five: Develop Strategies for Higher Team Performance

Working in teams requires leaders to acquire new knowledge and skills that they may not have developed earlier. Yet, if they hope to build high-performing teams, they'd better learn these skills. Just as in working with people one-on-one, it really helps team leaders if their people know what the leaders know. Team members need the same critical knowledge and skills as their team leader. For some people, that's revolutionary; when they're part of a team, they expect to be "done to." Thinking of a team as a partnership between team leader(s) and members is foreign to many.

When you ask most team leaders after a meeting how it went, they want to talk about the number of agenda items they got through and the decisions that were made. They are focused only on content. Very seldom do they comment on or even seem to care about how the team interacted. They are "process clueless." We have all been part of teams or groups where we dread going to meetings. Sometimes, this is driven by an egotistical leader who loves to hear his or her own voice, is not open to feedback, and wants everyone to endorse his or her agenda for everything. If you really want to find out what's going on with teams like that, go in the halls or toilets after a meeting, where everyone is holding "I should have said" meetings.

A conscious awareness of the dynamics occurring within a team is a critical factor in helping the team develop. Observing what is going on in the team while the team goes about its work is an important function of the team leader. This is when leaders can pick up information that will help them diagnose what the team needs to perform at the highest level. Over time, this role will be assumed by all team members.

By observing the team, leaders can develop strategies and skills to address issues confronting the team, such as conflict management, individual differences, problem solving, and decision making. For highest performance, leaders should encourage regularly scheduled team check-ups to review the charter, evaluate progress, discuss changes, and incorporate lessons learned.

The Miracle of Teamwork

The Team Performance Process gives you a purposeful way to look at teamwork and provides a framework for team development that helps you stay on track. Pay attention to the dynamics. Pay attention to the mechanics. If you have trouble along the way, chances are you may not have set up something well in the beginning. Developing a team charter is probably the most underappreciated step in the process. Skipping it is a shortcut to problems.

Building and maintaining high-performing teams requires two beliefs:

No one of us is as smart as all of us.

and

People have a right to be involved in decisions that affect them.

It is also essential that team members adopt community-building attitudes and perspectives.

First, team members must develop a learning attitude. Everything that happens in the team is "grist to the mill." There are no failures—only learning opportunities.

Second, the team must build a trust-based environment. Trust is built by sharing information, ideas, and skills. Building trust requires that team members cooperate rather than compete, judge, or blame. Trust is also built when team members follow through on their commitments. It is critical that team members communicate openly and honestly and demonstrate respect for others.

Third, the team must value differences. Team members should encourage and honour differences. Different viewpoints are the heart of creativity.

Fourth, people must view the team as a whole. By seeing the team as a living system rather than a collection of individuals, team members begin to think in terms of *we* rather than *I* and *you*.

When teams function well, miracles can happen. A thrilling and inspiring example of a high-performing team is the 1980 US's Olympic hockey team.[7] Twenty young men—many of whom had never played together before—came from universities all over the country. Six months later they won the Olympic gold medal, defeating the best teams in the world—including the Soviet Union, a team that had been playing together for years. No one expected this to happen. It is considered one of the greatest upsets in sports history and is labelled a miracle. When team members were interviewed, all without exception attributed their success to teamwork. The drive, commitment, cohesiveness, cooperation, trust, team effort, and a passionate belief in a common goal—"Go for the gold"—were the reason for their success.

A leader who has attained success at the team leadership level may be ready to move on to leading the organisation. After all, organisational leaders oversee a number of teams, departments, and/or divisions. The next chapter focuses on organisational leadership.

Chapter 11

ORGANISATIONAL LEADERSHIP

Pat Zigarmi, Judd Hoekstra, Ken Blanchard,
and Drea Zigarmi

Just as team leadership is more complicated than one-on-one leadership, leading an entire organisation is more complicated than leading a single team. Why? Because organisational leadership is all about leading change, and managing change is chaotic and messy.

Today we live in "permanent whitewater." What do we know about whitewater? It's both exhilarating and scary! You often have to go sideways or upside down to go forwards. The flow is controlled by the environment. There are unseen obstacles. Occasionally it's wise to use an eddy to regroup and reflect, but eddies are often missed because whitewater seems to create its own momentum.

The Importance of Managing Change

Once there was a time when you could experience change and then return to a period of relative stability. In that era, as things settled down, you could thoughtfully plan and get ready for another change. Kurt Lewin described these phases as unfreezing, changing, and refreezing. The reality today is that there is no refreezing. There's no rest and no getting ready.

In the midst of this chaos, it's hard for people to maintain perspective. The situation reminds us of the story about the little girl who comes home from school one day and asks her mother (although today it certainly could be her father), "Why does Daddy work so late every night?" The mother gives a sympathetic smile and replies, "Well, Daddy just doesn't have time to finish all his work during the day." In her infinite wisdom the little girl says, "Then why don't they put him in a slower group?" Alas, there are no slower groups. Constant change is a way of life in organisations today.

Mark Twain once said, "The only person who likes change is a wet baby." Like it or not, in the dynamic society surrounding today's organisations, the question of whether or not change will occur is no longer relevant. Change will occur. That is no longer a probability; it is a certainty.

The issue is, how do managers and leaders cope with the barrage of changes that confront them daily as they attempt to keep their organisations adaptive and viable?

They must develop strategies to listen in on the conversations in the organisation so that they can surface and resolve people's concerns about change. They have to strategise hard to lead change in a way that leverages everyone's creativity and ultimate commitment to working in an organisation that's resilient in the face of change.

Why Is Organisational Change So Complicated?

Consider what happens when people take a golf lesson. The instructor changes the golfers' swing in an effort to improve their score. However, golfers' scores typically get worse while they are learning a new swing. It takes time for golfers to master a new swing and for their scores to improve. Now, think about what happens when you ask each member of a team of golfers to change their respective swings at the same time. The cumulative performance drop is larger for the team than it is for any one golfer.

The same performance drop occurs in organisations where large numbers of people are asked to make behaviour changes at the same time. When one person on a team is learning a new skill, the rest of the team can often pick up the slack and keep the team on track. However, when everyone is learning new skills, who can pick up the slack?

When a change is introduced in an organisation, an initial drop in organisational performance typically occurs before performance rises to a level above the prechange level. Effective change leaders, being aware of this and understanding the process of change, can minimise the drop in performance caused by large numbers of people learning new behaviours at the same time. They can also minimise the amount of time taken to achieve desired future performance. Furthermore, they can improve an organisation's capacity to initiate, implement, and sustain successful changes. That's exactly what we hope you will be able to learn from this chapter.

When Is Change Necessary?

Change is necessary when a discrepancy occurs between an actual set of events—something that is happening right now—and a desired set of events—what you would like to happen. To better understand where your organisation might be in relation to needed change, consider the following questions.

- Is your organisation on track to achieve its vision?
- Are your organisation's initiatives delivering the desired outcomes?
- Is it delivering those outcomes on time?
- Is it delivering those outcomes on budget?
- Is your organisation maintaining high levels of productivity and morale?
- Are your customers excited about your organisation?
- Are your people energised, committed, and passionate?

If you find it difficult to say yes to these questions, your focus on leading change should be more intense.

Most managers report that managing change is not their forte. In a survey of 350 senior executives across 14 industries, 68 per cent confirmed that their companies had experienced unanticipated problems in the change process.[1] Furthermore, research indicates that 70 per cent of organisational changes fail, and these failures can often be traced to ineffective leadership.

Change Gets Derailed or Fails for Predictable Reasons

Our research and real-world experience have shown that most change efforts get derailed or fail for predictable reasons. Many leaders don't recognise or account for these reasons. As a result, they make the same mistakes repeatedly. As is often said:

Insanity is doing the same things over and over and expecting different results.

Fortunately, there is hope. If you recognise the reasons change typically gets derailed or fails, leadership can be proactive, thereby increasing the probability of success when initiating, implementing, and sustaining change.

Predictable Reasons
Why Change Efforts Typically Fail

1. People leading the change think that announcing the change is the same as implementing it.

2. People's concerns about change are not surfaced or addressed.

3. Those being asked to change are not involved in planning the change.

4. There is no compelling reason to change. The business case is not communicated.

5. A compelling vision that excites people about the future has not been developed and communicated.

6. The change leadership team does not include early adopters, resisters, or informal leaders.

7. The change is not piloted, so the organisation does not learn what is needed to support the change.

8. Organisational systems and other initiatives are not aligned with the change.

9. Leaders lose focus or fail to prioritise, causing "death by 1,000 initiatives."

10. People are not enabled or encouraged to build new skills.

11. Those leading the change are not credible. They undercommunicate, give mixed messages, and do not model the behaviours the change requires.

12. Progress is not measured, and/or no one recognises the changes that people have worked hard to make.

13. People are not held accountable for implementing the change.

14. People leading the change fail to respect the power of the culture to kill the change.

15. Possibilities and options are not explored before a specific change is chosen.

When most people see this list, their reaction depends on whether they have usually been the target of change or the change agent. Targets of change frequently feel as though we have been studying their organisation for years, because they have seen these reasons why change fails in action, up close and personal. The reality is that while every organisation is unique in some ways, they often struggle with change for the same reasons.

When change agents look at this list, they get discouraged, because they realise how complicated implementing change can be and how many different things can go wrong. Where should they start? Which of the 15 reasons why change fails should they concentrate on?

Over the years it has been our experience that if leaders can understand and overcome the first three reasons why change typically fails, they are on the road to being effective leaders of change.

Focus on Managing the Journey

In working with organisations for more than three decades, we have observed a leadership pattern that sabotages change. Leaders who have been thinking about a change for a while know why the change needs to be implemented. In their minds, the business case and imperative to change are clear. They are so convinced that the change has to occur that, in their minds, no discussion is needed. So they put all their energy into crafting their message and announcing the change and very little effort into involving others and managing the journey of change. They forget that:

Effective organisational leadership is more about managing the journey of change than announcing the destination.

In Situational Leadership® II terms, leaders who announce the change are using a directing style. They tell everybody what they want to have happen, and then disappear. Using an inappropriate delegating style, they expect the change to be automatically implemented. Unfortunately, that never happens. They are not managing the journey. As a result, the change gets derailed. Why?

Change gets derailed because people know they can outlast the announcement, or at least the person making the announcement. Because they haven't been involved up to this point, they sense that the organisation is concerned only with its own self-interests, not with the interests of everyone in the organisation. Change that is done to people creates more resistance. The moment vocal resistance occurs, the people leading the change break ranks. The minute they do, their lack of alignment signals that there's no need for others to align to the change, because it's going nowhere.

A poor use of directing style, followed by an inappropriate delegating style—announcing the change and then abdicating responsibility for the change—means that the change will never be successfully implemented. Rather, take time to practise partnering for performance and involve those impacted by the change in every phase of the change process.

Surfacing and Addressing People's Concerns

As we mentioned in Chapter 5, Situational Leadership® II applies whether you are leading yourself, another individual, a team, or an organisation. In the self and one-to-one context, the leader diagnoses the competence and commitment of a direct report on a specific task. In the team context, a leader diagnoses the team's productivity and morale. In the organisational context, the focus is on diagnosing the predictable and sequential stages of concern that people go through during change.

A US Department of Education project originally conducted by Gene Hall and his colleagues at the University of Texas[2] suggests that people who are faced with change express six predictable and sequential concerns (see Figure 11.1):

1. Information concerns
2. Personal concerns
3. Implementation concerns
4. Impact concerns
5. Collaboration concerns
6. Refinement concerns.

STAGES OF CONCERN

Figure 11.1   The Stages of Concern Model

People going through a change often ask questions that give leaders clues about which stage of concern they are in. Most of the time, the people managing a change don't hear these questions because there are no forums for people to express them. Or, if there are forums, the communication is one way. Those impacted by the change have little to no opportunity to question the reasons for the change or what the change will look like when it's implemented. So, instead of becoming advocates for the change because their concerns are surfaced and addressed, those impacted by the change become resistant to it.

Let's look at each stage of concern and the questions people are asking themselves and their peers.

Stage 1: Information Concerns

At this stage, people ask questions to get information about the change. For example: "What is the change? Why is it needed? What's wrong with the way things are now? How much and how fast does the organisation need to change?"

People with information concerns need the same information used by those who decided to move forward with the change. They don't want to know if the change is good or bad until they understand it. Assuming that the rationale for change is based on solid information, share this information with people, and help them see what you see. Remember, in the absence of clear, factual communication, people tend to create their own information about the change, and rumours become facts.

In a SAP[3] implementation where the change leadership team had done a good job explaining the business case, people said: "Fewer errors will occur with a single data entry. It will save money, because we will eliminate double entries. Fewer steps will be needed, and more functionality and collaboration will occur across work groups. It will be ten times easier to access information. In the long run, it will save time, because things will be done in the background. It will eliminate redundancy."

Their information concerns were largely answered by the data the leadership team provided them through multiple vehicles.

Stage 2: Personal Concerns

At this stage, people ask questions about how the change will affect them personally. For example: "What's in it for me to change? Will I win or lose? Will I look good? How will I find the time to implement this change? Will I have to learn new skills? Can I do it?"

People with personal concerns want to know how the change will play out for them. They wonder if they have the skills and resources to implement the change. As the organisation changes, existing personal and organisational commitments are threatened. People are focused on what they are going to lose, not gain.

These personal concerns have to be addressed in such a way that people feel they have been heard. As Werner Erhard often said, "What you resist, persists." If you don't permit people to deal with their feelings about what's happening, these feelings stay around. The corollary to this principle is that *if you deal with what is bothering you, in the very process of dealing with your feelings, the concerns often go away.* Have you ever said to yourself, "I'm glad I got that off my chest"? If so, you know the relief that comes from sharing your feelings with someone. Just having a chance to talk about your concerns during change clears your mind and stimulates creativity that can be used to help rather than hinder change efforts. This is where listening comes in. Leaders and managers must permit people to express their personal concerns openly, without fear of evaluation, judgement, or retribution.

Personal concerns are the most often ignored stage of concern during a change process.

In some cases, personal concerns are not resolved to an individual's satisfaction, but the act of listening to these concerns typically goes a long way towards reducing resistance to the change effort.

If you don't take time to address individual needs and fears, you won't get people beyond this basic level of concern. For that reason, let's look at some of the key personal concerns people often have with regard to change.

People are at different levels of readiness for change. Although almost everyone experiences some reluctance to change because they are not really sure how the change will impact them personally, some individuals may quickly get excited by an opportunity to implement new ideas. Others need some time to warm up to new challenges. This doesn't mean there's any one "right" place to be on the readiness continuum; it just means that people have different outlooks and degrees of flexibility about what they've been asked to do. Awareness that people are at different levels of readiness for change can be extremely helpful in effectively implementing any change effort. It helps you identify "early adopters" or change advocates who can be part of your change leadership team. This awareness will help you reach out to those who appear to be resisting the change. Their reasons for resisting may represent caution, or they could be clues to problems that have to be resolved if the change is to be successfully implemented.

People initially focus on what they have to give up. People's first reaction to a suggested change often tends to be a personal sense of loss. What do we mean by "losses"? These include, among other things, the loss of control, time, order, resources, coworkers, competency, and prestige. To help people move forward, leaders need to assist them in dealing with this sense of loss. It may seem silly, but people need to be given a chance to mourn their feelings of loss, perhaps just by having time to talk with others about how they feel. Remember, what you resist persists. Getting in touch with what you think you will be losing from the change will help you accept some of the benefits.

Ken Blanchard and John Jones, cofounder of University Associates, worked with several divisions of AT&T in the early 1980s during the break-up of the corporation into seven separate companies.[4] When they announced it, the leaders of this change started out by talking about the benefits. Ken and John realised that nobody could hear these benefits at that time, because people's personal concerns had not been dealt with. To resolve this, they set up "mourning sessions" throughout these divisions where people could talk openly about what they thought they would have to give up with this change. The following were the biggest issues that surfaced.

Loss of status. When you asked people at that time who they worked for, their chests would puff out as they said, "AT&T." It just had a much better ring to it than "Jersey Bell" or "Bell South."

Loss of lifetime employment. A classmate of Ken's, after he graduated from Cornell, got a job with AT&T. When he called home to tell his mother, she cried with joy. "You're set for life," she said. In those days, if you got a job with AT&T, the expectation was that you would work for them for 30 or 35 years, have a wonderful retirement party, and then ride off into the sunset. In these days of constant change, people have personal concerns about long-term employment.

Ken and John found that after people had expressed their feelings about these kinds of losses, they were much more willing and able to hear about the benefits of divestiture.

People feel alone even if everyone else is going through the same change. When change hits, even if everyone around us is facing the same situation, most of us tend to take it personally: "Why me?" The irony is that for the change to be successful, we need the support of others. In fact, we need to ask for such support. People are apt to feel punished when they have to learn new ways of working. If change is to be successful, people need to recruit the help of those around them. We need each other. This is why support groups work when people are facing changes or times of stress in their lives. They need to feel that their leaders, coworkers, and families are on their side in supporting the changes they need to make. Remember, you can't create a world-class organisation by yourself. You need the support of others, and they need your support, too.

People are concerned that they will have insufficient resources. When people are asked to change, they often think they need additional time, money, facilities, and personnel. But the reality today is that they will have to do more with less. Organisations that have downsized have fewer people around, and those that *are* around are being asked to accept new responsibilities. They need to work smarter, not harder. Rather than providing these resources directly, leaders must help people discover their own ability to generate them.

People can handle only so much change. Beyond a few changes—or even only one, if the change is significant—people tend to get overwhelmed and become immobilised. That's why it's probably not best to change everything all at once. Choose the key areas that will make the biggest difference.

Whatever you do, make sure people have some success experiences to build on before implementing more change.

In the SAP implementation mentioned earlier, what personal concerns were expressed, and how were they addressed? In interviews, people said: "I saw the databases yesterday and realise I don't have to do anything right now. It's less intimidating now that I've been able to play with it a little. I'm worried about the timing—the 'go live' date is in the middle of everything else. It will definitely take more time. I'm concerned that it will be hard to learn and use. I don't think my team leader can speak for us. She doesn't have a good enough view of our day-to-day work. I hope there will be one-on-one support, because the training won't create the sense of security I'll need to be able to use the system confidently. If things run smoother, what will we do with our time? We have to answer the question 'What does this mean for me?' now. I can't do this and my real job at the same time. When this project is over, I'll have to go back and fix everything else."

The SAP change leadership team in this company set up forums for people to express their personal concerns, and then systematically worked at providing responses to questions about timing, involvement, support systems, and managing multiple priorities.

Once people feel that their personal concerns have been heard, they tend to turn their attention to how the change will really shake out. These are called implementation concerns.

Stage 3: Implementation Concerns

At this stage, people ask questions about how the change will be implemented. For example: "What do I do first, second, third? How do I manage all the details? What happens if it doesn't work as planned? Where do I go for help? How long will this take? Is what we are experiencing typical? How will the organisation's structure and systems change?"

People with implementation concerns are focused on the nitty-gritty—the details involved in implementing the change. They want to know if the change has been tested. They know the change won't go exactly as planned, so they want to know, "Where do we go for technical assistance and solutions to problems that arise as the change is being implemented?" People with implementation concerns want to know how to make the best use of information and resources. They also want to know how the organisation's infrastructure will support the change effort (the performance management system, recognition and rewards, career development).

In the SAP implementation mentioned earlier, implementation concerns such as these were voiced: "I'm concerned that people will hold on to their pet systems. Some other applications may survive, and we'll end up with redundant systems. We don't have the hardware to run the software. I'm concerned that there won't be enough time to clean up the data or verify the new business processes we've designed. I want to touch it now, sooner rather than later. We need more information about what we can expect and when we can give suggestions. I could really use a timeline—what I've seen has been too detailed or too sparse. I need to know when I'll be involved/crunched. Will people really be held accountable for using the new system?"

These implementation concerns were best addressed when the people closest to the challenges of implementing the change were involved in planning the solutions to the problems that were surfaced.

Stage 4: Impact Concerns

Once the first three stages of concern are lowered, people tend to raise impact concerns. For example: "Is the effort worth it? Is the change making a difference? Are we making progress? Are things getting better? How?"

People with impact concerns are interested in the change's relevance and pay-off. The focus is on evaluation. This is the stage where people sell themselves on the benefits of the change based on the results being achieved. This is also the stage where leaders lose or build credibility for future change initiatives. If the change doesn't positively impact results—or if people don't know how to measure success—it will be more difficult to initiate and implement change in the future. Conversely, this is the stage where you can build change leaders for the future if you identify the early adopters and recognise their successes with the change.

Stage 5: Collaboration Concerns

People at the fifth stage of concern ask questions about collaboration during the change. For example: "Who else should be involved? How can we work with others to get them involved in what we are doing? How do we spread the word?"

People with collaboration concerns are focused on coordination and cooperation with others. They want to get everyone on board because they are convinced the change is making a difference. During this stage, get the early adopters to champion the change and influence those who are still on the fence.

Stage 6: Refinement Concerns

People at this stage ask questions about how the change can be refined. For example: "How can we improve on our original idea? How can we make the change even better?"

People with refinement concerns are focused on continuous improvement. During the course of an organisational change, a number of learnings usually occur. As a result, new opportunities for organisational improvement often come to the surface at this stage.

Impact, collaboration, and refinement concerns were barely audible in our SAP example, since it was still being planned. But we heard the following: "We expect a drop in productivity when we go live. We have to begin to define who owns which work processes and who upstream/downstream needs to change when we go live. SAP isn't just the implementation of new technology; it's business process redesign. We have to build the linkages and do the data conversions now. The experienced SAP users in the company haven't been tapped. I'm concerned we'll ship late when we make the conversion. Exceptions to usual flows are not being anticipated. Old-timers won't be able to take the shortcuts they are used to. Real-time processing will help us eventually, but at first it will add time. It's important to be thinking about integration across all processes now. I'm sure things will get worse in the first few weeks. What will the next phases focus on?"

We've learned that when people have refinement concerns with one change, they often are hatching the next change. The more you involve others in looking at options and in suggesting ways to do things differently, the easier it will be to build the business case for the next round of change.

While dealing with people's concerns about change may seem like a lot of hand-holding, each stage of concern can be a major roadblock to the change's success. Since the stages of concern are predictable and sequential, it is important to realise that, at any given time, different people are at different stages of concern. For example, before a change is announced, the leaders of the change often have information that others in the organisation don't. In addition, these change leaders typically have figured out how the change will affect them personally and even have gone so far as to formulate an implementation plan before others in the organisation are even aware of the proposed change. As a result, the change leaders have often addressed and resolved information, personal, and implementation concerns; now they are ready to address impact concerns by communicating the change's benefits to the organisation. Those in the rest of the organisation, however, still has not had a chance to voice their concerns. As a result, they will not be ready to hear about the change's benefits until their information, personal, and implementation concerns have been addressed.

Organisational Leadership Behaviours

If a leader can diagnose people's stage of concern, the leader can respond by communicating the right information at the right time to address and decrease or even resolve these concerns. This requires the flexibility to respond differently to the concerns that people have going through change.

Resolving concerns throughout the change process builds trust in the leadership team, puts challenges on the table, gives people an opportunity to influence the change process, and allows people to refocus their energy on the change.

To help people resolve the questions and concerns they have at each stage of the change process, it is most helpful to respond with the right combination of focusing (directive) and inspiring (supportive) behaviours. When you do so, the questions are answered, and people are prepared to move to the next stage of change. Not addressing the questions holds people back and delays, if not stops, the process of moving forward.

Focusing and inspiring behaviours are like directive and supportive behaviours in the Situational Leadership® II model as it's used with individuals and teams. Initially, leaders provide the focus or direction. They often spot the gaps between what is and what could be. They "direct" the change by creating a change leadership team and by committing resources to the change. They build the business case and set up the right experiments to determine best practices for implementing the change. At each stage of the planning process, though, it's critically important to involve others. Those impacted by the change, if involved in planning, will have vehicles to express their concerns. They will be able to work with those leading the change to inspire others to change. Let's look a little more closely at the two behaviours in Blanchard's organisational change leadership model.

Focusing (Directive) Behaviour for Organisational Change

Behaviours that provide direction in leading organisations are primarily related to *focusing energy on performance and making the change happen*. These directive behaviours, when applied to change leadership, help define and prioritise the changes required of the organisation. This includes explaining the business case for the change. In other words, why are we doing this? People also want to know who will be leading the change and whether they will be consulted or involved. Again, a clear vision is important here so that people can see where the organisation is headed and can determine if they fit into this picture of the future. They also want to see the implementation plan. They'll want direction about test-driving the change. They'll want to know how resources will be deployed. Leaders providing appropriate direction must see that the organisational structure and systems are aligned to support the desired change.

Finally, direction also involves holding everyone accountable for making the change. In successful change efforts, the responsibility for providing direction or focus is shared by a broad-based change leadership team that includes early adopters and advocates for the change from all levels of the organisation.

Inspiring (Supportive) Behaviour for Organisational Change

Behaviours that provide support in leading organisations are primarily related to *facilitating the change process and inspiring everyone to work together*. These inspiring or supportive behaviours, when applied to the organisation, help demonstrate that the change leadership team is passionately committed to the change.

They also make sure that people's concerns are surfaced and heard. The key here is involvement, involvement, and more involvement. Buy-in and cooperation are increased when change leaders listen to and involve others at each step of the change process. This means sharing information broadly across the organisation, asking for input, celebrating successes, and recognising people who are changing. The best support and most inspiration are provided when leaders throughout the organisation model the behaviours expected of others. When leaders walk the talk, they connect with the experience and concerns of those who are being asked to change. Connection leads to more collaboration and partnering.

Situational Leadership® II and Leading People Through Change

New work by Pat Zigarmi, Judd Hoekstra, and Ken Blanchard on the Situational Leadership® II and Leading People Through Change programmes provides guidance for diagnosing concerns and then using the appropriate change leadership strategy to address those concerns. That's where flexibility comes in, the second skill of a situational change leader. Remember, stages of concern are like stages of development at the individual and team levels.

For Information Concerns, Use a More Focusing or Directing Leadership Style

When a change is introduced, people often lack knowledge about it. They wonder what it's all about. They have information needs: "What will we be doing differently?" People need direction and focus much more than support or inspiration. To guide the process, the change leadership team should use focusing behaviours to explain the business case for the change. It's important to bring people face to face with data about the need to change and allow them to reach their own conclusions.

For Personal Concerns,
Use a Focusing and Inspiring Leadership Style

As information is shared and knowledge increases, people realise they need to develop new skills. Anxiety increases. They want to know, "How will the change affect me personally? Will I be successful?" People still need direction and focus, but there is a growing need for support and engagement.

Leaders can help people with personal concerns about the change by providing forums for team members to say what's on their minds. It is important at this stage to provide encouragement and reassurance. Leaders should continue to explain to team members why the change is important and provide consistent messages about the organisation's vision, goals, and expectations. They should ask people what it would take for them to see themselves as part of the future. They should create vehicles for early adopters in the organisation and users of the change outside the organisation to influence peer to peer. They should also provide resources that help resolve personal concerns—clear goals, time, management support, and coaching.

The outcome of the strategies that are high on focusing and inspiring behaviours is a compelling vision of the post-change future—a picture where people can see themselves succeeding.

For Implementation Concerns,
Use a Focusing and Inspiring Leadership Style

After personal concerns have been dealt with, people begin to question if enough planning has been done. They can often see what hasn't been done quicker than the people leading the change can, because they are closer to day-to-day reality. This is the time to set up small experiments, tests, or pilots to learn what still needs to be done. This is the time to broadly involve others—asking them to flesh out a robust implementation plan with you. This is the time to go forward with resisters to learn why they are resisting (beyond personal concerns). This is the time to increase the frequency of contact between change advocates and early adopters and people who are neutral. People still need both direction/focus and support/engagement to address their implementation concerns.

Leaders can help people through this phase in the change process by working to align systems—performance planning, tracking, feedback, and evaluation systems—with the change. They can offer perspective about how long the change should take and if performance is on track. Leaders can boost morale by walking the talk, modelling the behaviours they expect of others—openness, transparency, flexibility, responsiveness, and resilience. Leaders can also address discouragement by providing individual training and coaching, not mass training, on how to implement the change. By demonstrating that they want to listen and by responding honestly to the questions people raise, leaders build trust. At this stage, it is equally important to look for small wins, recognise progress, and share excitement and optimism about the change.

Remember that at each phase of the change process, the change leadership team includes change leaders from all levels of the organisation who can respond as peers with direction and support. They can gain the cooperation of others because they can speak first-hand of their experience and success with the change.

For Impact Concerns, Use an Inspiring Leadership Style

As the third stage of concern winds down, people begin to see the pay-off for using their new skills. There's a tipping point. There's some momentum—but only if information, personal, and implementation concerns have been surfaced and resolved and only if people have been asked to shape the change they are being asked to make. People begin to feel more confident that they will succeed. They want to know, "How are we doing on our change journey? Can we measure our progress to date?" The need for direction and focus can decline, but people continue to need support, engagement, and inspiration to let them know that progress is being made.

At this stage of the change, the change leadership team needs to collect and share information and success stories. By telling stories, they can anchor the change in the company's culture. Working together, the change leadership team can solve problems and remove barriers or obstacles to implementing the change. It is important at this stage for leaders to encourage people to keep up their effort and desire to change.

For Collaboration Concerns, Use an Inspiring Leadership Style

When people are firmly in the final stages of the change process, they can clearly see that their efforts are paying off, and they want to expand the positive impact on others. They begin to have more ideas that they want to share with others. The question on their minds is, "Who else should be involved in our change effort?" They need very little direction and focus but continue to need support and inspiration to encourage them to use the new talents they have developed and to leverage the success they have had.

The focus now should be on encouraging teamwork and interdependence with other teams. Leaders can support the change by cheerleading the improvements in the team's performance and encouraging people to take on even greater challenges.

For Refinement Concerns, Use an Inspiring Leadership Style

The destination is now in sight. People know new ways to behave and how to work in the changed environment. They are ready to ask questions such as "Can we identify new challenges and think of new ways to do things? Can we leverage what we've done so far?" The need for both direction/focus and support/inspiration is declining. This is where integration of everything they have learned during the change journey occurs.

Team members and leaders at this point need to support continuous improvement and innovation throughout the organisation. They should encourage each other to continue to challenge the status quo and to explore new options and possibilities.

The more that people throughout the organisation are involved in talking about options and possibilities, the easier it will be to build the business case for the next round of change.

Involvement and Influence in Planning the Change

As we have emphasised, once the change leadership team has diagnosed people's stages of concern, they must learn to flexibly use the appropriate change leadership strategy and corresponding behaviours to address the specific concerns people have in each stage of organisational change. Doing so significantly increases the probability of implementing successful change, because it creates a partnering for performance environment that expands opportunities for involvement and influence.

People often resent change when they have no involvement in how it should be implemented. So, contrary to popular belief, people don't resist change—they resist being controlled.

When leaders expand people's involvement and influence during a change, there is more buy-in for the change, because people are less likely to feel they are being controlled. When leaders expand opportunities for involvement and influence, they get a chance to hear people's concerns. When they've heard the concerns, they can often resolve them. This builds trust and increases the credibility of the change leadership team.

In this chapter, we have focused on how to use the Situational Leadership® II model to lead organisational change. We have shown how all three skills of a situational leader—diagnosis, flexibility, and partnering for performance—play out in leading people through change. We have also focused on the first three Predictable Reasons Why Change Efforts Typically Fail. In the next chapter, we introduce the Leading People Through Change model, which defines nine change leadership strategies. This will be helpful for overcoming the remaining reasons on the list of Why Change Efforts Typically Fail.

Chapter 12

STRATEGIES FOR LEADING A CHANGE

Pat Zigarmi and Judd Hoekstra

L eaders often get overwhelmed when they have to implement change. In many ways, they feel caught in a lose–lose proposition. If they try a necessary change, they risk unleashing all kinds of pent-up negative feelings in people. The resisters are seen as troublemakers trying to ruin something good. On the other hand, if leaders don't constantly drive change, their organisation will become obsolete, and everyone will lose their jobs. It's been said that if you don't change, you are dying.

Add to that lose–lose perspective a glance at the list of 15 Predictable Reasons Why Change Efforts Typically Fail, which we discussed in the preceding chapter, and leaders could be immobilised around change. That's why Pat Zigarmi and Judd Hoekstra developed the Leading People Through Change Model—to make the seemingly complicated simple (see Figure 12.1).[1]

Change Leadership Strategies

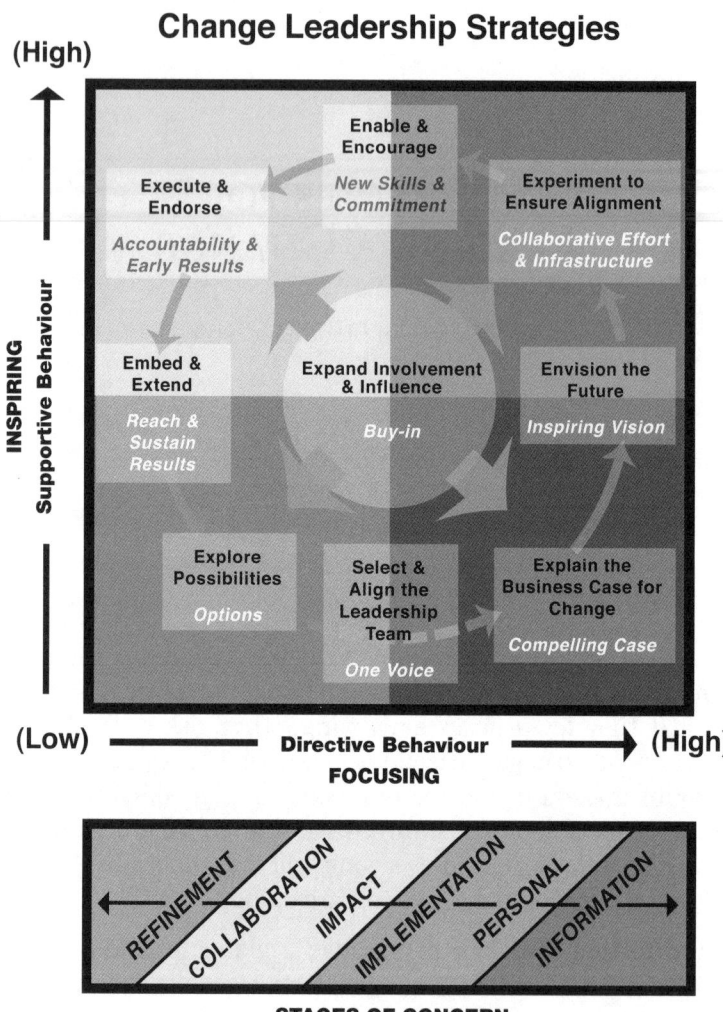

Figure 12.1   The Leading People Through Change Model

Nine Change Leadership Strategies

In Chapter 11, "Organisational Leadership," we focused on the first three predictable reasons why change efforts typically fail.

People leading the change think that announcing the change is the same as implementing it. People's concerns with change are not surfaced or addressed, and those being asked to change are not involved in planning the change.

The upper portion of the Leading People Through Change Model defines nine change leadership strategies and their respective outcomes. While these change leadership strategies are in response to the 6 stages of concern, their focus is on the remaining 12 reasons why change efforts typically fail. They also describe a process for leading people through change that differs dramatically from how change is introduced in most organisations.

Strategy 1: Expand Involvement and Influence

Outcome: Buy-In

As the Leading People Through Change Model shows, the first change leadership strategy, Expand Involvement and Influence, must be used consistently throughout the change process. It's at the heart of the change leadership strategies.

The core belief of our approach to leading organisational change is that the best way to initiate, implement, and sustain change is to increase the level of influence and involvement from the people being asked to change, surfacing and resolving concerns along the way. This was a key strategy in the preceding chapter, when we discussed dealing with the first three reasons why change efforts typically fail. Without this strategy, you cannot achieve the cooperation and buy-in you need from those responsible for making the changes you've proposed.

Which of the following are you more likely to commit to:
a decision made by others that is being imposed on you,
or a decision you've had a chance to contribute to?

What may seem obvious to you isn't obvious to many leaders trying to implement organisational changes. They believe changes will be implemented much faster if they make quick decisions, and it is quicker to make decisions with fewer people providing input into the decision-making process. *While it is true that decisions can be made faster when fewer people are involved, faster decisions do not usually translate into faster and better execution.* The "top-down, minimal involvement" leadership approach ignores the critical difference between compliance and commitment. People may comply with the new directive for a short time until the pressure is off and then return to old behaviour.

Providing opportunities for involvement and influence produces long-term, sustainable commitment to a new way of doing business, rather than short-term compliance. Keep Figure 12.2 in mind as you think about how much you want to involve people in the change process: Resistance increases the more people sense that they cannot influence what is happening to them.

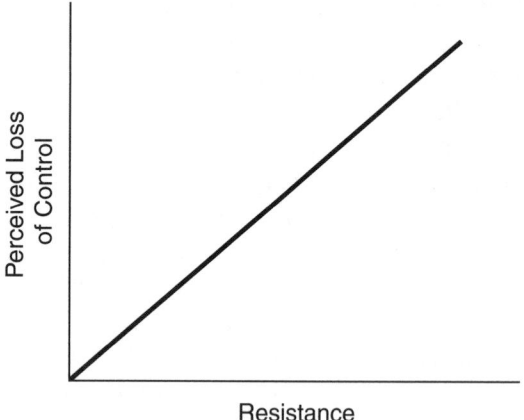

Figure 12.2   Perceived Loss of Control Increases Resistance to Change

If people aren't treated as if they are smart and would reach the same conclusion about the need to change as the change leadership team, they perceive a loss of control. Their world is about to change, but they have not been asked to talk about "what is," explore options, or consider possibilities. Their information concerns have not been addressed. Similarly, if personal concerns are not surfaced and acknowledged, people lose a sense of autonomy. They collude with others; they become anxious, and their resistance increases. Then, when T-shirts with a slogan are given out and everyone is sent to "one size fits all" training, people begin to believe that the organisation really is out of control. This puts their sense of control in jeopardy, which again increases resistance. The bottom line is that people have to influence the change they are expected to make, or, as Robert Lee said:

> *"People who are left out of shaping change have a way of reminding us that they are really important."*

Flexibility: Using a Number of Different Change Leadership Strategies to Successfully Lead Change

The 8 organisational change leadership strategies on the perimeter of the model proactively address the other 12 Predictable Reasons Why Change Efforts Typically Fail. They also illustrate a sequential process for initiating, implementing, and sustaining change.

To help make the remaining eight change leadership strategies come alive, we offer the following case study involving a problem that has plagued millions in America.

Case Study: Non-Support-Paying Parents

As many as 20 million children in America may have non-custodial parents who avoid their child support obligations. According to the Federal Office of Child Support, the total unpaid child support in the US is close to $100 billion; 68 per cent of child support cases were in arrears. An overwhelming majority of children—particularly minorities—residing in single-parent homes, where child support is not paid, live in poverty.

In the United States, child support enforcement is a loose confederation of state and local agencies with different guidelines that answer to the federal Office of Child Support Enforcement. Getting agencies to work together is the greatest challenge. While legislation exists to enforce child support payments, there is too much bureaucracy and not enough manpower to pursue non-support-paying parents across state lines and take them into custody. As a result, many of these parents have beaten the system.

Up until the 1990s, information on these parents was stored in paper files in clerks' offices in the county where the parent resided. County clerks were responsible for using this information to try to enforce the collection of child support. Often, as a county clerk got close to tracking down a parent not paying court-ordered child support payments, the parent would move to a different county or even a different state.

With the major challenge of sharing information stored in paper files across county lines or even state lines, it became nearly impossible to catch the non-support-paying parents. As a result, custodial parents and kids who were due to receive child support ended up losing.

As frustration grew over this situation, the federal government decided to take on the challenge. In the early 1990s, federal legislation mandated that each state implement an electronic tracking system that facilitated the sharing of current information across county and state lines to better enable the tracking of these parents. This may sound like a relatively simple change to make, considering that computers and the Internet are now commonplace in most businesses. However, many county clerks were in their fifties and sixties, lived in rural areas, had never used a computer, and had been trying to track non-support-paying parents with a notepad, pencil, and telephone for decades.

Do you think the county clerks being asked to change had concerns about the proposed change? Of course they did. Many of these county clerks had *information concerns*, such as how having a new computer would improve the situation in their county. In counties that were already doing a good job of collecting child support, people wondered if they needed to participate, or if they could continue using their paper files as long as they were successful. Counties that had been using a computer system for years to track cases wondered if they needed to use the new computer system, or if they could keep using their current system. People wondered how long it would take to move the information from their paper files to the computer.

Many of the county clerks had ***personal concerns*** as well. People said things like "I've never used a computer. Will I be taught how? Can I do it? If I can't learn to use the new computer system, will I still have a job? Besides using the new computer system, how else is my job changing? This sounds like a lot of extra work. I'm not ready for this." These questions are typical at this stage.

In addition, the clerks had ***implementation concerns***. They wanted to know when they would be trained on the new computer system. They wanted to know who to contact if they needed help after training. Many wondered if any counties were "going live" before they were, and they wondered if they could talk with people in those counties. They also wondered when the whole state would be up and running on the new system. Finally, they wondered what would happen if the computer system went down or was unavailable for a period of time.

Once the change was in motion, some of the clerks brought forward ***impact concerns***. For example, they wanted to know if they were catching any non-support-paying parents they wouldn't have caught without the new system. They wanted to know how much more money they were collecting compared to when they were doing things the old way. Many were curious to know if their customers (custodial parents) saw a positive change in how they were working with them and the results they were achieving.

In time, the clerks' ***collaboration concerns*** began to surface. Here are some of their comments: "I've seen the success of this new system first hand. Is there anybody who is not yet convinced that this is a good idea?"

"I'm so glad I got to be part of the pilot. I can't wait to go back to my county and share the good news. They are currently pretty sceptical about this new system."

"The system is working pretty well within the counties around us that have 'gone live.' Are there other counties or states we should be working with that we haven't connected with yet?"

Once the new system was up and running, the clerks brought forward their **refinement concerns**. While they acknowledged that the new system was an improvement over how things used to be, they suggested areas that might be improved. For example, a question came up about how they could connect their system to other systems (other county and state child support systems, the Department of Motor Vehicles, the new-hire database, the IRS) so that they could better track people and enforce the collection of child support.

Strategy 2: Select and Align the Leadership Team

Outcome: One Voice

The second change leadership strategy is Select and Align the Leadership Team. This strategy addresses the following reason why change efforts fail.

Why Change Efforts Typically Fail: Reason 6

6. The change leadership team does not include early adopters, resisters, or informal leaders.

Select the change leadership team. It is not possible to bring about change in an organisation with a single leader. As David Nadler says, "The scope of today's changes is too much for one CEO—even a very charismatic one—to pull off alone." Change requires a strong and broad-based change leadership team that is aligned and that speaks with one voice to the larger organisation. The outcome is a unified message that minimises ambivalence and confusion, a message that is compelling and inspiring.

In Chapter 10, "Situational Team Leadership," we described the importance of teamwork and how to build a high-performing team. How do you build a change leadership team?

First, it is important to select both sponsors and day-to-day change leadership team members. A sponsor is an executive who can legitimise the change and who has the formal authority to deploy resources to support the initiation, implementation, and reinforcement of the change. A member of the change leadership team is responsible for the day-to-day leadership of the change—the execution of the change leadership strategies described by the Leading People Through Change Model.

As you identify potential sponsors and members of the change leadership team, consider whether they possess the skills and traits required to lead change. Consider the following questions:

- Have they led or been part of successful change efforts in the past?
- Do they have the time and availability required of a change leader?
- Do they have the respect of their peers?
- Are they highly skilled?
- Are they willing to play the role of devil's advocate?
- Are they effective communicators who are willing to raise the concerns of colleagues who may be less inclined to play devil's advocate?
- Do they have the diversity necessary to think outside the box and come up with the best solutions to challenges that arise?

In our child support example, it was critical that the change leadership team include county clerks representing a diverse set of counties across the state: rural and urban counties, a county already using computers to track non-support-paying parents, a county using only pen and paper to track non-support-paying parents, a county with good performance regarding collection of child support, and a county with poor performance regarding collection of child support.

The change leadership team should be a representative sample of the organisation—advocates and resisters, formal and informal leaders, and leaders at all levels of the organisation.

It's important to embrace the resisters of a change effort. We once worked with a company where a manager appeared to be very resistant to the changes being proposed by the executive team. This manager had lots of credibility within his department and could sway people to support or block the change. Once the executive proposing the changes allowed this manager to be involved in many of the decisions regarding the change and to take an active leadership role, this manager ended up being one of the strongest supporters and leaders of the change. It's been said that

---

Those who plan the battle rarely battle the plan.

It's also important to include a variety of perspectives and roles that represent the entire organisation on the change leadership team. This way, various perspectives can be surfaced and worked through before final decisions are made. Although it may feel uncomfortable at first, it is very helpful to include at least one or two people who would be considered "resistant" and who can articulate the concerns of those who share that perspective.

When you include a representative sample of the organisation, people throughout the organisation feel that their point of view and concerns are being heard. A diverse team also means that there are more opportunities for advocates to be in contact with people who are neutral, before they become resistant. When resisters have a forum to surface and address their concerns, they often become the most effective problem solvers and spokespeople for the change.

Align and build a high-performing change leadership team. Once the change leadership team is selected in a way that increases opportunities for involvement and influence, consider how important it is for this to be a high-performing team. It is extremely damaging to an organisation when its leaders are not on the same page and communicate inconsistent messages to the organisation during times of change.

We worked with an organisation where the top executive was trying to get buy-in from his executive team for a series of changes. Some of his team did not agree with what was proposed. Although there were meetings to discuss the changes, one executive did not voice his concerns. By being silent, he implied that he supported the change leadership team's recommendations and that he would communicate a consistent message to his people. Instead, the team member chose to publicly criticise the top executive and the changes that were being proposed to members of his department. He tried to subvert the change outside the change leadership team.

When people see a lack of alignment at the top, they know they don't have to align. In addition, they know that without alignment, the change will stall or derail and that they can outlast it. In this example, as a result of his actions, the subversive executive was fired. The team members agreed to this action during the team chartering session. It sent a strong message about alignment to the whole organisation. It is important to note that the executive was fired as much for not voicing his concerns to his team as for disparaging the top executive and the proposed changes.

While it may not always lead to someone being fired, communication of inconsistent messages during a change effort results in people freezing and waiting for the leaders to sort out the inconsistencies. Negative spin from one member of a change leadership team will kill a change effort. Again, with a broad, diverse team, there are more people to communicate, but the challenge is to get them to communicate one message and to get them to listen as much as talk when they communicate. Remember: Sustainable organisational change happens through conversation and collaboration, not by unilateral action by a few.

Strategy 3: Explain the Business Case for Change

Outcome: Compelling Case for Change

The third change leadership strategy, Explain the Business Case for Change, addresses ***information concerns***.

When leaders present and explain a rational reason for the change, the outcome is a compelling case that helps people understand the change being proposed, the rationale for the change, and why the status quo is no longer a viable option. This change leadership strategy addresses the following reason why change efforts fail.

Why Change Efforts Typically Fail: Reason 4

4. There is no compelling reason to change. The business case is not communicated.

Expect that many people in the organisation will not understand the need for a change; they will feel good about the job they are currently doing. As a result, they will have information concerns and likely will ask questions such as "What is the change? Why is it needed? What's wrong with the way things are now? How much and how fast does the organisation need to change?"

Most likely, those initiating the change were frustrated by something that was wrong with the status quo or were anxious about an opportunity that would be lost by continuing with business as usual. This spirit of discontent with the status quo needs to be shared and felt by those being asked to change.

Suppose a leader mistakenly attempts to create and communicate a change-specific vision to the organisation before demonstrating that the status quo is no longer a viable option. The inertia of the status quo will likely prove too strong, and the very people whose cooperation the leader needs are much less likely to embrace the picture of the future the leader intends to create. As John Maynard Keynes said:

---

*"The difficulty lies not so much in developing
new ideas as in escaping from old ones."*

In the child support example described earlier, it was critical to have custodial parents and county clerks share their stories about the frustration and hopelessness they felt in trying to track down and enforce the collection of child support from non-support-paying parents with only pen-and-paper support from government agents. Without county clerks feeling this frustration in some way, shape, or form, it was very unlikely that they would be willing to learn a new computer system and adopt new ways of working just because it was mandated by federal legislators.

As you build the case for change, one of the best ways to get buy-in from employees is to share information broadly and then ask people at all levels in the organisation to tell you why they believe the organisation needs to change. Ask people for their reasons why the organisation needs to change even if you already think you know the answers. By doing so, your case for change will be more compelling in people's eyes, because they came up with it. As a result of their ownership in the case for change, people are much more likely to leave the status quo behind.

Returning to the example we cited in Chapter 4, "Empowerment Is the Key," The Ken Blanchard Companies needed to make a number of changes as a result of the economic downturn following the terrorist attacks on September 11, 2001. The leaders shared information broadly with the organisation regarding projected revenue, current expenses, and break-even figures. This brought people face to face with the reality of the situation and ensured that the organisation understood that "business as usual" was no longer a viable option. Then the leaders asked associates what would happen if the status quo were maintained. The associates clearly stated that the company's survival was at stake. As a result of their involvement in building the case for change, associates bought into a number of cost-cutting initiatives, even when the initiatives weren't in their own best interest.

Strategy 4: Envision the Future

Outcome: Inspiring Vision

The fourth change leadership strategy, Envision the Future, addresses both **information** and **personal concerns**. To quote Proverbs 29:18, "Where there is no vision, the people perish."

When leaders envision the future, they create an inspiring vision that motivates people in the organisation and that unleashes their power and potential. This change leadership strategy addresses the following reason why change efforts fail.

Why Change Efforts Typically Fail: Reason 5

5.   A compelling vision that excites people about the future has not been developed and communicated.

It is critical for the organisation to have a compelling vision that inspires and excites people and makes them want to stay. When any organisational change is considered, it is always important to revisit the organisation's vision to provide rationale for the change. At times, this may mean modifying the organisation's vision or creating a new one, such as what happened when Louis Gerstner took over IBM. A new, compelling picture of the future when the proposed change is implemented must support the organisation's vision, including its purpose and values.

The process used to create a vision, whether it is for an entire organisation or for a specific change initiative, is the same. This process was described in detail in Chapter 2. As Ken Blanchard and Jesse Stoner point out in *Full Steam Ahead!: Unleash the Power of Vision in Your Company and Your Life*, the process you use to develop a vision is as important as the vision itself. In other words, if people are involved in the process and feel the vision is theirs— as opposed to some words on a poster from an executive retreat— they are more likely to see themselves as part of the future organisation. When this happens, people are more likely to show the tenacity needed during the challenging times that inevitably accompany change.

Getting people involved in the visioning process is also a key way to help them resolve the *personal concerns* they experience during a change. The more you can get people involved in the visioning process, the more likely it is they will want to be part of the future organisation. They need to be able to see themselves in the picture of the future for it to inspire them.

In our earlier child support example, the change leadership team was responsible for drafting the initial vision. Because there was no existing vision for the state's child support programme to compare it to, they needed to create a vision for the entire programme, not just for the implementation of an electronic tracking system. Next they took the draft vision to the county clerks across the state and asked them for input. The result was the creation of a shared vision that was compelling for the vast majority of those being asked to change:

> Our state's Child Support Programme helps children thrive by providing financial stability to their families and offering the highest-quality service as a nationally recognised model of excellence for child support enforcement.

While a small group of leaders could have come up with these words, giving county clerks an opportunity to provide input ensured that the vision was understood and embraced.

Strategy 5: Experiment to Ensure Alignment

Outcome: Collaborative Effort and Infrastructure

The fifth change leadership strategy, Experiment to Ensure Alignment, is for *personal* and *implementation concerns*.

When leaders engage others in planning and experimenting, they encourage collaborative effort and help build the infrastructure that is needed to support the change. The Experiment to Ensure Alignment strategy addresses the following reasons why change efforts fail.

Why Change Efforts Typically Fail: Reasons 7, 8, and 9

7. The change is not piloted, so the organisation does not learn what is needed to support the change.

8. Organisational systems and other initiatives are not aligned with the change.

9. Leaders lose focus or fail to prioritise, causing "death by 1,000 initiatives."

Involve others in planning and pilots. We've all seen or been part of changes that have not gone well. In most of these cases, the implementation plan was not developed by people anywhere near the front line. As a result, the plan did not account for some real-world realities and was shrugged off as flawed, unrealistic, and lacking the details required for action—or, worse yet, flat-out wrong.

As with the earlier change leadership strategies we described, when you involve people and give them a chance to influence, you get not only their buy-in, but also a better outcome. Also, your planning process needs to account for the fact that you won't have it all figured out ahead of time. Run some experiments or pilots with early adopters in an effort to work out the kinks and learn more about the best way to implement the change with the larger organisation. Ensure that your change implementation plan is dynamic.

By getting others involved in the planning process, you can resolve a number of **personal** and **implementation concerns**. Test drives, pilots, or experiments can also teach you what else needs to change in terms of policies, procedures, systems, and structures so that the probability of successful implementation across the larger organisation improves. The positive outcomes of engaging others at this stage of the change process are collaborative effort and the right infrastructure.

Many change plans underestimate the momentum generated by short-term wins. Short-term wins are improvements that can be implemented within a short time frame—typically three months—with minimal resources, at minimal cost, and at minimal risk. Short-term wins have several benefits. First, they proactively address ***impact concerns*** (such as "Is the change working?"). Second, they provide good news early in the change effort, when good news is hard to come by. Third, they reinforce behaviour changes made by early adopters. Fourth, they help sway those who are "on the fence" towards action.

In the child support case study pilot described earlier, it was critical to select counties that had the greatest probability of seeing significant short-term results from implementing the new electronic tracking system. This would help grease the skids and build momentum for post-pilot implementations with other counties where the impact was more in question.

Avoid death by 1,000 initiatives. With limited resources, it is critical to make choices about what change initiatives will allow your organisation to achieve its vision most effectively and efficiently. Individual change initiatives need to be scheduled and implemented in light of other activities and initiatives competing for people's time, energy, and mind share.

During times of change, it is critical to provide your people with direction on priorities. Like a sponge, after a certain amount of change, people cannot absorb any more, no matter how resilient and adaptive they are.

Decide what not to do. While it is important to provide direction on what to do, it is just as important to provide direction on what not to do. Ask the following questions when deciding what to do and what not to do: "What project or initiative will have the greatest impact on your vision? What provides the greatest value for resources expended (money, people, time)? Can the people responsible for working on the project handle it in light of all the other things they have been assigned to do? Are there enough qualified people who can dedicate time to work on the project? Are there any synergies between this project and other critical projects?"

Once you have prioritised and sequenced a list of possible change projects, recognise that, because we live in a dynamic environment, priorities can shift and resources can become more abundant or scarce. This may shift the type and number of projects an organisation undertakes at any point in time as well.

Decide how and when to measure and assess progress. The adage is true: What gets measured gets done. Because it is difficult to predict human behaviour with absolute certainty—especially in the face of major change—assess the progress being made on a number of fronts in an effort to identify potential risks to the change's success. These areas include sponsor commitment, employee commitment and behaviour change, achieving project milestones, and interim business results.

The plan crafted at this step of the change process needs to describe what will be measured, how it will be measured, and the frequency of measurement. To increase the probability of successful change, consider using an organisational change readiness assessment to determine what's working well and what requires additional work.

Communication, communication, communication. Much has been written about the importance of communication during times of change. Why is it so important? A significant amount of resistance encountered during organisational change is caused by a lack of information, especially the what and why types of information. In the absence of honest, passionate, and empathetic communication, people create their own information about the change, and rumours begin to serve as facts.

For example, we worked with an organisation going through a tremendous amount of change. As we started our work, we quickly realised that little or no rationale was being provided for key decisions that affected a large number of people. Without supporting rationale, the facts appeared harsh to team members:

- The development project I am working on was stopped.
- My budget was cut.

Based on these facts alone, many people assumed that the company's future was bleak. As a result, tremendous effort was required to overcome the rumour mill that led to drops in productivity and morale and that caused some people to begin looking for other jobs.

Let's consider these same facts, only this time with supporting rationale. Can you see how providing this rationale could have prevented the rumours and resistance that occurred?

- The project I am working on was stopped because we found that customer safety was at risk. Customer safety is our highest-priority value, so we made a decision in line with our values.

- My budget was cut because the organisation is reallocating these funds towards another drug development project based on a recent licensing agreement we signed.

Some of the strongest resistance to change occurs when reality differs from expectations. Therefore, understanding the current expectations of those affected by the change is critical if leaders are to manage and shape or transform those expectations effectively.

Recognise that covert resistance kills change. Effective leaders not only tolerate the open expression of concerns, they actually reward their people for sharing their concerns in an open, honest, and constructive manner. It is critical that leaders provide opportunities for two-way communication, because concerns cannot be surfaced and resolved without give-and-take dialogue.

It is also important to recognise that communicating your message once is not enough for most people to act on it. People in organisations are so bombarded with information that one of the best ways to sort out what requires action versus what does not is to listen for the messages that are communicated repetitively over time. These can be distinguished from the flavour-of-the-month messages that come and go. Communicate your key messages at least seven times in seven different ways. Better yet, at least ten times in ten different ways.

Strategy 6: Enable and Encourage

Outcome: New Skills and Commitment

The sixth change leadership strategy, Enable and Encourage, is for ***implementation*** and ***impact concerns***. When leaders enable and encourage people throughout the organisation to embrace the change, associates can develop new skills and make a deeper commitment to the organisation. This change leadership strategy addresses the following reason why change efforts fail.

Why Change Efforts Typically Fail: Reason 10

10. People are not enabled or encouraged to build new skills.

Our experience has shown that most organisations jump into this change leadership strategy much too soon. In many cases, executives announce the change and try to get people into training as soon as possible. Unfortunately, people's ***information*** and ***personal concerns*** have not been addressed, so the results of the training are less than optimal. Also, training often is delivered before all the kinks are worked out, contingencies are planned for, help desks are created, or systems are aligned. Finally, early training usually fails because it's "one size fits all." After the learnings from pilots and experiments are culled and the right infrastructure is in place, training for the change should be done in as individualised a way as possible. Ideally, a training strategy for each individual should be delivered at just the right time.

Notice how many other change leadership strategies precede the Enable and Encourage change leadership strategy in our model. Our model is front-loaded for a reason—namely, because most organisations don't do a good job on the early work that needs to be done to set up a successful change. The rallying cry we often hear in our work with organisations going through change is, "We're raising the bar!" This rallying cry is not bad in and of itself. However, nothing kills motivation faster than telling people to raise their performance but failing to provide them with new skills, tools, and resources required to leap over the height of the recently raised bar. As a result, people's reaction to leadership's statement that "We're raising the bar!" is often along the lines of "What does that mean? I'm not doing a good job now?"

After the roles, responsibilities, and competencies required for lasting change are determined, skill gaps need to be closed. As

Situational Leadership® II would suggest, leaders need to use a directing style 1 (with high direction and low support) or, more likely, a coaching style 2 (with high direction and high support) to build people's competence and commitment. Leaders need to use mistakes as opportunities for further learning, and they need to praise progress.

In the child support case study we described earlier, a group of county clerks involved in the pilots were chosen to train other county clerks on the new electronic tracking system and new work processes. This brought county clerk trainees face to face with others in similar positions who had gone down the path before them. Because the trainers were speaking from a position of experience, they were credible and could set realistic expectations for what other county clerks could expect when their county "went live."

In addition, the county clerks facilitating the training used the sessions as opportunities to gather additional input and ensure that the implementation plan was as strong as it could be.

Strategy 7: Execute and Endorse

Outcome: Accountability and Early Results

The seventh change leadership strategy, Execute and Endorse, is for **impact** and **collaboration concerns**. James Champy articulates this strategy well:

"A leader needs to attract followers ... but if the mobilisation process is to succeed, those followers must become leaders too, finding their own sense of purpose in the shared challenge and spreading the call and vision of the change."

When leaders execute and endorse the change, they create conditions for accountability and early results. This change leadership strategy addresses the following reasons why change efforts fail.

Why Change Efforts Typically Fail: Reasons 11, 12, and 13

11. Those leading the change are not credible. They undercommunicate, give mixed messages, and do not model the behaviours the change requires.

12. Progress is not measured, and/or no one recognises the changes that people have worked hard to make.

13. People are not held accountable for implementing the change.

Much has been written about the importance of execution. We do not argue with the emphasis being placed on execution. That being said, execution is much easier if you lead the change using the strategies we've described up to this point. If you don't, you will fight an uphill battle.

Walking the talk. Although it is critical for the change leadership team to communicate with one voice, it is even more important that the change leaders walk their talk and model the behaviours they expect of others.

It is estimated that a leader's actions are at least three times as important as what he or she says. Leaders need to display as much or more commitment to the change as the people they lead. People will assess what the leader does and doesn't do to assess the commitment to the change. The minute that associates or colleagues sense that their leader is not committed or is acting inconsistently with the desired behaviours of the change, they will no longer commit themselves to the effort.

Measure, praise progress, and redirect when necessary. As stated earlier, what gets measured gets done. Keep in mind that people's thoughts and actions are leading indicators of business and financial performance. Leading indicators allow you to drive by "looking through the windscreen" rather than by relying solely on lagging indicators such as financial performance, which is akin to driving while looking in the rear-view mirror.

Once measurement occurs, praise the progress that is being made. Don't wait for perfect performance. If you do, you'll be waiting a long time. This concept has been key to our teachings for decades:

---

*The key to developing people and creating
great organisations is to catch people doing things right
and to accentuate the positive.*

Because you've planned for short-term wins, you should be able to find and share success stories as a means of influencing people who remain on the fence. Follow through on your promise to recognise and reward the behaviour you expect, and follow through on your promise to impose consequences for anyone attempting to derail the change programme. This is the stage where you get rid of the people who are still resisting.

In our child support case study, the state government called monthly meetings for county clerks across the state with similar "go live" dates. During these meetings, each county was asked to share a success story as well as any challenges they were having. The idea of holding each county accountable for sharing a success story in front of their peers created some healthy competition to make the new tracking system work. It allowed early-adopting counties to sway those that were on the fence. Discussing the challenges also provided opportunities for learning that could be fed back into the design of the tracking system, the planning process, and the training of county clerks.

In another example, a change leadership team we worked with instituted the use of a "performance dashboard" to continually measure progress against a set of key performance indicators. The change leadership team met twice a month to discuss the plan's progress, as seen by green, yellow, and red indicators on the performance dashboard. If a key performance indicator was green, this was praised and celebrated. If a key performance indicator was yellow or red, the team would discuss how best to respond to get that indicator back on track. This process held people accountable for performance and also ensured that people got the direction and support they needed to get back on track.

Strategy 8: Embed and Extend

Outcome: Reach and Sustain Results

The eighth change leadership strategy, Embed and Extend, is for **collaboration** and ***refinement concerns***. Here's a good rule of thumb:

Organisations should spend ten times more energy reinforcing the change they just made than looking for the next great change to try.

When leaders embed and extend the desired change, they can reach and sustain the desired results. This change leadership strategy addresses the following reason why change efforts fail.

Why Change Efforts Typically Fail: Reason 14

14. People leading the change fail to respect the power of the culture to kill the change.

Culture can be defined as the predominating attitudes, beliefs, and behaviour patterns that characterise an organisation's functioning. While a high-performing change leadership team can generate enthusiam and short-term success during times of change, it is critical that the change be embedded in the organisation's culture if it is to be sustainable over the long haul.

If a change is introduced that is not aligned with the current culture, you must alter the existing culture to support the new initiative or accept that the change may not be sustainable in the long term. The best way to alter the culture is to go back to the organisation's vision and examine its values. Identify which values support the new culture and which don't. Choose the most critical values. Then define the behaviours that are consistent with the values, and create rewards and accountability for behaving consistently with the values. It is energising for an organisation to do this in the context of implementing change.

In many cases, a change is implemented within one business unit before other business units are engaged. The change process defined by the Leading People Through Change Model needs to be repeated for the new units that have not yet gone through the process.

Citing our child support case study again, it was critical to ensure that all obstacles to using the new tracking system were removed. While there were some common obstacles to overcome for most counties, many obstacles differed by county. As a result, embedding the change on a local level required attention at the local level. Because ongoing support was provided, obstacles were removed, and the counties themselves sold each other on the benefits of implementing the new tracking system. Doing so allowed the initiative to be extended across an entire state and eventually the entire country.

Strategy 9: Explore Possibilities

Outcome: Options

The ninth change leadership strategy, Explore Possibilities, is for **refinement concerns**. By involving others in exploring possibilities, you immediately lower information concerns as a new change is announced, because people are "in the loop" about deciding what needs to change. This change leadership strategy addresses the following reason why change efforts fail.

Why Change Efforts Typically Fail: Reason 15

15. Possibilities and options are not explored before a specific change is chosen.

Ideally, those who are closest to the problems and opportunities in an organisation are the ones who come up with the options to be considered by the change leadership team. To ensure face validity and inclusion of the best options, the options identified should be reviewed by a representative sample of those being asked to change.

In our child support case study, non-custodial parents and county clerks across the country expressed frustration with the fact that non-support-paying parents were getting harder to track and more elusive than ever. As a result, the federal government took this input, explored the root causes of the problem, and identified a number of possible responses. A number of change projects were chosen as part of an integrated strategy to enforce the collection of child support payments. These projects included but were not limited to withholding income from the non-custodial parent's employer and intercepting income tax refunds (state and federal), unemployment compensation benefits, and lottery winnings. The projects also included credit bureau reporting, driving and professional licence suspension, financial institution data match (locating bank assets), cross-matching new-hire reporting, hunting and fishing licence suspension, passport denial, liens, federal loan data matching, and computer automation of child support operations, including interfaces with numerous other state agency systems.

Some of these options were potentially more feasible and would have more impact than others. By simply having options, people felt they had choices and could influence what changed.

Since 1995, annual child support collections in the state where the enforcement tracking system was implemented have increased from $177 million to more than $460 million. Increased collections means that more children are receiving the child support they deserve, and fewer families will have to resort to public assistance to survive.[2]

It is our hope that instructing change leadership teams how to address each stage of concern during organisational change has taken much of the mystique out of the process and shown you how you can lead at a higher level. Responding to others' concerns and paying attention to how you increase involvement and influence at each step in the change process is the best way we know to build future change receptivity, capability, and leadership.

To get sustainable results over the long term from a change effort, it is critical that the change be embedded in the organisation's culture. It's worth repeating that if a change is introduced that is not aligned with the current culture, you must alter the existing culture to support the new initiative or accept that the change may not be sustainable. Given the importance of culture, in the next chapter we will help you understand how to build or transform an organisational culture.

Chapter 13

MANAGING A SUCCESSFUL CULTURAL TRANSFORMATION

Garry Demarest, Chris Edmonds,
and Bob Glaser

Look closely at the operations of any high-performing organisation, and you are bound to find a strong and distinct culture. While most people have heard the term and it has been written about widely,[1] culture can be a slippery concept to describe. As we indicated in Chapter 2, "The Power of Vision," we define culture as the context in which all practices exist. It is the organisation's personality; it's "how things are done around here." When we talk about an organisation's culture, we are referring to the values, attitudes, beliefs, behaviours, and practices of the organisational members.

In our experience, most members of an organisation typically find it difficult to describe their company's culture, often because they are so immersed in it. They have not thought about the unique elements, symbols, rituals, stories, events, and demonstrated behaviours that make their organisation's culture what it is.

New members of an organisation often learn about the culture the hard way, by bumping into it—literally and figuratively—as they attempt to navigate their way through it. Experienced members are quick to correct the newcomers and educate them about the "expected behaviour." For example, when teaching a class at one of American Honda's manufacturing plants several years ago, one of our consulting partners was reprimanded by a manager for bringing food into the classroom. He was told that no associate was allowed to eat in the classrooms, and he was expected to follow the same rule.

Every organisation has a culture; it can be formally defined or evolve entirely by default. The company's culture will enable organisational performance and employee passion—or erode it. Culture can be complex. Within an organisation, different divisions, regions, or departments can have slightly—or hugely—different cultures. Those intact cultures may, as with the broad organisation, help, hinder, or hurt organisational performance and employee passion.

Culture underlies all that an organisation does. As we learned in the preceding chapter, it also determines the organisation's readiness for change. When organisations seek greatness, they often find aspects of their organisational culture that need change.

Leaders begin to consider a culture change when they know something in their organisation is not working or is broken. It may be a single incident that raises eyebrows—or requires a costly recovery—or patterns of behaviour that demonstrate a low threshold of trust, respect, and confidence across the organisation. Perhaps a series of low scores on employee morale surveys tells leaders the organisation is less than healthy.

Gung Ho!: A Starting Point

We recognised for a long time that culture has a profound effect on the behaviour of organisational members, the trust and respect that exist between them, and ultimately the organisation's success. However, we didn't spend much time studying culture until after the publication of Ken Blanchard and Sheldon Bowles's book *Gung Ho!: Turn on the People in Any Organisation*. It was the story of two unlikely characters—Peggy Sinclair, a new top manager, and Andy Longclaw, an often-criticised manager. They went on an unconventional journey to successfully change the culture in their manufacturing plant.[2]

We received many calls and e-mails from organisation leaders about their efforts and hopes for putting the Gung Ho!® story into practice. Some had attempted to implement the key principles based on the book—needing worthwhile work (the Spirit of the Squirrel), being in control of achieving the goal (the Way of the Beaver), and cheering each other on (the Gift of the Goose). But they found that the results and changes were not sustainable or didn't produce the anticipated results. Some who focused on the Gift of the Goose "Cheering Each Other On" principle found that the positive feelings generated were short-lived and didn't change their people's behaviour in the long term.

Interacting with these leaders, we realised we had to get smarter about culture—both how to create a strong and distinct culture, and how to change a culture that is hindering the implementation of a major initiative. Early on, we learned four things. First, there is no one "right" culture. Second, most organisations do not consciously create their culture. Third, senior leaders often don't understand the impact of culture on performance. Finally, a strong, focused culture starts with a compelling vision.

One "Right" Culture?

There is no "right" or "correct" organisational culture. We've seen high-performing organisations in a variety of industries around the world. They have slightly different value descriptions, and different behaviours that are expected, but one thing is true among all of them—the culture serves their people, customers, and stakeholders equally.

The biggest question everyone faces is, "What is the right culture for our organisation?" The answer depends on several factors. What principles do you want demonstrated, day in and day out, in your organisation? What behaviours will consistently create the desired high-performance while enabling strong trust and respect across all employees and customers? What behaviours do star performers consistently demonstrate? How do you want managers and employees to treat each other? What would you like customers to consistently say about your products and services, and about their interactions with your staff?

Culture by Default, Not by Design

Our extensive experience with a wide variety of organisations has led us to conclude that most organisations do not *consciously* create their culture. Their company's culture simply emerged as the organisation's products and services were developed, then purchased by customers and delivered by the organisation. Culture, therefore, typically happens by default, not by design.

If your current organisational culture does not serve customers well, maintain passionate employees, and create profits for your enterprise to continue growing and serving, you must consider revising the organisation's way of operating by embracing cultural transformation.

The key question for senior leaders is:

Does your culture serve your organisation?

If it doesn't, it is time to become proactive about building a culture that serves the needs of the entire organisation, not just the leaders.

Senior Leaders Are Sceptical About Culture

Very often leaders cannot diagnose a sick culture. For example, they attribute low morale or poor performance to poor management skills, inconsistent teamwork, or outside influences. They don't see that these issues may be a result of a culture that needs attention.

One reason that culture is not at the top of leaders' minds is the prevailing notion that culture is not relevant to bottom-line business—not linked to an organisation's performance. This belief has been reinforced by the fact that much of the business press over the past 20 years has focused on increasing organisational performance. Very few books—and even fewer consultants—have focused on the power of culture to positively impact both performance and employee passion.

"Culture Drives Performance"

The reason business writers have focused primarily on organisational performance is completely rational. Most senior leaders will tell you their primary performance metric is organisational performance (sales, productivity, and profits). Financial performance is of critical importance to senior leaders because *that's how they get evaluated and rewarded*. Unfortunately, this situation produces a single-minded focus on short-term results at the expense of longer-term outcomes that contribute to and drive performance, such as employee passion, customer service, and consistent quality. These are all things that a high-performing culture can impact after a culture change process has been implemented.

For example, Merck, one of the world's most successful pharmaceutical companies, experienced a remarkable turnaround in a sales division that embraced a culture change process. The division was one of the poorest performers at the time, and the division vice president had left for another opportunity in the company. This transition presented a "great opportunity to think about the culture we wanted," related Tim Schmidt, then director of sales training and professional development. The management team internalised, applied, and modelled a culture change process, with particular emphasis on teamwork, responsibility, and accountability for everyone in the division. Within a year, and still without a vice president at the helm, the division rose to the number two performer in the country. Senior business director of the division at the time, Janet Crawford, stated that their culture change process had "a direct link to our success."

A culture change can improve the bottom line—and quickly. Under the guidance of president Mark Deterding and his senior leadership team, Banta Catalog Group's transformed culture increased employee engagement by 20 per cent, increased employee retention by 17 per cent, and improved profitability by 36 per cent—all within 18 months.

Bowater Pulp and Paper in Gatineau, Ontario, Canada, attributed over $50 million in cost reductions to their culture change process. They noted, among other positive changes, a 40 per cent improvement in clarity of work objectives and responsibilities, a 44 per cent improvement in managerial follow-up to employee suggestions, and a 24 per cent improvement in interdepartmental relations.

The culture change process of Minera El Tesoro, a copper mining operation in Chile, helped the mine generate production levels 29 per cent over design capacity by the fourth year. After the culture change, accidents were reduced by 40 per cent, and the company was recognised as one of the ten best places to work in Chile.

The Importance of a Compelling Vision

As we discussed in Chapter 2, a strong, focused organisational culture starts with a compelling vision that tells everyone who you are (your purpose), where you're going (your picture of the future), and what will guide your journey (your values).

Of these three key elements, the most impactful one for a high-performing culture is values, because they should guide behaviour and decisions on a daily basis. Most senior leadership teams are not clear about the values and behaviours that are expected of their members. In fact, most organisations have not even defined values, such as "what a good citizen looks like around here." Yet understanding an organisation's core values is vital to decoding an organisation's culture. Corporate values, if they exist, typically are communicated during a new member's introduction to the company. Those values may be described in the annual report, posted in the lobby or on hallway walls, or even printed on the backs of business cards. But these espoused or stated values may not be well communicated or understood by employees or visible to customers.

Try this test: ask a few frontline employees if they can recite your company's values. In many organisations around the globe, you won't get a confident, clear answer—you'll get a blank look!

Even if an organisation's desired values are clear, senior leaders typically are not disciplined in examining the extent to which members of their organisation are living these espoused organisational values. If the lived values are not aligned with the espoused values, you will not see desired behaviours demonstrated in the organisation. In fact, you'll see undesirable behaviours that cause you to cringe and that undermine your organisation's success and integrity. Enron is an example of an organisation whose lived values were inconsistent with its espoused values. Enron's "integrity" value was displayed for all to see and was even behaviourally defined. However, it was not a lived value (at least in the executive suites), as we so sadly learned.

From Gung Ho! to a Proven Cultural Transformation

If senior leaders are to effectively transform their organisation's culture, they need to create a foundation of clear performance expectations, behaviourally defined values, and accountability for demonstrating both. To help them build such a foundation, we created a Gung Ho! culture training programme that teaches leaders and managers the best practices of high-performing, values-aligned organisations. The programme helps leaders identify gaps that exist in their organisation's current culture and take steps to turn their cultural vision into reality. In 2002 the Gung Ho! programme was recognised as one of the top ten training programmes of the year by *HR Executive* magazine.[3]

One of the most important aspects of the Gung Ho! training programme was that it helped leaders decide if they were ready to commit to a full-blown culture change. As with so many corporate initiatives, the training programme alone would not generate the traction needed to make long-term culture change happen. True change required a deeper commitment.

Once we analysed the issues and problems that senior leaders faced in managing a full-blown cultural transformation, the core issue was obvious: most organisational leaders have not experienced successful culture change and didn't see the impact that the culture was having on performance and results. Fewer still had *led* successful culture change. We realised that to effectively lead culture change, we needed to build both **competence** (knowledge and skills) and **commitment** (motivation and confidence) in these senior leaders. We needed to create structure, educate about steps and phases, and provide ongoing coaching to ensure that senior leaders—who must be the primary drivers and champions of the initiative—keep the process on track. This required a consulting intervention, not just a training programme.

Managing a Successful Cultural Transformation

The process we use to help organisations and their leaders successfully manage cultural change was developed before the Leading People Through Change model discussed in the preceding chapter, yet the two approaches are compatible. For example, senior leaders *must* be the champions of the culture change. They alone have the power to define the desired culture and create or refine systems, policies, and procedures to reinforce that desired culture. They must "walk the talk," modelling the behaviour expected of all organisation members.

A quick fix is rarely possible. It takes years for any organisational culture to reach its current stage. With consistent, focused effort, leaders can expect to spend two to five years successfully transforming their organisation's culture. It took Jack Welch nearly ten years to turn around General Electric in the mid-1980s.

Keep in mind that people resist change. Even if the present isn't fun, people prefer the known to the unknown. Patience and persistence will pay off. Senior leaders need to continually communicate the need for change, celebrate progress, and reinforce the desired behaviours.

If cultural change is to be successful, everyone—senior leaders, managers, supervisers, team leads, frontline staff—should be held accountable for achieving performance and living the organisational values. Remember, organisational culture will change when individuals change their behaviour.

Don't embark on this cultural transformation journey casually. The promise of culture change raises hopes in the hearts and minds of staff members that department silos, unethical behaviour, and inconsistent policies will go away. If the senior leadership team does not follow through on declared commitments for transforming the culture, credibility and trust will be eroded. If you're not certain that this is the right path for your organisation, and you're unwilling to commit to a multiyear initiative, *don't start*.

The Gung Ho! culture change process has four distinct phases: ***discovery***, ***immersion***, ***alignment***, and ***refinement***. These usually occur in chronological order. However, some overlap occurs as an organisation moves into the later phases. This process has been proven over many years. We've seen consistent positive results when these steps are followed—and inconsistent results when the steps are not followed.

Phase One: Discovery

This initial phase allows us to learn about the current organisational culture and understand the issues and opportunities senior leaders are concerned about. During this phase we focus on the present reality. We find out from senior leaders and selected frontline staff what performance outcomes are expected. We discover what values, if any, are defined, known, or acted on. We talk to frontline staff and sometimes even customers to assess the degree of employee passion that exists. And, probably most importantly, we find out what accountability systems are in place to ensure that people's behaviour matches the organisation's values.

At the end of the discovery phase we make specific recommendations that address the organisation's issues and gaps. For example, it is rare to find organisations with clearly defined values, let alone organisations with accountability systems in place to ensure that those values are practised. In such organisations, it's not surprising to find that employees lack passion and that performance is lagging. When we point out this dynamic to senior leaders, they're often amazed that we nailed their issues so quickly. They're also relieved that we can provide a logical approach to addressing these problems. This often motivates them to continue the culture change process.

Phase Two: Immersion

The immersion phase focuses on giving senior leaders, managers, and supervisers thorough exposure to the best practices of high-performing, values-aligned organisational cultures. Because senior leaders are the key players in this initiative and will be the champions and banner carriers throughout, we will start with their immersion.

The two-day culture process kick-off workshop shows senior leaders how their organisation fares on our Purposeful Culture Assessment (PCA). During the kick-off, leaders learn the elements of the culture change process, identify consensus issues to address, and decide whether to move forward with the initiative.

The assessment is a vital tool for the process kick-off workshop. Done as work in advance of the session, the assessment compares best practices of high-performing, values-aligned organisations to the practices of the team's organisation. The assessment profile is scored during the workshop and serves as the basis for identifying issues and culture gaps. It also helps senior leaders begin action planning during the session.

Once they've completed the culture process workshop, senior leadership teams typically agree that they have some clear gaps to address, short-term and long-term. Yet before those action plans can be created or prioritised, the senior leaders must decide if they are ready to move forward with this initiative. The time commitment and scrutiny they will undergo are heavy burdens. In some cases, either the team or the organisation is not ready to take the steps necessary for the change.

A quick word about the scrutiny the senior leaders will face. As this team takes the lead on defining the values and behaviours the new culture will require, the individual members immediately will be held to those standards. The employee expectation of senior leaders will be "If they declare these values, they'd better live by them!" How senior leaders live their lives will be watched closely. If they run a red light driving home from work one night, that might be perceived as "not living the company values." This scrutiny is natural and will diminish as leaders model the values consistently and credibly as the initiative builds.

Several other action items come out of the culture kick-off session. Now the senior leadership team must agree on a process for formalising the organisation's new vision, purpose, and values. They must decide how to manage performance with greater discipline, with clear goal agreements and accountability for performance. They must manage values with greater discipline as well, describing what it will look like when people are living the new values and how people will be held accountable when they don't live up to those values. They must develop a communication plan that clearly describes the reasons for the change initiative and that fully explains the desired values and behaviours. They must invite staff members to provide thoughts and insights as the new organisational vision, purpose, and values are developed.

As the senior leadership team focuses on these action steps, the process kick-off sessions are cascaded throughout the management hierarchy. In these sessions, managers get feedback about how their teams are functioning compared to best practices. They also get to give feedback on the initial work done by the senior leadership team. The managers' action plans typically are more tactical and day-to-day in nature than the action plans of the senior leaders, which are usually more strategic and across-the-organisation in nature.

Some companies are highly creative about the **immersion** process. For example, ASDA, a successful supermarket chain across the UK, transformed the grounds of a conference centre into a retreat, featuring the elements of the Gung Ho! story. The interior of the main tent looked like a forest, with a set that included a beaver dam and lake, with geese flying across the ceiling. Beanbag chairs represented rocks, and the ASDA mission and values were carved in stone. Additional tents were set up like log cabins around a forest lake, with each cabin housing three session participants. Participants were literally immersed in the culture story. Cabin groups were paired throughout the three-day event, cooking and serving dinner to their cabinmates each evening and learning servant leadership along the way.

"The approach seemed slightly off the wall to the reserved Brits," said ASDA president and project leader Philip Horn.

The event had a long-lasting effect. Graduates of the programme took the *Gung Ho!* principles back to their business units and inspired employees to build high-performing, values-aligned teams in their workplaces. In 2004, ASDA was named Britain's number-one employer of choice. Horn and his team believe this could not have happened without immersing the company in the culture change.

Phase Three: Alignment

Alignment is the phase in which structures and systems in the organisation are re-engineered to be consistent with the new culture. Without this phase, it's impossible for members of an organisation to walk the talk and be held accountable for the new vision and desired changes. Accountability can happen only when expectations are clear. All staff members must understand what's expected of them in terms of performance and values. Only after these expectations have been defined and agreed on can coaching, celebrating, or redirecting occur.

During the alignment phase, the senior leadership team must identify key metrics for the culture change initiative. These are often items such as performance gains, efficiency, growth, and employee engagement or passion. These metrics need to be published and measured regularly—monthly is best—with the results published throughout the organisation. Everyone needs to know what the targets are and how well they are meeting them.

One of the bindery supervisers at the Banta Catalog Group created a simple graph of each team's (and each shift's) targets and progress. This graph became the bindery "dashboard" referred to in team meetings and during team huddles at the start of each shift. That graph proved so valuable that when the team was able to purchase a computerised system to display these key metrics, the dashboard elements were displayed exactly as the original graph had displayed them.

Systems need to be assessed for needed modifications to ensure that staff members are delivering on performance expectations *and* are demonstrating desired values. If systems are not aligned, people get confused. Competing systems and procedures frustrate staff and reduce employee passion.

One example of the power of alignment came from an all-company meeting facilitated by Mark Deterding, the president of Banta Catalog Group. The senior leaders had done a great job of seeking feedback and input on the proposed plant values and valued behaviours. Mark reviewed the final draft of the values for all staff in this meeting and made a statement that shocked the attendees. "From this day forward, I am no longer the boss around here. These values and behaviours are the boss!" Mark invited everyone in attendance to hold him accountable for modelling these values and to do the same with their managers and supervisers. That commitment made a strong impression on the plant staff about how important the values were to Mark and his team.

The benefits and outcomes of the alignment phase cannot be underestimated. It is during this time that positive cultural changes begin to appear. For example, after we worked with Aetna Production Services to help guide a department-wide culture change initiative, the company found significant improvement not only in productivity and service levels but also in corporate employee morale. For example, 84 per cent of the staff scored their unit as a good place to work—39 per cent better than the overall national score for the company. Ninety-two per cent scored their job satisfaction as favourable—26 per cent higher than the national score. Ninety-two per cent also ranked the appropriate use of rewards and recognition (other than money) as favourable—46 per cent better than the national score.

Senior leaders must be democratic about the alignment process, inviting thoughts, ideas, and insights from people across the organisation. Inviting everyone to chime in creates buy-in. It usually takes two to three months to finalise the initial[4] draft of the values and behaviours on which the values survey will be based.

The Employee Survey

Once the values and behaviours have been formulated and blessed by the entire workforce, accountability systems must be created and tested. The single most effective tool for values accountability is the employee survey, preferably one that's been customised to the organisation's unique values definitions and observable valued behaviours.

In the first run of the survey, employees are asked to assess the degree to which organisational senior leaders, managers, and supervisers demonstrate the valued behaviours. Employee perceptions of how well they and their peers demonstrate these valued behaviours are measured in successive runs of the survey.

It is important to assess employee perceptions with the initial values survey within six months of finalising the draft vision, purpose, and values. The survey should be distributed to all employees with an invitation for them to complete the survey.

Making the survey mandatory will skew employee attitudes about the survey and even about the culture change.

Once survey responses have been submitted, senior leadership team members must analyse the results for gaps in values alignment and develop tactical plans for quickly addressing the gaps. Employees might identify gaps in systems and procedures, providing insights into specific supervisers or managers who may not consistently demonstrate the desired valued behaviours. It is of the utmost importance to share the resulting data, coach leaders to refine their behaviour, and fix broken systems as soon as possible after the first survey is completed.

The second run of the survey—and all successive runs—should invite employees to assess not only the organisation's leaders but also their peers and themselves. The survey process is ongoing; once you start, you never stop. Best practices for values suggest surveying the employee community every six months. After each round, a summary of successes and gaps should be published, and staff members should be made aware of what is being done to address those gaps.

The final element of this alignment phase is exposing frontline staff to the culture change workshop. Because most frontline employees cannot be pulled off their jobs for a two-day session, team members and supervisers go through modular sessions lasting about two hours each. These sessions allow frontline staff members to clarify and formalise their team's purpose and refine the organisation's values into team norms that are relevant to their work and customers.

Phase Four: Refinement

The **refinement** phase is in essence an ongoing project. Senior leaders must continue to refine systems and policies—and at times even "refine" staff members—to reinforce the desired behaviour and values. Through surveys and feedback, monitoring of key metrics continues, ideally featuring grand celebrations of accomplishments. This is also the time when additional leadership training is scheduled to continue building the skills to keep the cultural change alive and breathing. The organisation should create a new employee orientation process to include the newly clarified purpose, values, and performance expectations.

As we noted earlier, it is likely that you will need to refine the organisational values and valued behaviours over time. As you experience how your valued behaviours are embraced or tested, some tweaking will help ensure that the day-to-day culture continues to reflect the desired vision.

Critical Success Factors for Cultural Transformation

Organisations that successfully create high-performing, values-aligned cultures share five critical success factors:

- **The senior leadership team must demonstrate commitment to the long-term process.** The culture change process must be embraced and championed by the senior leadership team. They will be held to high standards as the values are defined and communicated. Cultural transformation is an ongoing project that will never go away.

- **Values must be defined in behavioural terms.** This is the only approach that makes your desired behaviours observable, tangible, and measurable.

- **Accountability for delivering promised performance and demonstrating valued behaviours is paramount.** Consequences must be swift and consistent. Positive consequences for meeting performance and values expectations must be described and demonstrated, and agreed-to negative consequences must be applied when performance is below standards or valued behaviours are not demonstrated.

- **It is vital that all staff are involved in and buy into the culture transformation at every phase.** This process is not about "managing by announcements," where leaders tell everyone what the new expectations are but don't invite thoughts or hold people—including themselves—consistently accountable. For everyone to embrace the desired culture, they must be included in the process. They must help define and commit to what the new culture will demand of them in their roles.

- **The elephant must be eaten one bite at a time.** Find a manageable scope for the change initiative. Don't try to change the entire organisation at once. Start with a distinct part of the organisation—a department, division, plant, or regional office—to learn how the process flows. Then, with learnings clearly in mind, select another distinct part of the organisation, and begin the change process there. Continue until you've digested the entire elephant.

Changing an organisational culture is not easy. Leaders whose motto is "My way or the highway" will have trouble getting buy-in throughout the organisation. The most successful culture changes we've seen are those in which the top managers are servant leaders. They help establish a compelling vision and clear goals and then become the head cheerleaders for helping everyone live the dream. The next section discusses the right kind of leadership.

section IV

HAVE THE RIGHT KIND OF LEADERSHIP

Chapter 14

SERVANT LEADERSHIP

Ken Blanchard,
Scott Blanchard, and Drea Zigarmi

When people lead at a higher level, they make the world a better place, because their goals are focused on the greater good. This requires a special kind of leader: a servant leader.

Robert Greenleaf first coined the term "servant leadership" in 1970 and published widely on the concept for the next 20 years.[1] Yet it is an old concept. Two thousand years ago, servant leadership was central to the philosophy of Jesus, who exemplified the fully committed and effective servant leader.[2] Mahatma Gandhi, Dr Martin Luther King, Jr, and Nelson Mandela are more recent examples of leaders who have exemplified this philosophy.

What Is Servant Leadership?

When people hear the phrase servant leadership, they are often confused. They immediately conjure up thoughts of the inmates running the prison, or trying to please everyone. Others think servant leadership is only for church leaders. The problem is that they don't understand leadership. They think you can't lead and serve at the same time. Yet you can if you understand—as we have emphasised a number of times—that leadership has two parts: vision and implementation. In the visionary role, leaders define the direction. It's their responsibility to communicate what the organisation stands for and wants to accomplish.

Max DePree, legendary chairman of Herman Miller and author of *Leadership Is an Art,* compared this role to that of a primary school teacher who keeps repeating the basics. "When it comes to vision and values, you have to say it over and over and over again until people get it right, right, right!"

As you now know, the responsibility for this visionary role falls to the hierarchical leadership. Kids look to their parents, players look to their coaches, and people look to their organisational leaders for direction. *The visionary role is the leadership aspect of servant leadership.*

Once people are clear on where they are going, the leader's role shifts to a service mindset for the task of implementation— the second aspect of leadership. How do you make the dream happen? *Implementation is where the servant aspect of servant leadership comes into play.* In a traditional organisation, managers are thought of as responsible, and their people are taught to be responsive to their boss. "Boss watching" becomes a popular sport, and people get promoted on their upward-influencing skills. That activity doesn't do much for accomplishing a clear vision. All people try to do is protect themselves rather than move the organisation in the desired direction.

Servant leaders, on the other hand, feel their role is to help people achieve their goals. They constantly try to find out what their people need to perform well and live according to the vision. Rather than wanting people to please their bosses, servant leaders want to make a difference in the lives of their people and, in the process, impact the organisation. With its emphasis on bringing out the magnificence in people, Situational Leadership® II is a servant leadership model.

Applying Servant Leadership

To help you realise that servant leadership can occur in any organisation, consider the following example from the USA's Department of Motor Vehicles (DMV). The DMV has such a multitude of people to take care of—basically, everybody with a driving licence—that it's no surprise they sometimes treat you like a number instead of a person. In most states, after you have passed your initial tests, you can avoid the DMV for years if you fill out the proper form and mail it in.

Ken Blanchard had avoided his local DMV like the plague. But several years ago, he lost his driving licence about three weeks before he was scheduled to leave on a trip to Europe. He knew he had to go to the DMV and get a new licence to back up his passport on his trip. So he said to his executive assistant, "Dana, would you put three hours on my calendar next week sometime so I can go to the DMV?" In Ken's experience, that's about how long it usually took to get anything done there. He'd wait for a long time, and then they'd tell him he was in the wrong line, he'd filled out the wrong form, or he'd done something that meant he had to start all over.

As a result, Ken headed over to the DMV with low expectations. (Remember, he hadn't been there in years.) He knew immediately something had changed when he walked in the front door, because a woman spoke to him and said, "Welcome to the Department of Motor Vehicles! Do you speak English or Spanish?"

"English," Ken replied.

She said, "Right over there." The guy behind the counter smiled and said, "Welcome to the Department of Motor Vehicles! How may I help you?" It took Ken nine minutes to get his replacement licence, including having his picture taken. He said to the woman who took his picture, "What are you all smoking here? I mean, this isn't the Department of Motor Vehicles that I used to know and love."

She asked, "Haven't you met the new director?"

"No," he said.

So she pointed to a desk behind all the counters, right out in the open. Clearly the director had no privacy. His office was in the middle of everything. Ken went over, introduced himself, and said, "What's your job as the director of the Department of Motor Vehicles?"

What the man said is the best definition of management we've ever heard:

"My job is to reorganise the department on a moment-to-moment basis, depending on citizen (customer) need."

The director obviously had a compelling vision for this department. The point of their business was to serve the citizens and their needs, and to serve them well.

What did this director do? He cross-trained everybody in every job. Everyone could handle the front desk; everyone could take the pictures. You name it—everyone could do it! Even the people in the back, who normally weren't out in front, could do every job. Why? Because if suddenly there was a flood of citizens, why have people in the back doing bookkeeping, accounting, or secretarial work when there were customers who needed help? So he'd bring them out when they were needed.

The DMV director also insisted that nobody go to lunch between 11:30 and 2:00. Why? Because that's when the most customers showed up. Ken told this story at a seminar one time, and a woman came up to him at the break and said, "Where is your Department of Motor Vehicles? I can't believe what you've been telling us." She continued, "I recently waited in line for about 45 minutes at our DMV, and I was almost at the front of the line when the woman announced, 'It's break time.' We had to stand around for 15 minutes while they all went for coffee and stretched their legs."

That didn't happen at this "new" Department of Motor Vehicles, where the director had created a motivating environment. Those team members were really committed. Even employees Ken recognised from past visits who had joined in on the "fun" of abusing the customers were now excited about serving.

Often you see people at one point and they are so excited about their work. Then you see them three months later and they're discouraged. In 90 per cent of these cases, the only thing that has changed is that they have a new boss. Someone who jerks them around, who doesn't listen to them, who doesn't involve them in decision making, and who treats them as if they really are *subordinates*. The reverse is also true. People can be unhappy in a job situation when suddenly a new leader comes in and their eyes brighten, their energy increases, and they are really ready to perform well and make a difference.

When leaders make a positive difference, people act like they own the place, and they bring their brains to work. Their managers encourage their newfound initiative. Another example from the "new" DMV underlines this point.

Great Leaders Encourage Their People to Bring Their Brains to Work

Just about the time Ken had his inspiring experience with the DMV, Dana, his executive assistant, decided to buy a big scooter and whizz around southern California. When she got this beauty, somebody told her, "You have to get a licence." She had never thought about needing a licence for a scooter. So, she went to the DMV to do the right thing. The woman behind the counter went into the computer and found Dana's name and driving record. It turns out that Dana had a perfect driving record. She never had a traffic violation.

"Dana," the woman said, "I noticed that in three months you have to retake your written driving test. Why don't you take both tests today?"

Caught off guard, Dana said, "Tests? I didn't know I was supposed to take a test." And she started to panic.

The woman reached over the counter, patted Dana's hand, and said, "Oh, Dana, don't worry. With your driving record, I'm sure you can pass these tests. And besides, if you don't, you can always come back."

Dana took the tests. She went back to the woman, who marked them. Dana fell one correct answer short of passing each test, so officially she failed both. But, in a kind way, the woman said, "Oh, Dana. You are so close to passing. Let me try something. Let me re-ask you one question on each test to see if you can get it right so I can pass you." Not only was this a wonderful offer, but the fact was, each question had only two possible answers. So the woman said, "Dana, you chose B. What do you think would be the right answer?"

When Dana said, "A," this helpful woman said, "You're right! You pass!"

Ken once told this story at a seminar, and a bureaucrat came racing up to the platform during the break. He started yelling, "Why are you telling this story? That woman broke the law! Your assistant failed both of those tests!"

So Ken went back to see his DMV director friend. He told him about this bureaucrat, and the director said, "Let me tell you one other thing. When it comes to decision making, I want my people to use their brains more than rules, regulations, or laws. My person decided that it was silly to make someone like your assistant Dana, with her perfect driving record, come back to retake a test on which she missed only one question. I guarantee you, if she had missed four or five questions, my person wouldn't have given her the same deal. And to show you how important I think this is, *I would back that person's decision with my job.*"

Would you like to work for this kind of leader? You'd better believe it. Why? Because he is a servant leader. In Rick Warren's best-selling book *The Purpose Driven Life*, the first sentence is "It's not about you."[3] Just like our DMV director, servant leaders realise that leadership is not about them. It's about what and who they are serving. What's the vision, and who's the customer? The vision answers Hayes and Stevens' question, "What's the point?" As the authors of *The Heart of Business* insist, "profit can be a by-product of the pursuit of a higher purpose and even part of the planned process in pursuit of that higher purpose, but it should never be the purpose and motive itself."[4] If profit is your reason for being an organisation, it will eventually drive your people and customers to be self-serving, too. As we argued in Chapter 3, "Serving Customers at a Higher Level," everyone has a customer. Who is a manager's customer? The people who report to that manager. Once the vision and direction are set, managers work for their people.

What Impacts Performance the Most?

To find out what kind of leadership has the greatest impact on performance, Scott Blanchard and Drea Zigarmi worked with Vicky Essary to study the interaction between organisational success, employee success, customer loyalty, and leadership.[5] In their year-long study, which included an exhaustive literature review of hundreds of studies from 1980 to 2005, they examined two kinds of leadership: **strategic leadership** and **operational leadership**.

Strategic leadership is the "what" that ensures everyone is going in the same direction. It's where the answer to the question "What's the point of your business?" is found. Strategic leadership includes activities such as establishing a clear vision, maintaining a culture that aligns a set of values with that vision, and declaring must-do initiatives or strategic imperatives that the organisation needs to accomplish. Vision and values are enduring, whereas strategic imperatives are short-term priorities that could last a month or two, or a year or two. An example of a strategic initiative is David Novak, chairman and CEO of Yum! Brands, declaring a customer mania focus for all the company's restaurants around the world. Strategic leadership is all about the vision and direction aspect of leadership, or the *leadership* part of servant leadership.

Operational leadership is everything else. It provides the "how" for the organisation. It includes the policies, procedures, systems, and leader behaviours that cascade from senior management to the frontline employees. These management practices create the environment that employees and customers interact with and respond to on a daily basis. Operational leadership is all about the implementation aspect of leadership, or the *servant* part of servant leadership.

Blanchard and Zigarmi discovered that employee success included things like employee satisfaction (I am happy), employee loyalty (I will stay at my job), employee productivity (how I am performing), perceptions of one's relationship with his or her manager and the teamwork in the environment, and more tangible measures, like absenteeism, tardiness, and vandalism. They identified all these factors as ***employee passion***.

When it came to customers, their reactions to the organisation's environment fell into three bodies of research: satisfaction (I am happy with how this organisation serves me), loyalty (I will continue doing business with this organisation), and advocacy (I am willing to speak positively about my experience with this company). The net result of these three factors they labelled ***customer devotion***.

Blanchard and Zigarmi combined all the hard measures of organisational success (profitability, growth over time, and economic stability) and soft measures (trust in the company and a sense of its integrity) into a concept they called ***organisational vitality***. In many ways, organisational vitality depicts that triple bottom line—being the provider of choice, employer of choice, and investment of choice—we discussed in Chapter 1, "Is Your Organisation High-Performing?"

If leadership is the engine that drives a high-performing organisation, Blanchard and Zigarmi were interested in how the two aspects of leadership—strategic leadership and operational leadership—interact with and impact employee passion, customer devotion, and organisational vitality. Figure 14.1 shows the leadership–profit chain of events.

Figure 14.1   The Leadership–Profit Chain

Interestingly, Blanchard and Zigarmi found that while strategic leadership is a critical building block for setting the tone and direction, it has only an indirect impact on organisational vitality. The real key to organisational vitality is operational leadership. If this aspect of leadership is done effectively, employee passion and customer devotion will result from the positive experiences and overall satisfaction people have with the organisation.

It is also interesting to note that positive employee passion creates positive customer devotion. At the same time, when customers are excited about and devoted to the company, this has a positive effect on the work environment and the employees' passion. People love to work for a company where customers are raving fans. It makes them gung ho, and together the customers and employees directly impact organisational vitality.[6]

The big-picture conclusion from the research of Blanchard and Zigarmi is that the *leadership* part of servant leadership (strategic leadership) is important—because vision and direction get things going—but the real action is with the *servant* aspect of servant leadership (operational leadership). If the vision and direction are compelling and motivating, and leaders do a good job of implementing them in the eyes of the employees and customers, organisational vitality and success are ensured.

To do a good job, effective servant leaders must be environmentalists whose job is to create and maintain a culture that turns on employees so that they can turn on customers. These leaders do that by looking down the traditional hierarchy and saying, "What can I do for you?" rather than their people looking up the hierarchy and saying, "What can we do for you?" That's why Yum! Brands calls its corporate headquarters "The Support Centre" and has changed all manager titles to "coach."

When managers focus only on organisational indicators of vitality—such as profit—they have their eyes on the scoreboard, not the ball. Profit, a key aspect of organisational vitality, is a by-product of serving the customer, which can be achieved only by serving the employee. *So profit really is the applause you get from taking care of your customers and creating a motivating environment for your people.*

If the servant aspect of servant leadership has a greater impact on organisational vitality, how do leaders develop their serving qualities?

Being a Servant Leader Is a Question of the Heart

Most of our work in the past has focused on leadership behaviour and how to improve leadership style and methods. We have attempted to change leaders from the outside. In recent years, though, we have found that effective leadership is an inside job. It is a question of the heart. It's all about leadership character and intention. Why are you leading? Is it to serve or to be served? Answering this question truthfully is so important. You can't fake being a servant leader. We believe that if leaders don't get the heart right, they simply won't ever become servant leaders.

The most persistent barrier to being a servant leader is a heart motivated by self-interest that looks at the world as a "give a little, take a lot" proposition. Leaders with hearts motivated by self-interest put their own agenda, safety, status, and gratification ahead of those affected by their thoughts and actions.

In a sense, we all entered this world with a self-focus. Is there anything more self-centred than a baby? A baby doesn't come home from the hospital asking, "How can I help around the house?" As any parent can attest, all children are naturally self-ish; they have to be taught how to share.

You finally become an adult when you realise that life
is about what you give rather than what you get.

The shift from self-serving leadership to leadership that serves others is motivated by a change in heart.

Driven Versus Called Leaders

When we talk about servant leadership and ask people whether they are a servant leader or a self-serving leader, no one admits they're a self-serving leader. Yet we observe self-serving leadership all the time. What's the difference?

In his book *Ordering Your Private World*, Gordon MacDonald discusses an interesting distinction that can help us understand the difference between servant leaders and self-serving leaders.[7] MacDonald contends that there are two kinds of people: "driven" people and "called" people. Driven people think they own everything. They own their relationships, they own their possessions, and they own their positions. Driven people are self-serving. Most of their time is spent protecting what they own. They run bureaucracies and believe the sheep are there for the benefit of the shepherd. They want to make sure that all the money, recognition, and power move up the hierarchy and away from the frontline people and the customers. They're great at creating "duck ponds."

Called people are very different. They think everything is on loan—their relationships, possessions, and position. Do you know your relationships are on loan? One of the tough things about 9/11 was that some loans got called in early. If you knew you might not see someone important in your life tomorrow, how would you treat that person today? Margie Blanchard has a wise saying: "Keep your I-love-yous up to date."

Called people understand that possessions are only temporary, too. In tough economic times, a lot of people get uptight about losing their toys. They think "He who dies with the most toys wins." The reality is, "He who dies with the most toys dies." It's great to have nice things when things are going well, but you might have to give up some of them in hard times. Possessions are on loan.

Called leaders also understand that their positions are on loan from all the stakeholders in the organisation, particularly the people who report to them. Since called leaders don't own any-thing, they figure their role in life is to shepherd everybody and everything that comes their way.

Self-serving leaders give themselves away in two ways. The first is how they receive feedback. Have you ever tried to give feed-back to someone up the hierarchy, and that person killed the messenger? If that has ever occurred, you were dealing with a self-serving leader. They hate feedback. Why? Because if you give them any negative feedback, they think you don't want them to lead any more. And that's their worst nightmare, because they *are* their position. The second giveaway for self-serving leaders is their unwillingness to develop other leaders around them. They fear the potential competition for their leadership position.

Called leaders have servant hearts, and they love feedback. They know the only reason they are leading is to serve, and if anybody has any suggestions on how they can serve better, they want to hear them. They look at feedback as a gift. When they receive feedback, their first response is, "Thank you. That's really helpful. Can you tell me more? Is there anybody else I should talk to?"

Called leaders also are willing to develop others. They think leadership is not the province of just the formal leaders. To them, leadership should emerge everywhere. Since they believe their role in life is to serve, not to be served, they want to bring out the best in others. If a good leader rises, servant leaders are willing to partner with that person, and even step aside and take a different role if necessary. They thrive on developing others and the belief that individuals with expertise will come forward as needed throughout the organisation.

Robert Greenleaf said it well: "The true test of a servant leader is this: Do those around the servant leader become wiser, freer, more autonomous, healthier, and better able themselves to become servant leaders?"[8]

The Plight of the Ego

What keeps people from becoming servant leaders? The human ego. We believe that ego can stand for **e**dging **g**ood **o**ut and putting yourself in the centre. That's when we start to get a distorted image of our own importance and see ourselves as the centre of the universe. The greater good is a foreign thought.

Our ego gets in the way in two ways. One is *false pride*, when you start thinking more of yourself than you should. That's when you start pushing and shoving for credit and thinking leadership is about you rather than those who are led. You spend much of your time promoting yourself. Your ego also gets in your way through *self-doubt* or *fear*—thinking less of yourself than you should. You are consumed with your own shortcomings and are hard on yourself. You spend a great deal of time protecting yourself. With both false pride and self-doubt, you have a hard time believing you are okay. To borrow the title from an old song, you are "looking for love in all the wrong places." Now you think that, as Robert S. McGee warns, "your self-worth is a function of your performance plus others' opinions."[9] Since your performance varies from day to day and people are often fickle, with that belief your self-worth is up for grabs every day.

It's easy to understand that self-doubt comes from lack of self-esteem, because people afflicted with it on a daily basis act as if they are worth less than others. It is less obvious with people who have false pride, because they behave as if they are worth more than others. People with false pride, who act as if they are the only ones who count, are really trying to make up for their lack of self-esteem. They overcompensate for their "not okay" feelings by trying to control everything and everybody around them. In the process, they make themselves unlovable to those around them.

It's interesting to see how false pride and self-doubt play out in managers. When managers are addicted to either ego affliction, it erodes their effectiveness. Managers dominated by false pride are often called "controllers." Even when they don't know what they are doing, they have a high need for power and control. Even when it's clear to everyone that they are wrong, they keep on insisting they are right. These folks aren't much for supporting their people, either. If everyone is upbeat and confident, controllers throw out the wet blanket. They support their bosses over their people because they want to climb the hierarchy and be part of the bosses crowd.

At the other end of the spectrum are fear-driven managers, who are often characterised as "do-nothing bosses." They are described as "never around, always avoiding conflict, and not very helpful." They often leave people alone even when those people are insecure and don't know what they are doing. Do-nothing bosses don't seem to believe in themselves or trust in their own judgement. They value others' thoughts more than their own—especially the thoughts of those they report to. As a result, they rarely speak out and support their own people. Under pressure, they seem to defer to whoever has the most power.

If any of this sounds a bit too close for comfort, don't be alarmed. Most of us have traces of both false pride and self-doubt, because the issue is really ego. We are stuck, all alone, focusing only on ourselves. The good news is that there is an antidote for both.

Ego Antidotes

The antidote for false pride is humility. True leadership—the essence of what people long for and want desperately to follow—implies a certain humility that is appropriate and elicits the best response from people.

Jim Collins supports this truth in *Good to Great*.[10] He found two characteristics that describe great leaders: *will* and *humility*. Will is the determination to follow through on a vision/mission/goal. Humility is the capacity to realise that leadership is not about the leader; it's about the people and what they need.

According to Collins, when things are going well for typical self-serving leaders, they look in the mirror, beat their chests, and tell themselves how good they are. When things go wrong, they look out the window and blame everyone else. On the other hand, when things go well for great leaders, they look out the window and give everybody else the credit. When things go wrong, these servant leaders look in the mirror and ask questions like "What could I have done differently that would have allowed these people to be as great as they could be?" That requires real humility.

One of the keys, therefore, to becoming a servant leader is humility. We have found two compelling definitions of humility. The first one appeared in a book by Ken Blanchard and Norman Vincent Peale, *The Power of Ethical Management*:[11]

People with humility don't think less of themselves; they just think about themselves less.

So, people who are humble have solid self-esteem.

The second definition of humility comes from Fred Smith, author of *You and Your Network:*[12]

People with humility don't deny their power; they just recognise that it passes through them, not from them.

Too many people think that who they are is their position and the power it gives them. Yet that's not true. Where does your power come from? It's not from your position; it's from the people whose lives you touch. Most people would like to make the world a better place. But how many actually have a plan for how they will do that? Very few. And yet we all can make the world a better place through the moment-to-moment decisions we make as we interact with the people we come into contact with at work, at home, and in the community.

Suppose as you leave your house one morning, someone yells at you. You have a choice: You can yell back, or you can hug the person and wish her a good day. Someone cuts you up on your way to work. You have a choice: Will you chase him down and give him an obscene gesture, or will you send a prayer towards his car? We have choices all the time as we interact with other human beings. Humility tames your judgemental nature and motivates you to reach out to support and encourage others. That's where your power comes from.

What's the antidote for fear? It's love. Do you have kids? Do you love your kids? Does this love for your kids depend on their success? If they're successful, you love them; if they're not, you won't? Few people would agree with this. You love your kids unconditionally, right? What if you accepted that unconditional love for yourself? You know God doesn't make junk. He unconditionally loves each one of us. Did you know that you can't control enough, sell enough, make enough money, or have a high-enough position to get any more love? You have all the love you need. All you have to do is open yourself to it.

What Servant Leaders Do

The Secret: What Great Leaders Know and Do[13]—a book Ken Blanchard wrote with Mark Miller, vice president of training and development for Chick-fil-A—illustrates that great leaders *serve*. This book is built around the acronym SERVE. In fact, Chick-fil-A organises its management training programme around the five fundamental ways in which every great leader serves. And since Chick-fil-A has less than 5 per cent turnover among its restaurant managers in more than 1,100 restaurants, this programme has a pretty good track record.

S stands for See the Future. This has to do with the visionary role of leaders that we discussed in detail in Chapter 2, "The Power of Vision." Leadership is about taking people from one place to another. We can't say enough about the importance of having a compelling vision. Once a clear vision is established, goals and strategies can be developed within the context of the vision.

E stands for Engage and Develop People. That's what Section III, "Treat Your People Right," was all about. We took you on a transformational journey from self leadership to one-on-one leadership, to team leadership, to organisational leadership. As a leader, once the vision and direction are set, you have to turn the hierarchical pyramid upside down and focus on engaging and developing your people so that they can live according to the vision. You also must take care of your customers in a way that creates customer maniacs and raving fans.

R stands for Reinvent Continuously. Reinventing continuously has three aspects. First, great leaders reinvent continuously on a personal level. They are always interested in ways to enhance their knowledge and skills. The very best leaders are learners. Great leaders find their own approach to learning— some read, some listen to audio books or downloads, some spend time with mentors. They do whatever it takes to keep learning. We believe if you stop learning, you stop leading. We feel that everyone in every organisation, every year, should have at least one learning goal. What do you hope will be on your resumé next year that's not on it this year? For example, maybe you want to learn Spanish this year, since more and more of your customers are Spanish-speaking. You might want to learn some new computer programme that will make your life simpler and help you retrieve the information you need to make effective decisions. Whatever it is, focus on learning something new every year.

Leaders must also work to instil the desire for improvement into the people doing the day-to-day work. The leader may champion this cause, but the people make it happen—or not.

The third part of Reinvent Continuously is the idea of structural invention. Many people assume that an organisational structure is permanent. In many cases, the organisational structure no longer serves the business—the people are serving the structure. Great leaders don't change the structure just to have something to do. They understand that their organisational structure should be fluid and flexible. That belief is key to creating the energising structures and systems that are characteristic of high-performing organisations. Other, less proficient leaders tend to let the structure drive their decisions rather than adapting the structure to meet the business's ever-changing demands.

Don Shula, the famous NFL coach and coauthor with Ken Blanchard of *Everyone's a Coach*, was a great believer in this. He said great teams are "audible-ready." Suppose a football quarterback calls "halfback right." When he gets to the line of scrimmage, he sees that the defence is all to the right. He doesn't turn to the halfback and say, "Hold on; I think they'll kill you." He decides to call a new play. Why? Because the structure and what they've set up are no longer appropriate. Shula always felt it was important to realise that you don't call an audible for nothing. It's good to have a plan; it's good to have your structure in place. But always be watchful, and determine whether it's serving you, your customers, and your people well. If it's not, change it.

V stands for Value Results and Relationships. Great leaders—those who lead at a higher level—value both results and relationships. Both are critical for long-term survival. Not either/or, but both/and. For too long, many leaders have felt that they needed to choose. Most corporate leaders have said it's all about results. In reality, there are two tests of a leader. First, does he or she get results? Second, does he or she have followers? By the way, if you don't have followers, it's very hard to get long-term results.

The way to maximise your results as a leader is to have high expectations for both results and relationships. If leaders can take care of their customers and create a motivating environment for their people, profits and financial strength are the applause they get for a job well done. You see, success is both results and relationships. It's a proven formula.

E stands for Embody the Values. All genuine leadership is built on trust. Trust can be built in many ways. One way is to live consistently with the values you profess. If I say customers are important, my actions had better support that statement. If I choose to live as if customers are unimportant, people will have reason to question my trustworthiness. In the final analysis, if my people deem me untrustworthy, I will not be trusted—or followed as a leader. Embody the Values is all about walking your talk. The leader, above all, has to be a walking example of the vision. Leaders who say "Do as I say, not as I do" are ineffective in the long run.

The SERVE acronym builds a wonderful picture of how servant leaders operate. But it's a tough act to follow. Continually doing a good job in each of these areas is a significant task, but it's worth it. Servant leadership is about getting people to a higher level by leading people at a higher level.

Servant Leadership: A Mandate or a Choice

We believe that servant leadership has never been more applicable to the world of leadership than it is today. Not only are people looking for deeper purpose and meaning as they meet the challenges of today's changing world, but they are also looking for principles that actually work. Servant leadership works.

As Blanchard and Zigarmi found in their research, when the "what" (the *leadership* aspect of servant leadership) gets things started in the right direction and the "how" (the *servant* part of servant leadership) excites employees and customers, organisational vitality and success are almost guaranteed. If that's true, why wouldn't everyone—even self-serving leaders who are focused only on making money or their own power, recognition, and status—want to be servant leaders? Doesn't servant leadership benefit their motives, too? The answer is yes, but not for long. Self-serving motivations can't be hidden forever. Your heart will be exposed. As Blanchard and Zigarmi found, there is a direct correlation between bad senior leadership and organisational failure. What happened at Enron, WorldCom, and other companies speaks volumes.

Servant leadership is not just another management technique. It is a way of life for those with servant hearts. In organisations run by servant leaders, servant leadership becomes a mandate, not a choice, and the by-products are better leadership, better service, a higher-performing organisation, and more success and significance.

Servant leadership provides better leadership. Organisations led by servant leaders are less likely to experience poor leadership. In studying bad leadership, Barbara Gellerman found seven different patterns, falling along a continuum ranging from ineffective to unethical leadership. Ineffective leadership just does not get the job done because of incompetence, rigidity, and lack of self-control or callousness. Unethical leadership, in contrast, is about right and wrong. "Unethical leadership can be effective leadership, just as ineffective leadership can be ethical," Gellerman states. "But unethical leadership cannot make even the most basic claim to decency and good conduct, and so the leadership process is derailed."[14]

Organisations led by servant leaders ward off unethical leadership. When the vision and values are clearly defined, ethical and moral dilemmas are less likely to emerge. Drea Zigarmi, coauthor of *The Leader Within*,[15] contends that a moral dilemma exists when no guidelines for decision making exist, forcing an individual to rely on his or her own values and beliefs. An ethical dilemma arises when the organisation has clearly established guidelines for behaviour and the individual must consciously decide to either go along with or violate those guidelines.

Organisations work more effectively if clear vision and values are established up front, as they are under servant leadership. When unethical leadership occurs, it is often the result of the moral confusion created by the organisation's lack of clearly established guidelines that a compelling vision provides.

Servant leadership provides a cure for ineffectiveness as well. Suppose someone who is unqualified accepts a leadership position. What will it take for this person to become effective and get the job done? The key is humility. True servant leadership embraces a humble sincerity that brings out the best in leaders and those they serve. Because servant leaders have solid self-esteem, they are willing to admit when they have a weakness or need assistance. Put in positions over their heads, they can reach out to their people for help.

We had a beautiful example of this in our own company. Because of a leadership crisis, we needed Debbie Blanchard, one of the owners, to take over our sales department. The only sales experience she had was working at Nordstrom in the summer while at university. When she had her first meeting with all her salespeople, her humility showed through. She told them that she needed their help if she were to be effective. She flew around the country, met with her team, found out what their needs were, and figured out how she could help them. Responding to her humility, the salespeople reached out to make sure she had the knowledge she needed to be effective. With Debbie at the helm, the sales department has produced the highest sales in the history of the company, far exceeding its annual goals.

Servant leadership provides better service. Organisations led by servant leaders are more likely to take better care of their customers. As we've pointed out, if you don't take care of your customers today, somebody is waiting, ready and willing to do it. Again, the only thing your competition can't steal from you is the relationship your people have with your customers. Under servant leadership these relationships can really grow, because the people closest to the customer are given the power to soar like eagles rather than quack like ducks. As we pointed out in Chapter 3, the great customer service experiences created by Southwest Airlines and the Ritz-Carlton were a direct result of servant leadership. Leaders like Herb Kelleher and Horst Shultze set up their organisations to empower everyone—including the frontline people—to make decisions, use their brains, and be servant leaders who could carry out the vision of high-quality customer service.

Servant leadership helps create a high-performing organisation. When we discussed HPO SCORES in Chapter 1, we said that if becoming a high-performing organisation is the destination, leadership is the engine. And the kind of leadership we want is servant leadership. The one HPO SCORES element that best characterises a servant leader is *Shared Power and High Involvement*. It goes hand in hand with leaders who realise it's not about them.

Is being a servant leader just about being nice for the sake of niceness? No—it works. Practising shared power and high involvement strongly impacts financial results through productivity, retention, and employee satisfaction. Using US Department of Labour data and surveys of over 1,500 firms from various industries, Huselid found that such participative practices significantly improved employee retention and financial performance and increased productivity. In fact, he was able to quantify the financial impact of participative practices with enough confidence to say that each standard deviation in the use of participative practices increased a company's market value between $35,000 and $78,000 per employee.[16]

The servant leaders in high-performing organisations understand that day-to-day decision making should occur closest to the action and on the front lines by those directly involved with the customer. Being involved in decisions that affect their lives reduces people's stress and creates a healthier, happier workforce. Involvement in decision making increases their ownership and commitment as well as effectiveness.

For example, Chaparral Steel does not use quality inspectors. The people in their plants are responsible for the products they produce and the quality of those products. Given the power and responsibility for decision making, they act as they are expected to: as owners.

Servant leaders in high-performing organisations involve their people at all levels and from multiple areas of the business in complex and strategic decision making. Research demonstrates that decisions and action plans are more effective when people whose commitment is required are part of the planning.[17] Effectiveness increases in quality, quantity, and implementation. These kinds of decisions are often made in a team environment where everyone involved is in the room at the same time, able to benefit from and react to each other's thinking and to arrive at "collective wisdom." W.L. Gore, a company whose watchwords are "commitment, empowerment, and innovation," recognises the importance of personal contact. Gore even goes so far as to limit the size of its facilities. They will build a new plant rather than expand one where associates would lose contact with each other.

High-performing organisations do not depend on a few peak performers to guide and direct, but have broadly developed leadership capacities. This allows for self-management, ownership, and the power to act quickly as the situation requires. Pushing decision making to those closest to the action is an empowering practice. Servant leaders in high-performing organisations create environments where people are free to choose to empower themselves.

The benefit of shifting power from top management leaders to the people closest to the action is illustrated by the journey of

Summit Pointe, a large state and locally funded behavioural health organisation. Eunice Parisi-Carew, one of the HPO SCORES researchers, had the opportunity to collaborate with Erv Brinker, the CEO—a wonderful example of a servant leader. When Erv took his position, he determined that it was critical to share the power concentrated at the top. He decided to allow those involved on the front lines to make decisions that impacted their lives and the service they provided. His first step was to hire Dev Ogle, a talented senior consultant, to act as his guide. Dev began by training his senior leaders using an approach that emphasised the importance of sharing leadership and power. Brinker's expectation was that the senior leaders would act as models as he moved the organisation from a hierarchical to a team-based culture. The journey was successful. Summit Pointe is now an organisation that supports team performance. For example, each team sets its own performance standards, monitors its progress, and receives pay incentives based on its accomplishments. They use a "pay-for-performance" approach to compensation. Now that they are in control, teams are actually setting higher goals for themselves than had previously been set for them. A collection of both hard and soft data revealed the exceptional results of servant leadership.

- Administrative overhead has been reduced significantly while the number of customers served has increased. It went from 230 staff serving 2,000 customers per year to 100 staff serving 8,000 customers with a $1.5 million cost savings.
- New services such as prevention have been added, with increased revenue of $5 million.
- Communication across departments has increased dramatically.
- Employee morale has increased, and the isolation that is common in this stressful field has decreased dramatically.
- Whereas the industry average for turnover is 29 per cent, Summit Pointe has averaged 9 per cent.

Servant leaders think differently than self-serving leaders. It is not possible to share power without believing that people can and will manage power and decision making responsibly if given the proper training, information, and opportunity. It is also not possible to create a high-involvement culture without including everyone. Servant leaders in high-performing organisations not only appreciate but capitalise on cultural diversity; style diversity; social diversity; and diversity in race, religion, sexual orientation, and age. They realise that effective decision making, problem solving, and innovation come from utilising different perspectives.

Servant leadership brings more success and significance. In his classic book *Halftime*, Bob Buford reveals that most people, later in life, want to move from success to significance—from getting to giving.[18] Organisations led by servant leaders are more likely to create environments where people at all levels can experience both success and significance.

Too many leaders today focus only on success. They think success depends only on how much wealth they have accumulated, the amount of recognition they have received, and their power and status. Nothing is inherently wrong with any of those things, as long as you don't identify those things as who you are. As an alternative, we'd like you to focus on the opposite of each of those as you move from success to significance. What's the opposite of accumulating wealth? It's generosity of time, talent, treasure, and touch (reaching out to support others). What's the opposite of recognition? It's service. What's the opposite of power and status? It's loving relationships.

We've found over the years that when you focus only on success, you will never reach significance. That's the problem with self-serving leaders—they never get out of their own way. On the other hand, if you focus on significance—generosity, service, and loving relationships—you'll be amazed at how much success will come your way. Take Mother Teresa. She couldn't have cared less about accumulating wealth, recognition, and status. Her whole life was focused on significance. And what happened? Success came her way. Her ministry received tremendous financial backing, she was recognised all over the world, and she was given the highest status wherever she went. She was the ultimate servant leader. If you focus on significance first, your emphasis will be on people. Through that emphasis, success *and* results will follow.

An amazing story of significance occurred during the 100-yard dash at the Special Olympics several years ago in Spokane, Washington. Nine contestants waited anxiously for the starting gun to fire. When it did, they raced towards the finish line as fast as they could, given their physical disabilities. About a third of the way down the track, one of the boys fell. He tried to get up, but he fell again. In frustration, he lay on the track, sobbing. While six of the other racers continued to push towards the finish line and possible victory, two of the youngsters, hearing the sobs of their opponent, stopped, turned around, headed back towards their fallen competitor, and helped him up. The three boys held hands, walked down the track, and crossed the finish line together, well after the others had finished the race. The crowd was surprised. When they realised what had happened, they rose in unison and gave these youngsters a longer and louder ovation than they'd given the winner of the race.

Life is all about the choices we make as we interact with each other. We can choose to be self-serving or serving. Most of the youngsters in the race chose to focus on their own success—victory—but two tossed aside their dreams in favour of serving someone else. The crowd responded with enthusiasm, because we all yearn to live at a higher level, and these young people modelled what that means. They made a different choice—they were true servant leaders.

We hope you make these kinds of choices. Life constantly presents leaders with opportunities to choose to love and serve one another. Someone once said to Margie Blanchard, "You've lived with Ken for almost 45 years. What do you think leadership is all about?" She said:

"Leadership is not about love—it is love."

She continued, "It is loving your mission, it's loving your customers, it's loving your people, and it's loving yourself enough to get out of the way so that other people can be magnificent."

That's what leading at a higher level is all about.

Chapter 15

DETERMINING YOUR LEADERSHIP POINT OF VIEW

Ken Blanchard, Margie Blanchard,
and Pat Zigarmi

A ll right, you've heard from us. Throughout this book, we have essentially shared with you our leadership point of view—our thoughts about leading and motivating people. Our leadership point of view is based on a belief that, to create a great organisation, leaders have to make sure everyone's aiming at the right target and vision. They need to make sure everyone is treating both their customers and their people right. As leaders, they need to focus on serving, not being served.

Now it's your turn.

The goal of this chapter is to help you develop your own leadership point of view. Not only will this help you clarify your thoughts on leadership, but it will also prepare you to teach your leadership point of view to others.

Why is developing a clear leadership point of view important? Ken Blanchard was sold on this idea after reading Noel Tichy's book *The Leadership Engine* and talking with Noel while they were doing consulting work with Yum! Brands. Noel's extensive research has shown that effective leaders have a clear, teachable leadership point of view and are willing to share it with and teach it to others, particularly the people they work with.[1]

This realisation so impacted Ken that he and his wife, Margie, created a course called "Communicating Your Leadership Point of View" as part of the Master of Science in Executive Leadership (MSEL) course jointly offered by The Ken Blanchard Companies and the College of Business at the University of San Diego. As we have said, effective leadership is a journey beginning with self-leadership, moving to one-on-one leadership, then team leadership, and ending with organisational leadership. This course is the final focus of the self-leadership portion of the degree. The course culminates in all of the students making presentations to the class that embody their leadership points of view. The students deliver their leadership points of view as though they are talking to those who report to them in their organisational leadership positions.

If you can teach people your leadership point of view, they will not only have the benefit of understanding where you're coming from, but they'll also be clear on what you expect from them and what they can expect from you. They may also begin to solidify their own thinking about leadership so that they can teach others, too. Tichy feels strongly that learning, teaching, and leading are intricately intertwined and therefore should be considered inherent parts of everyone's job description. Why everyone's? Because, as we emphasised in the preceding chapter, we are all leaders in some part of our lives.

Elements of a Leadership Point of View

In determining your leadership point of view, you should be guided by the following questions:

1. Who are the influencers (key people) in your life who have had a positive (or, in some cases, negative) impact on your life, such as parents, teachers, coaches, mentors, or bosses, and what did you learn from these people about leadership?

2. What key events in your life have had an impact on how you lead others? Think back to events and turning points during your childhood, school years, and early career. How did these events impact your thinking about leadership?

3. Think about your life purpose. Why are you here, and what do you want to accomplish?

4. What are your core values that will guide your behaviour as you attempt to live your life "on purpose?"

5. Given what you've learned from past influencers, life events, your life purpose, and core values, what is your leadership point of view—your beliefs about leading and motivating people?

6. What can your people expect from you?

7. What do you expect from your people?

8. How will you set an example for your people?

When you finally share your leadership point of view, your listeners will often be particularly interested in questions 6 and 7. Sometimes that is where we ask people to start with their leadership point of view—with expectations. Think of an example of yourself or someone behaving consistently with your expectations. Real examples are better than platitudes.

Once your expectations are clear and are supported by examples, think about your background. Where did those expectations come from? Was it from modelling by your parents or a coach or boss? What did they do, and what did it mean to you? Perhaps a significant life event shaped your expectations. Get in touch with that story. People remember and respond more to stories and examples than to glittering generalities, and usually, less is more.

The idea in your leadership point of view is to share some meaningful information about yourself—what that information taught you about leadership and development, and what it means to your listeners. By sharing your leadership point of view, you are revealing some important background about yourself, harvesting key lessons from that background, and letting others know how they can accomplish their goals and meet your expectations.

What follows are some ways to think about your leadership point of view and where your key beliefs and expectations might have come from. Each of these examples may give you ideas about your life and help you decide what you want to share. It is helpful to think through all the areas and then select the most powerful or insightful ones to put into your leadership point of view. Your leadership point of view is to help others relate to you. By giving examples, you allow people to do that.

Your Leadership Role Models

When we ask people who most impacted their lives, sometimes they mention bosses or other organisational leaders. More often they talk about their parents, grandparents, friends, coaches, or teachers. When Ken Blanchard is asked this question, he is quick to mention his mother and father:

> My mum was the ultimate positive thinker. She told everyone that I laughed before I cried, I smiled before I frowned, and I danced before I walked. With those kinds of messages, how could I have ended up anything but a positive thinker? My dad was a career naval officer who retired as an admiral. He was a powerful leadership role model for me. He didn't think leadership was choosing between people or results. He thought leadership was a 'both/and' relationship—both people and results were important to him. He taught me that position power and 'my way or the highway' are not the way to lead. I'll never forget when I was elected president of the seventh grade and came home all excited. Dad said, 'It's great, Ken, that you're president of your class. But now that you have a position, don't use it.

Great leaders are followed not because they have position power, but because they're respected and trusted as individuals.' He always supported and involved his people, yet he demanded high-performance.

My mum instilled in me a strong belief in God. That helped me keep things in perspective. Mum said, 'Ken, don't act like you're better than anybody else. But don't let anyone act like they are better than you, either. We are all children of God.' The one-two punch I received from my mum and dad gave me the belief that, in life, I was here to serve, not to be served."

In crafting your leadership point of view, first think about who influenced your life and your beliefs about leadership. Then think about which key events gave you a sense of what leadership is all about. Think about the milestones in your life. Where were the major transitions? What were the sliding doors—those moments in time where you made a choice to go one way versus another and that, as Robert Frost said, "made all the difference"? Choose three to four key events and reflect on what these events taught you about leading or influencing others.

Your Life Purpose

Next, think about your life purpose. Why are you here? What business are you in? As we suggested in Chapter 2, "The Power of Vision," if an organisation doesn't have a clear purpose and sense of what business it's in, we think something is wrong. Yet few people have a clear sense of their life's purpose. How can you make good decisions about how you should use your time if you don't know what business you're in?

The following is a simple process that will help you create a good first draft of your life purpose.[2] First, list some personal characteristics you feel good about. Use nouns, such as:

computer expertise	enthusiasm
physical strength	wit
sense of humour	sales ability
intellect	happiness
people skills	charm
problem-solving skills	diplomacy
teaching skills	artistic ability
role model	creativity
energy	patience

For example, Ken chose sense of humour, people skills, teaching skills, and role model.

Next, list ways you successfully interact with people. These will be verbs, such as:

teach	inspire
produce	manage
educate	motivate
encourage	plan
stimulate	act
lead	sell
love	coach
help	write

Ken picked educate, help, inspire, and motivate.

Finally, visualise what your perfect world would be. What would people do or say? Write a description of this perfect world.

> To Ken, a perfect world is where everyone is aware of the presence of God in their lives and realise they are here to serve, not to be served.

Now combine two of your nouns, two of your verbs, and your definition of your perfect world, and you'll have a good start on a definition of your life purpose.

Ken's life purpose is to be "a loving teacher and a role model of simple truths who helps and motivates myself and others to be aware of the presence of God in our lives and realise we are here to serve, not to be served."

One of our MSEL students said his life purpose was "to use my humour and people skills to help and inspire others to be successful in achieving their goals." He went on to say, "I would like our company to become a place where people want to come to work and where they can grow to feel better about who they are and what they are accomplishing."

Your Core Values

Values are beliefs you feel strongly about because you choose them over other alternatives. It has been said that:

The most important thing in life is to decide what's most important.

When you were a kid, your parents and other adults tended to dictate your values, but at some point in life we all choose what is important to us. Your leader at work might value results more than people. You might be the opposite. People don't all value the same things. Some people value wealth and power, and others are more concerned with safety or survival. Success is a value; integrity and relationships are values as well. The following is a sample list of personal values:

truth	wisdom
power	commitment
courage	recognition
excitement	learning

creativity	honesty
happiness	originality
service	respect
freedom	order
integrity	spirituality
peace	cooperation
loyalty	humour
security	resources
love	excellence
fun	responsiveness
relationships	success

In trying to determine what your values are, you might start with a long list. You probably like a lot of the values listed above, plus others you might think of. But fewer are better, particularly if you want your values to guide your behaviour. In *Managing by Values*, Ken Blanchard and Michael O'Connor contend that more than three or four values is too many and can become immobilising.[3] So, see if you can pick out what you think are your most important values. If you're having trouble narrowing down your top values, you might combine a couple. For example, Ken combined two words to create "spiritual peace" as his number one value, followed by "integrity," "love," and "success."

Your number-one value is often your core value—something you want to be present no matter what you're doing. So, if your number one value is integrity, living without integrity is not an option.

In talking about core values, the implication is that your values should be rank-ordered. Why? Because values live in dynamic tension with one another, as we discussed in Chapter 2. For example, if you value financial growth but integrity is your core value, any activities that could lead to financial gain must be checked against your integrity value.

How do you know when you're living according to a particular value? You have to define that value as specifically as possible.

Without defining your values, the people you work with might not really understand what's important to you. Pat can remember a conversation in which three people defined the value of "justice" differently. For Pat, it meant equal opportunity. For another person, it meant fair process. For the third, it meant "getting my due share."

Let's take something that you might not think is easy to define, like love. According to Ken, "I value love. I know I am living by this value any time I feel loving towards myself and others, any time I have compassion, any time I feel love in my heart, any time I feel the love of others, any time my heart fills with love, and any time I look for the love of others."

Your Beliefs About Leading and Motivating People

Your beliefs are where you will find the essence of your leadership point of view. These should flow naturally from the people and key events that have influenced you, and your purpose and values.

For example, let's look at some of the beliefs about leading and motivating people that Ken shares with others. You'll recognise that his beliefs represent some of the key themes in this book:

> I believe people who produce good results feel good about themselves. Therefore, my leadership role as your manager is to help you win—to accomplish your goals. I want you to get an A. If things are going in the right direction, I should cheer you on with an 'attaboy' or 'attagirl.' If progress is not being made, I should redirect your efforts and get you back on course. In other words, you should know when you are getting 'wrong answers' so that we can discuss what would make a 'good answer.' Everything I do as a manager with you should be geared towards helping you produce good results and, in the process, feel good about yourself.

What People Can Expect from You

Letting people know what they can expect from you underscores the idea that good leadership is a partnership. It gives people a picture of how things will look under your leadership.

For example, one of the students on the MSEL course at the University of San Diego described what his people could expect from him:

> Knowing that I like building things will help you understand what you can expect from me. In fact, I look at many different things in the context of building. I like building houses. I like building my family. I like building businesses, and I like building and developing people. I'm happy to roll up my sleeves to help build most anything. It's what I enjoy most. So you can expect that I will give you plenty of my time, I will listen to you when you see the need, and I will help you access what you already know.
>
> Just the other day, I noticed that Jack had stayed late at work and was looking a little frustrated. When I asked him how things were going, he shared that our building permits for the new office were held up, putting the whole project behind. Through our conversation, he figured out another person to call and approach to take. He had the answer all along; I just helped him ask different questions.

What You Expect from Your People

Because leading is a partnership process, it is perfectly reasonable—in fact, it's imperative—that you let people know what you expect from them. This gives people a picture of what their behaviour will look like under your leadership.

Here is another example from one of the students of the MSEL course at USD:

My expectations of you can be combined into a saying known as the Golden Rule: *Do unto others as you would have them do unto you.* What do I mean by that? I expect you all to act ethically in everything you do. You'll have many opportunities to take short cuts and do things that will result in short-term gains. Plenty of business examples in recent years have shown how disastrous this can be. I expect you to stand tall on this issue and to not allow anyone to think that you tolerate fraud or anything unethical. You manage hundreds of employees. While each of them may not know you that well, they need to know your feelings on this topic by way of your word and example.

How You Will Set an Example

Your leadership point of view should let others know how you will set an example for the values and behaviours you are encouraging. As most parents know, people learn from your behaviour, not from your words. Leaders must walk their talk.

For example, the MSEL student just mentioned made clear how he would set an example for his people:

All of you know that I released our company's top salesperson about nine months ago for questionable activities. He thought that he was untouchable due to his status as a top-producing account executive. However, no one, including me, is above the ethical standards that are expected of someone working at our company.

Developing Your Own Leadership Point of View

Now it's your turn to create your own leadership point of view. To serve as a guide, we'll share a couple of examples. The first example comes from Colleen Barrett, the former president of Southwest Airlines.

My Background

I grew up poor, with an alcoholic father and a mother who raised the kids. My mother was the most influential person in my life. She was uneducated and didn't have money, but she had a huge heart. Her hard work and determination set a great example for me, and she was a great people person as well. Although she didn't actually use the expression, she modelled the Golden Rule. Her guiding belief in life was that as long as you were respectful of others and treated people the way you would like to be treated, you would get that back in kind. My alcoholic dad was not a good role model. I learned a lot from that, as well. Good teachers or bad teachers—you can learn from both.

A series of setbacks across my life also have shaped my leadership point of view. When I was about 15 in secondary school, my home burned down. I have survived breast cancer and a number of personal attacks. These challenges taught me to think about my priorities and not to judge others, because you never know what's going on in their lives.

An incident at secondary school taught me why it's not a good idea to judge others. I was working as the receptionist at a paper company. My superviser told me to minimise my interaction with the big, burly truck drivers who delivered the paper, because she thought they were "too scruffy, too dangerous, too tough." But, after my house burned down, the truck drivers got together and bought me a winter coat. They knew more about what was going on with me than my manager did. That experience also taught me to reach out when people are going through horrendous times. Every time an employee has a fire or is battling cancer, I reach out by sending a care parcel or note.

My *Purpose and Values*

My life purpose is to make a positive difference by fighting for a good cause. For example, Southwest Airlines is a cause. We did something no airline has ever done. In 1971, when flying was for the elite, we wanted to open up the skies to everyone. We believed flying could be fun. Only 13 per cent of Americans were flying regularly when we started; today, 97 per cent are. We got people flying with low fares at night and on weekends.

My mum had a tremendous impact on my values, particularly her do-unto-others philosophy. I think all good leaders really enjoy and value people. Mum encouraged me to believe I could do anything I wanted to do and that in the process I would make a positive difference. Her do-unto-others attitude about people, her belief that I could be whatever I wanted to be, and her confidence that I could make a positive difference are values that guide me to this day. I also value determination, passion, patience, tolerance, and teamwork—which translates into my desire to be inclusive and egalitarian.

My *Beliefs about Leading and Motivating People*

I believe that in leading and motivating people, you treat them with respect, practise the Golden Rule, and love people for who they are. Leadership is about mentoring. I believe mentoring has to evolve naturally; it has to happen every day. My leadership beliefs actually mirror Southwest's. Every day I want to show a servant heart, demonstrate a warrior spirit, and project a fun, loving attitude.

I learned a lot about leadership from my mentor, Herb Kelleher. When I was a young secretary, we had a mailer that had to get out. Everything that could go wrong with it went wrong. It had to be in the post the next day but the printer broke down and the postage was somehow wrong. All the envelopes had to be stuffed and retyped—and this was back when you couldn't just push a button and it would happen. It was 8:00 at night and we had to start all over. Herb sat right there with me until 4:00 in the morning, on the floor, licking envelopes and putting stamps on them, because we didn't have a franking machine. I'll never forget it. He could have thought it was my fault that the mailing had gone wrong but he didn't. He just jumped right in there with me. That was a valuable lesson for me about leading and motivating people.

What You Can Expect from Me

I think if you were to talk to any of my people they would tell you, "She's a bottom-line-orientated person and she's always going to tell you what she thinks. Whether you like it or not, you're going to hear it." That doesn't bother me because I want people to expect that from me. I do have a few nicknames; one of them is "mum." I think people know I will be there for them; I'm their biggest supporter; I believe in them and trust them. But it goes both ways.

What I Expect from You

I won't expect you to do anything I won't do myself. I expect a give-and-take relationship. We both need to give back when it's needed. I don't like surprises. I like to hear bad news first so we can fix the situation. If I don't hear about it, we can't fix it. I want you to see problems, use good judgement, and bring me solutions. I believe in absolute truthfulness. I want passion; I want you to believe in what you do and to care.

I want all decisions to be made from a servant's heart. After all, Southwest is in the customer service business. We just happen to provide airline transportation. So if people don't want to serve others, they're not bad people—but they don't belong at Southwest Airlines. For example, we have pilots who have paid for hotel rooms for passengers without money who had to get off at different cities than they'd intended for the night. The pilots don't call and ask, "Is it OK? Will I get reimbursed?" They do these things because that's the kind of people they are.

How I Will Set an Example for You?

I will set an example for you by following our philosophy of leadership at Southwest Airlines: Treat your people right and good things will happen. I will do my best to be a servant leader who ensures that you have a good, strong work environment and the tools to do your jobs. I will do my best to assure that you feel loved, appreciated, and supported, so that you can in turn give our passengers that same warmth, caring, and fun spirit.

Our second example of a leadership point of view is from Eddie Hiner, an MSEL student who is an officer in the Navy SEALs. We include this for a couple of reasons. Although Eddie doesn't follow the seven elements perfectly, he talks from his heart and makes it clear to his people where he comes from, what he believes, and how his beliefs will impact them. So, don't get hung up on following our formula to a T. Your leadership point of view is about who you are and how you intend to be with your people. We also included Eddie's leadership point of view because it illustrates how a military officer can be a servant leader in the context of a hierarchical organisation. We believe that servant leadership should be the foundation of *all* leadership, no matter where you find yourself leading.

How I Learned My Leadership Point of View

By the time I was 11, both my parents had moved away, leaving my brother and me with our grandmother. We lived in a remote town in the Blue Ridge Mountains of Virginia, where my grandmother had lived her entire life. My grandfather had passed away about seven years earlier, so it was only my grandmother, my brother, and I. She was retired and living on Social Security. Needless to say, we were not wealthy.

My brother and I grew up without parental guidance. We made our own decisions in life, learning by trial and error. My brother was my first mentor—and by far my most influential one. Even though he was only 13 at the time, he had vision and was wise beyond his years. He knew that life had a lot to offer us. He constantly encouraged me to strive to be better and not let my situation determine my future. He taught me what I later learned in the SEAL teams was the "offensive mindset." Offensive mindset is being the cause of the effect, not the effect that was caused. Essentially, it means controlling your own destiny rather than letting your environment control it.

My brother was two years older than I, so he taught me the hard lessons he had learned. We were a *team*. These two concepts are extremely important in my current profession.

My final year I met my next mentor when I received a baseball scholarship. Coach Guzzo taught me discipline, teamwork, honour, and how to be a winner. He didn't care how good a player you were; if you weren't a team player, you didn't play. During one game he benched one of our best players because he ignored the signal to sacrifice bunt and decided, on his own, to swing at the pitch. His hit scored the winning run, but Coach Guzzo benched him for not being willing to sacrifice himself for the team.

Shortly after leaving school, I decided I wanted to be a Navy SEAL. From the moment I found out about the SEAL teams, I knew that was where I needed to be. I have learned nearly my entire leadership point of view from living it in the teams. The training is centred on core values and team values. Part of the selection requires you to adopt the team's values. Your character is stressed more than your skills or physical ability. I don't know of any other organisation in the world that is as good at training character as this one.

My Leadership Point of View

I approach my job as a responsibility and a privilege; I work for you. I compare myself to a stagecoach driver. By driving the stagecoach, I am responsible for leading the team of horses, but without the team, I'm a pedestrian. Without me, you would still be pulling the stagecoach, and you would still be a team. The bottom line is, without you, I don't have a job. Without me, you still have a job. Therefore, I am here because of you, not the other way around.

I realise that everyone makes mistakes. If you make a mistake or use poor judgement because of lack of experience, own up to it and move on. I can deal with that. If it's a character issue, that's a different story. When making a decision, I find it useful to ask myself a few questions. Does it look right? Sound right? Feel right? If I answer no to any of these, I know it probably isn't the right thing to do. I also consider if the decision supports the mission and if I would be willing to walk into the commanding officer's office and tell him about my decision. If I am unwilling to do that, I reconsider my decision.

Remember that we are all here for the same reason: to accomplish the mission. This means that sometimes I'll have to make decisions that not all of you agree with. I don't expect you to. If we are all thinking alike, none of us is thinking at all. It is crucial that each one of you think for himself. But sometimes I will make decisions that may not be popular. That is my job and my responsibility. Remember, you fight for a democracy; you don't work for one—and neither do I. We all take orders. Just keep in mind that I am always trying to do the best for the team and that I will shield you from the top. Most of the time, I will leave the decisions up to you. I trust your judgement, because you are the experts. You have the authority to use that judgement. I'm here to guide you; I'm not a dictator. On the rare occasion when I do need to give a direct order, I expect it to be followed both in practice and in spirit. Remember that there is a reason for it.

These past ten years with the teams have had the greatest influence on my leadership perspective. The adversity I have encountered in the teams has helped stimulate a powerful bond between me and the men I work with. The sense of brotherhood that comes from that bond has really influenced how I approach leadership.

Every leader I have worked for has given me the same advice: Take care of your men. That's why the concept of servant leadership is not new to me. This concept is deeply rooted in the SEAL teams.

As a platoon commander, I am not only responsible for my team's performance at work; I am also accountable for helping you deal with your personal lives. Being a team is not a part-time job. The whole man goes into combat, not just the one at work.

When you finally make it into the teams, you realise why the character traits we value are crucial to our success. It's simple: We either live by them, or we might die by not doing so.

During the writing of the first edition of this book, Eddie was in Iraq. No matter how dangerous the assignment, wouldn't you like to have him as your leader?

In writing *Leading at a Higher Level*, we've done our best to give you the leadership point of view that we have been developing over the last 30 years. So, as you develop your own leadership point of view, don't be hard on yourself. This might be your first time thinking about your beliefs about leading and motivating people. Feel free to incorporate any of the ideas you have learned in these pages.

The world needs more leaders who are leading at a higher level. As we said in the Introduction, our dream is that some day everyone will know someone who is leading at a higher level. We dream of the day when self-serving leaders are history, and leaders serving others are the rule, not the exception.

You can be a leader who makes a positive difference on our planet. So, go out and do it! We're counting on you.

ENDNOTES

Introduction

1 Matt Hayes and Jeff Stevens, *The Heart of Business* (Bloomington, IN: Author House, 2005).

2 Robert Greenleaf, *Servant Leadership: A Journey into the Nature of Legitimate Power and Greatness, 25th Anniversary Edition,* (New Jersey: Paulist Press, 2002).

Chapter 1

1 Ken Blanchard and Don Shula, *Everyone's a Coach* (Grand Rapids, MI: Zondervan, 1995).

2 John Elkington uses the phrase "triple bottom line accounting" in his 1998 book, *Cannibals with Forks.* Elkington's use of the phrase includes environmental and social responsibility measures in accounting reports. Our use of the phrase "triple bottom line" has a different focus: success with customers, employees, and investors.

3 Ken Blanchard and Sheldon Bowles, *Raving Fans: A Revolutionary Approach to Customer Service* (New York: William Morrow, 1993).

4 For more information on the HPO SCORES model and the research conducted, see "High Performing Organizations: SCORES" by Don Carew, Fay Kandarian, Eunice Parisi-Carew, and Jesse Stoner, The Ken Blanchard Companies, 2001.

5   The HPO SCORES Profile is a psychometrically sound organisational assessment, with strong validity and reliability, that provides feedback on the extent to which the practices in your organisation are similar to those in high-performing organisations. Developed by Don Carew, Fay Kandarian, Eunice Parisi-Carew, and Jesse Stoner, The HPO SCORES Profile is published by The Ken Blanchard Companies.

6   Supplement to the HPO SCORES quiz.

Chapter 2

1   Jesse Stoner, *Visionary Leadership, Management, and High Performing Work Units* (doctoral dissertation, University of Massachusetts, 1988).

2   Jesse Stoner and Drea Zigarmi, "From Vision to Reality" (Escondido, CA: The Ken Blanchard Companies, 1993). The elements of a compelling vision were also described by Stoner in "Realizing Your Vision" (Provo, UT: *Executive Excellence*, 1990)

3   Charles Garfield and Hal Bennett, *Peak Performance: Mental Training Techniques of the World's Greatest Athletes* (New York: Warner Books, 1989).

4   Ken Blanchard and Michael O'Connor, *Managing by Values* (San Francisco, CA: Berrett-Koehler, 1997).

5   Ford Motor Company documents indicate that company officials had data that Firestone tyres installed on Explorer four-wheel drive vehicles had little or no margin for safety in top-speed driving at the tyre pressures that Ford recommended. The papers were part of a collection of documents that Congressional investigators released before the third round of Congressional hearings investigating Ford's and Bridgestone/Firestone Inc.'s handling of tyre failures.

6 Jim Collins and Jerry Porras, *Built to Last: Successful Habits of Visionary Companies* (New York: HarperCollins, 1994).

7 Research studies described in *Leaders: The Strategies for Taking Charge* by Warren Bennis, 1985, and *The Leadership Challenge* by James Kouzes and Barry Posner, among others.

8 *The New York Times*, 2 August 1995.

9 Ken Blanchard and Jesse Stoner, *Full Steam Ahead!: Unleash the Power of Vision in Your Company and Your Life* (San Francisco, CA: Berrett-Koehler, 2003).

Chapter 3

1 Rick Sidorowicz, "Back to the Beginning—Core Values," *The CEO Refresher*, Ontario, Canada: Refresher Publications, Inc., 2002.

2 Marshall Goldsmith, "Retain Your Top Performers," Marshall Goldsmith Library online (www.marshallgoldsmithlibrary.com/cim/articles_display.php?aid=162).

3 Ken Blanchard and Sheldon Bowles, *Raving Fans: A Revolutionary Approach to Customer Service* (New York: William Morrow, 1993).

4 Thomas Peters and Nancy Austin, *A Passion for Excellence* (New York: Random House, 1995).

5 Ken Blanchard and Don Shula, *Everyone's a Coach* (Grand Rapids, MI: Zondervan, 1995).

6 Ken Blanchard and Sheldon Bowles, *Gung Ho!: Turn on the People in Any Organization* (New York: William Morrow, 1998).

Chapter 4

1 The Sarbanes-Oxley Act of 2002 is a US federal law also known as the Public Company Accounting Reform and Investor Protection Act of 2002. It's commonly called SOX or SarbOx.

2   Edward Lawler, *Creating High Performance Organizations: Practices and Results of Employee Involvement and Total Quality Management* (San Francisco, CA: Jossey-Bass, 1995).

3   In a more recent and rigorous research study, S. R. Silver investigated the relationship between organisational empowerment and "hard" measures of team performance for 50 teams of applied research engineers. The study found that organisational empowerment had a positive impact on the quality, timeliness, and financial outcomes of the team's performance.

S. R. Silver, "Perceptions of Empowerment in Engineering Workgroups: The Linkage to Transformational Leadership and Performance," unpublished doctoral dissertation, 1999, Washington, DC, George Washington University.

In a highly rigorous study, S. E. Siebert, S. R. Silver, and W. A. Randolph analysed data collected from 375 employees in 50 work teams in one division of a Fortune 100 manufacturer of high-technology office and printing equipment. They determined that a climate of empowerment was positively related to manager ratings of work unit performance and job satisfaction.

S. E. Siebert, S. R. Silver, and W. A. Randolph, "Taking Empowerment to the Next Level: A Multiple-Level Model of Empowerment, Performance, and Satisfaction," *Academy of Management Journal* 47 (2004).

4   T. W. Malone, "Is Empowerment Just a Fad? Control, Decision Making, and IT," *Sloan Management Review*, Winter (1997): 23–35.

5   Inaugural address of John Fitzgerald Kennedy, 20 January 1961.

6   Ken Blanchard, John Carlos, and Alan Randolph, *Empowerment Takes More Than a Minute* (San Francisco, CA: Berrett-Koehler, 1996).

7 As described in the HPO SCORES model in Chapter 1, "Is Your Organisation High Performing?"

8 Jim Harris, "Five Principles to Revitalize Employee Loyalty and Commitment," *R&D Innovator* 5, No. 8 (August 1996).

9 Thomas H. Davenport and Laurence Prusak, *Working Knowledge* (Boston, MA: Harvard Business School Press, 2000).

10 Jim Harris, ibid.

11 Ken Blanchard, Alan Randolph, and Peter Grazier, *Go Team: Take Your Team to the Next Level* (San Francisco, CA: Berrett-Koehler, 2005).

12 Ken Blanchard, Jim Ballard, and Fred Finch, *Customer Mania!: It's Never Too Late to Build a Customer-Focused Company* (New York: Simon & Schuster/Free Press, 2004).

13 Barney Bunnell and Marcelina Gilliam, two of the shift leaders, presented this story with Don Carew at the 2000 Blanchard Client Conference. They got a standing ovation.

Chapter 5

1 The original Hersey-Blanchard model gained prominence in 1969 in the authors' classic text *Management of Organizational Behavior*, now in its eighth edition. After finding that some critical aspects of the model were not being validated in practice by thousands of users and that it didn't fit the research on team development, Ken and the founding associates of The Ken Blanchard Companies—Margie Blanchard, Don Carew, Eunice Parisi-Carew, Fred Finch, Drea Zigarmi, and Patricia Zigarmi—created Situational Leadership® II. *Leadership and the One Minute Manager*, coauthored with Drea Zigarmi and Patricia Zigarmi, marked a new generation of Situational Leadership® II for managers everywhere.

2 Derived from Leadership Behaviour Analysis II (LBAII), an instrument designed to measure both self and others' perceptions of leader flexibility, as well as the leader's effectiveness at choosing an appropriate leadership style. Drea Zigarmi, Carl Edeburn, and Ken Blanchard, *Getting to Know the LBAII: Research, Validity, and Reliability of the Self and Other Forms*, 4th Edition (Escondido, CA: The Ken Blanchard Companies, 1997).

3 The application of the original Situational Leadership® II model was advanced when Don Carew and Eunice Parisi-Carew developed the team leadership programme; Susan Fowler and Laurie Hawkins championed Situational Self-Leadership; and Drea Zigarmi, Pat Zigarmi, and Judd Hoekstra focused energy on organisational leadership.

Chapter 6

1 See the HPO SCORES model in Chapter 1, "Is Your Organisation High Performing?"

2 Ken Blanchard, Jim Ballard, and Fred Finch, *Customer Mania!: It's Never Too Late to Build a Customer-Focused Company* (New York: Simon & Schuster/Free Press, 2004).

3 Jim Belasco and Ralph Stayer, *Flight of the Buffalo: Soaring to Excellence, Learning to Let Employees Lead* (New York: Warner Books, 1994).

4 Robert Slater, *The New GE: How Jack Welch Revived an American Institution* (New York: McGraw-Hill, 1993).

5 Based on the Situational Self-leadership programme, which was developed to teach Situational Leadership® II skills to direct reports and other associates.

6 Ken Blanchard, Susan Fowler, and Laurence Hawkins, *Self Leadership and The One Minute Manager* (New York: William Morrow, 2004).

Chapter 7

1 Ken Blanchard and Garry Ridge, *Helping People Win at Work: A Business Philosophy Called "Don't Mark My Paper, Help Me Get an A"* (Upper Saddle River, NJ: Pearson Prentice Hall, 2009).

2 Jim Belasco and Ralph Stayer, *Flight of the Buffalo: Soaring to Excellence, Learning to Let Employees Lead* (New York: Warner Books, 1994).

3 Doing an Internet search for "handling performance problems" provides excellent insight into the content of the literature and training courses.

4 Marjorie Blanchard and Garry Demarest, *One on One Conversations* (Escondido, CA: The Ken Blanchard Companies, 2000).

Chapter 8

1 Ken Blanchard and Spencer Johnson, *The One Minute Manager* (New York: William Morrow, 1982 and 2003).

2 An introduction to the research on goal setting can be found in E. A. Locke and G. P. Latham, *Goal Setting: A Motivational Tool That Works* (New Jersey: Prentice Hall, 1984). Two excellent quick summaries can be found in Gary P. Latham, "The Motivational Benefits of Goal Setting" (New York: *Academy of Management Executive*, 2004, Vol. 18, No. 4, pp. 126–129). Also see Stephan Kerr and Landauer Steffen, "Using Stretch Goals to Promote Organizational Effectiveness and Personal Growth" (New York: *Academy of Management Executive*, 2004, Vol. 18, No. 4, pp. 134–138).

3 Scott Meyers, *Every Employee a Manager* (New York: McGraw-Hill, 1970).

4   Gerard Seijts and Gary Latham, "Learning Versus Performance Goals: When Should Each Be Used?" (New York: *Academy of Management Executive*, 2004, Vol. 18, No. 4, pp. 124–131).

5   David McClelland, J. W. Atkinson, R. A. Clark, and E. L. Lowell, *The Achievement Motive* (Princeton, NJ: Van Nostrand, 1953).

6   "Management by Wandering Around" was developed by executives at Hewlett-Packard in the 1970s. It was popularised in a book written by Tom Peters and Robert Waterman in the early 1980s, *In Search of Excellence*. Their research revealed that managers of the most successful companies in America stayed close to the customers and the people doing the work; they were involved in rather than isolated from the business's daily routines.

7   Ken Blanchard, Jim Ballard, Thad Lacinak, and Chuck Tompkins, *Whale Done!: The Power of Positive Relationships* (New York: Free Press, 2002).

8   Ken Blanchard and Robert Lorber, *Putting the One Minute Manager to Work* (New York: William Morrow, 1984).

9   Ken Blanchard and Margret McBride, *The Fourth Secret of the One Minute Manager: A Powerful Way to Make Things Better* (New York: William Morrow, 2008). William Morrow originally published this book in 2003 as *The One Minute Apology*.

Chapter 9

1   "Coaching: A Global Study of Successful Practices," American Management Association, 2008, www.amanet.org/training/whitepapers/Coaching-A-Global-Study-of-Successful-Practices-02.aspx.

2 Goldsmith, "Retain Your Top Performers," Marshall Goldsmith Library online (www.marshallgoldsmithlibrary.com/cim/articles_display.php?aid=162).

3 Madeleine Homan and Linda J. Miller, *Coaching in Organizations: Best Coaching Practices from The Ken Blanchard Companies* (Hoboken, NJ: John Wiley & Sons), 2008.

Chapter 10

1 Ken Blanchard, Sheldon Bowles, Don Carew, and Eunice Parisi-Carew, *High Five!: The Magic of Working Together* (New York: William Morrow, 2001).

2 C. Southers, E. Parisi-Carew, and D. Carew, *Virtual Teams Handbook* (Escondido, CA: The Ken Blanchard Companies, 2002).

3 J. V. Johnson, W. Stewart, and E. M. Hall, "Long Term Psychological Work Environment and Cardiovascular Mortality," *American Journal of Public Health* (March 1996).

4 J. Despain and J. B. Converse, *And Dignity for All* (New Jersey: Financial Times/Prentice Hall, 2003).

5 B. Tuckman, "Developmental Sequence in Small Groups," Psychological Bulletin, 1964; R. B. Lacoursiere, *The Life Cycle of Groups: Group Development Stage Theory* (New York: Human Science Press, 1980); J. Stoner and D. Carew, "Stages of Group Development and Indicators of Excellence" (unpublished manuscript, 1991); S. A. Whelan and J. M. Hochberger, "Validation Studies of Group Development Questionnaire" (Thousand Oaks, CA: Small Group Research, 1996).

6 Adapted from R. B. Lacoursiere, ibid.

7   ABC Video Enterprises, *Do You Believe in Miracles?*, 1981. Also, Disney's *Miracle* is a 2004 film that tells the story of Herb Brooks and the 1980 US hockey team.

Chapter 11

1   International Consortium for Executive Development Research.

2   Gene E. Hall and Susan Loucks, "Teacher Concerns as a Basis for Facilitating and Personalizing Staff Development," Lieberman and Miller, eds., *Staff Development: New Demands, New Realities, New Perspectives* (New York: Teachers College Press, 1978).

3   SAP stands for Systems, Applications, Products. It is a mainframe system that provides users with a soft real-time business application.

4   In an interesting development, in 2005 SBC Communications purchased AT&T, thus reuniting the venerable phone company with three of its offspring (SBC was composed of Southwestern Bell, Pacific Telesis, and Ameritech). The merged company is named AT&T, Inc.

Chapter 12

1   For some of the pioneering work on change leadership, see Warren Bennis, *Managing the Dream: Reflections on Leadership and Change* (New York: Perseus Book Group, 2000), John Kotter, *Leading Change* (Boston, MA: Harvard Business School Press, 1996), and Daryl R. Conner, *Managing at the Speed of Change* (New York: Random House, 1993).

2   Indiana Department of Child Services website: www.in.gov/dcs

Chapter 13

1 Notable scholars that have contributed to our understanding of culture include Edgar Schein, Jim Collins, John Kotter, James Heskett, Max DePree, Richard Lieder, Stephen Covey, and Jim Kouzes.

2 Ken Blanchard and Sheldon Bowles, *Gung Ho!: Turn on the People in Any Organization* (New York: William Morrow, 1998).

3 This was only the second time in Blanchard's history that one of their programmes won this award.

4 This first release of the valued behaviours is called "initial" because it is extremely likely that revision of the values and/or behaviours will occur as the organisational change begins to take hold. In the refinement phase, the senior leadership team continually assesses if the initial valued behaviours need clarification or modification to better define what a good citizen looks and acts like in their organisation.

Chapter 14

1 A collection of Greenleaf's most mature writings on the subject can be found in *The Power of Servant Leadership* (San Francisco, CA: Berrett-Koehler, 1998). The Greenleaf Center for Servant Leadership (www.greenleaf.org) is a source of all his writings.

2 Ken Blanchard and Phil Hodges, *Lead Like Jesus: Lessons from the Greatest Leadership Role Model of All Time* (Nashville, TN: Thomas Nelson, 2005).

3 Rick Warren, *The Purpose Driven Life: What on Earth Am I Here For?* (Grand Rapids, MI: Zondervan, 2002).

4 Matt Hayes and Jeff Stevens, *The Heart of Business* (Bloomington, IN: Author House, 2005).

5   Scott Blanchard, Drea Zigarmi, and Vicky Essary, "The Leadership–Profit Chain," *Perspectives* (Escondido, CA: The Ken Blanchard Companies, 2006).

6   Ken Blanchard and Sheldon Bowles, *Gung Ho!: Turn on the People in Any Organization* (New York: William Morrow, 1998).

7   Gordon MacDonald, *Ordering Your Private World* (Nashville, TN: Nelson Books, 2003).

8   Robert Greenleaf, *The International Journal of Servant Leadership*, Vol. 1, No. 1 (Spokane, WA: 2006).

9   Robert S. McGee, *The Search for Significance* (Nashville, TN: W. Publishing Group, 2003).

10 Jim Collins, *Good to Great: Why Some Companies Make the Leap—and Others Don't* (New York: Harper Collins, 2001).

11 Ken Blanchard and Norman Vincent Peale, *The Power of Ethical Management* (New York: William Morrow, 1988).

12 Fred Smith, *You and Your Network* (Mechanicsburg, PA: Executive Books, 1998).

13 Ken Blanchard and Mark Miller, *The Secret: What Great Leaders Know and Do* (San Francisco, CA: Berrett-Koehler, 2004 and 2009).

14 Barbara Gellerman, "How Bad Leadership Happens," *Leader to Leader*, No. 35 (Winter 2005).

15 Drea Zigarmi, Ken Blanchard, Michael O'Connor, and Carl Edeburn, *The Leader Within: Learning Enough About Yourself to Lead Others* (Upper Saddle River, NJ: Prentice Hall, 2004).

16 M. A. Huselid, "The Impact of Human Resource Management Practices on Turnover, Productivity, and Corporate Financial Performance," *Academy of Management Journal*, 38 (1995).

17 E. Trist, "The Evolution of Socio-technical Systems," Ontario Quality of Working Life Centre, 1981.

18 Bob Buford, *Halftime* (Grand Rapids, MI: Zondervan, 1997).

Chapter 15

1 Noel Tichy, *The Leadership Engine: How Winning Companies Build Leaders at Every Level* (New York: HarperCollins, 1997).

2 Susan Fowler developed this process for the Situational Self-Leadership programme offered by The Ken Blanchard Companies. For more information, see www.kenblanchard.com.

3 Ken Blanchard and Michael O'Connor, *Managing by Values* (San Francisco, CA: Berrett-Koehler, 1997).

ACKNOWLEDGEMENTS

This is one of the biggest and most significant writing projects in which I have ever been involved. As I indicate in the Introduction, this book pulls together the thinking from The Ken Blanchard Companies over the past 30 years. This certainly wasn't a solo flight. Many people contributed to bringing to reality the dream of *Leading at a Higher Level*.

Let me start with my coauthors. The idea for creating an organisation where *we could work with people we love and care about and make a difference in organisations* was born in the early 1970s by eight of us who were faculty members or doctoral students at the University of Massachusetts in Amherst. This group, including **Margie** and me, **Don Carew**, **Eunice Parisi-Carew**, **Fred Finch**, **Laurie Hawkins**, **Drea Zigarmi**, and **Pat Zigarmi**, is what we call the Founding Associates of The Ken Blanchard Companies.

In the early 1980s, this group changed the original Situational Leadership® theory to Situational Leadership® II, which is the cornerstone of the Blanchard leadership programmes. These Founding Associates are the people I went to when I first thought of writing this book. Without their encouragement and important contributions, this book would have remained a dream.

After the Founding Associates got underway on the book, we invited a number of other consulting partners and associates to join us in writing it, because of the major part they have played in the development of our work. Big hugs and appreciation to **Scott Blanchard**, **Madeline Homan Blanchard**, **Kathy Cuff**, **Garry Demarest**, **Chris Edmonds**, **Susan Fowler**, **Bob Glaser**, **Lael Good**, **Vicki Halsey**, **Judd Hoekstra**, **Fay Kandarian**, **Linda Miller**, **Alan Randolph**, and **Jesse Stoner**, who have made important contributions to this book.

One other writer was instrumental in this book's becoming a reality. Without **Martha Lawrence**, the senior editor on my team, we would still be talking about this book. She made it happen. She nurtured every section, every chapter, and every word. Martha hates attention and recognition, but she has no choice. Everyone who has worked on this book loves her and recognises the important role she has played. Martha and I could never do what we do without the support of the other members of our team: **Margery Allen**, **Anna Espino**, and **Renee Broadwell**. They all light up my life.

Another Blanchard person has been key to the creation of this book. **Richard Andrews** is a miracle worker when it comes to writing win–win contracts. Not only does he believe "among friends, clear accounts," but he is always making sure that our intellectual property is protected.

As an editor, **Tim Moore** is every author's dream—brilliant, insightful, and always encouraging. A huge thank you to Tim and his top-notch publishing team at Pearson/FT Press: **Gina Kanouse**, **Amy Neidlinger**, **Lori Lyons**, **Kristy Hart**, **Gayle Johnson**, and **Gloria Schurick**.

I have had the pleasure of coauthoring books with a number of other authors. Several deserve special mention:

Paul Hersey, my partner in developing the original Situational Leadership® model that led to Situational Leadership® II, the foundational concept for our company.

Spencer Johnson, my coauthor on *The One Minute Manager*, the book that catapulted my career and our company to a new level.

Sheldon Bowles, my coauthor on *Raving Fans* and *Gung Ho!*, two bestsellers that have taken our company in new directions.

Jim Ballard, a key writing partner who worked with me on *Managing by Values* (coauthored with Michael O'Connor), *Everyone's a Coach* (coauthored with Don Shula), and *The Heart of a Leader*. We also wrote two books together: *Whale Done!* (coauthored with Thad Lacinak and Chuck Thompkins) and

Customer Mania! (coauthored with Fred Finch). Jim has made me a better writer and has been a constant spiritual encouragement.

Bob Lorber, my coauthor on *Putting the One Minute Manager to Work*, the follow-up book that started The One Minute Manager Library.

Margret McBride, my coauthor on *The Fourth Secret of the One Minute Manager* and the literary agent who introduced me to mainstream publishing.

Norman Vincent Peale, my coauthor on *The Power of Ethical Management* and a wonderful inspiration for my spiritual growth.

Phil Hodges, my coauthor on *Leadership by the Book* (with Bill Hybels), *The Servant Leader*, and *Lead Like Jesus*, books that began my writing about Jesus as one of the greatest leadership role models of all time and led to our founding of the Lead Like Jesus ministries.

My work with Paul, Spencer, Sheldon, Jim, Bob, Margret, Norman, and Phil is cited throughout this book. They all have had a major impact on my thinking and my life.

ABOUT THE AUTHORS

Ken Blanchard

Few people have impacted the day-to-day management of people and companies more than Dr Ken Blanchard. A prominent, gregarious, sought-after author, speaker, and business consultant, Dr Blanchard is universally characterised by his friends, colleagues, and clients as one of the most insightful, powerful, and compassionate individuals in business today.

From his phenomenal best-selling book *The One Minute Manager*®, coauthored with Spencer Johnson (which has sold more than 15 million copies and has remained on best-seller lists for more than 25 years), to the library of books he has coauthored with Sheldon Bowles (including the blockbuster best sellers *Raving Fans* and *Gung Ho!*), Ken's impact as a writer is far-reaching. In July 2005, he was inducted into the Amazon Hall of Fame as one of the top 25 best-selling authors of all time.

Dr Blanchard is the chief spiritual officer of The Ken Blanchard Companies, an international management training and consulting firm that he and his wife, Dr Marjorie Blanchard, founded in 1979 in San Diego. He is also a visiting lecturer at his alma mater, Cornell University, where he is a trustee emeritus of the Board of Trustees. Along with his wife, he teaches a course in leadership for the Master of Science in Executive Leadership course at the University of San Diego. He is also cofounder of Lead Like Jesus, a non-profit organisation.

The National Speakers Association awarded Dr Blanchard its highest honour, the Council of Peers Award of Excellence, and the College of Business at Grand Canyon University in Phoenix, Arizona bears his name.

Marjorie Blanchard

Dr Marjorie Blanchard has earned a reputation worldwide as a compelling motivational speaker, an accomplished management consultant and trainer, a best-selling author, and an entrepreneur. She was the corecipient with her husband, Dr Ken Blanchard, of the Entrepreneur of the Year award from Cornell University.

Coauthor of *The One Minute Manager Gets Fit* and *Working Well: Managing for Health and High-Performance*, Dr Blanchard is well versed in a variety of topics and often speaks on leadership, balance, managing change, and life planning. As cofounder of The Ken Blanchard Companies, she works diligently with Ken, developing the company into one of the world's premier management consulting and training companies.

Dr Blanchard now heads the firm's Office of the Future, a think tank charged with shaping the future of both the training industry and the company.

Dr Blanchard received her bachelor's and master's degrees from Cornell University and her doctorate from the University of Massachusetts. Along with Ken, she teaches a course in leadership for the Master of Science in Executive Leadership course at the University of San Diego.

Scott Blanchard

Mr Scott Blanchard is a stimulating author, motivational speaker, accomplished corporate trainer, and passionate champion of coaching in the workplace. He founded Coaching.com, a Web-enabled corporate coaching and personal development service. Under his leadership, his organisation is revolutionising corporate coaching by offering the most advanced, accessible, and research-driven services in the industry. His personal philosophy is based on a fundamental shift occurring in the discipline of leadership: Great leaders do not succeed by doing what they are good at; instead, they succeed by getting things done with and through others.

Mr Blanchard is senior vice president of The Ken Blanchard Companies. As a Blanchard family member and part owner, he represents the "next generation" charged with leading the business into the future. In addition, he is the principal architect of Blanchard's strategic alliance with Ninth House® Network.

Mr Blanchard is the coauthor of *Leverage Your Best, Ditch the Rest*, a book on corporate coaching. As a senior consulting partner for more than six years, he has led major training interventions at numerous Fortune 500 companies.

Mr Blanchard was educated at Cornell University and received his master's degree in organisational development from American University in Washington, DC.

Madeleine Homan Blanchard

Madeleine Homan Blanchard is vice president of Coaching Services for The Ken Blanchard Companies. She is a founder of Coaching.com, which was acquired by The Ken Blanchard Companies in 2002, and coauthor of the Internet platform (the Coaching Management System) used to support large coaching initiatives. With more than 19 years of experience, Madeleine was instrumental in developing the core curriculum for Coach University, where she was a founding advisory board member and senior trainer.

Madeleine has been a pioneer in the coaching profession. In 1994 she founded Straightline Coaching, a coaching service firm devoted to work satisfaction for creative geniuses. She is the designer and facilitator of *The Manager as Coach*, which was the core coaching curriculum for several companies worldwide, including Boston Consulting Group and Capital One. She is also a coauthor of The Ken Blanchard Companies' coaching skills course, *Coaching Essentials for Leaders*. Madeleine was a founding board member of the International Coach Federation, where she served on the board for six years, founded the Organisational Coach Committee, and was the VP of Professional Development.

Madeleine's expertise in coaching has been highlighted on ABC, NBC, CBS, and Fox News Channel. Her presence in the marketplace extends into press articles in *The New York Times, London Times, Training & Development Magazine, ASTD Publications,* and *Women's Media.* She is a regular keynote speaker at leadership and corporate conferences around the world. She is the coauthor of two books: *Leverage Your Best: Ditch the Rest* and *Coaching in Organizations.*

Donald K. Carew

Dr Don Carew is a founding associate of The Ken Blanchard Companies and a professor emeritus at the University of Massachusetts, Amherst. He is an accomplished and respected management consultant, trainer, educator, and author whose primary academic and consulting interests are in the areas of leadership and building high-performing teams and organisations.

Dr Carew met Ken Blanchard when they were young faculty members at Ohio University in 1966. Don moved to the University of Massachusetts in 1969, and Ken joined the faculty in 1970. It was Don Carew's and Eunice Parisi-Carew's research on group development that led the Founding Associates of The Ken Blanchard Companies to change the Situational Leadership® II model so that it could be used with groups and teams as well as with individuals.

In addition to being a full-time faculty member at the University of Massachusetts, Dr Carew has been a faculty member at Trenton State University, Princeton University, and the University of San Diego. He is coauthor of two best-selling books: *The One Minute Manager Builds High-Performing Teams*, with Ken Blanchard and Eunice Parisi-Carew, and *High Five*, with Ken, Eunice, and Sheldon Bowles. He is also a coauthor of the article "High-Performing Organizations: SCORES."

Dr Carew holds a bachelor's degree in business from Ohio University, a master's degree in human relations from Ohio University, and a doctorate in counselling psychology from the University of Florida. He is an associate of the NTL Institute and a licenced psychologist in Massachusetts.

Eunice Parisi-Carew

Dr Eunice Parisi-Carew is the coauthor of two best-selling books: *The One Minute Manager Builds High-Performing Teams*, with Ken Blanchard and Don Carew, and *High Five*, with Ken Blanchard, Don Carew, and Sheldon Bowles. She is also cocreator of the High-Performing Teams product line offered by The Ken Blanchard Companies.

An accomplished management consultant and trainer and a sought-after motivational speaker, she has led training and consulting projects for a number of top corporations, including Merrill Lynch; AT&T; Hyatt Hotels; Transco Energy Company; and the Department of Health, Education, and Welfare. Team building, leadership, organisational change, and life management are among the many topics she addresses in seminars, speeches, and articles.

Dr Carew has directed a graduate course in group dynamics and leadership at the University of Hartford, and she was a part-time faculty member at American University. She is also a member of the Board of Directors of the NTL Institute. She has also served as vice president of Professional Services at The Ken Blanchard Companies.

She received her doctor of education in behavioural sciences from the University of Massachusetts and is also a licenced psychologist in the state of Massachusetts.

Dr Carew now serves as a senior researcher with the Office of the Future at The Ken Blanchard Companies, where she studies trends that occur five to ten years out and summarises their implications for leaders, organisations, and business practices.

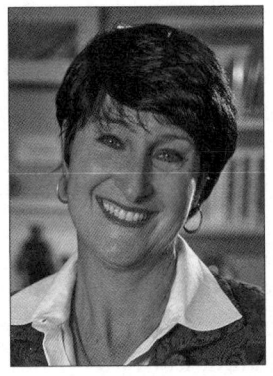

Kathleen Riley Cuff

Ms Kathy Cuff is an energetic motivational speaker, trainer, and consultant for many organisations. The enthusiasm and humour she brings to every presentation are complemented by her positive attitude and sincere commitment to meeting the specific needs of each client.

For 22 years Ms Cuff has been with The Ken Blanchard Companies, where she now serves as a senior consulting partner. Drawing from her broad base of experience in leadership, management, and customer service, she has designed and implemented training and consulting projects for a client list that includes Charles Schwab, Medtronic, TaylorMade-Adidas Golf, and W.L. Gore.

She is coauthor of The Ken Blanchard Companies' Legendary Service customer service programme, as well as coauthor of the revised Raving Fans® programme.

Ms Cuff received her degree from San Diego State University and has participated in numerous educational seminars and courses over the years.

S. Chris Edmonds

Mr Chris Edmonds is an expert on creating high-performing, values-aligned organisational cultures. He serves as an executive coach for senior leaders engaged in culture change initiatives, helping them understand their responsibility to clarify expectations, refine systems, consistently demonstrate desired values, and hold leaders and staff accountable for demonstrating those values. His clients include American Honda, Clorox, Deloitte, Federal Reserve Bank, Genentech, IBM, Merck, New Belgium Brewery, Northwest Airlines, Pfizer, Taylor Corporation, T-Mobile, Toyota Motor Corporation, and YMCA of the USA.

Mr Edmonds coauthored Blanchard's culture change process, which is based on Ken Blanchard's bestselling book *Gung Ho!*® The process was recognised as one of the Top Ten Training Courses of 2000 by *Human Resource Executive* magazine.

A graduate of Whittier College with a degree in education, Mr Edmonds holds a secondary teaching credential from California Lutheran College. He received his master's degree in human resources and organisational development from the University of San Francisco. He is a faculty member of the Master of Science in Executive Leadership course at the University of San Diego.

Fred Finch

Dr Fred Finch is the author of *Managing for Organizational Effectiveness: An Experiential Approach.* A founding associate of The Ken Blanchard Companies, he has been a consultant and leadership educator at Harvard University, Merrill Lynch, IBM, Shell International, and many other high-profile organisations. He received his doctorate from the Graduate School of Business at the University of Washington. He served as a professor of management and organisational behaviour for 14 years in the Graduate School of Management at the University of Massachusetts.

Dr Finch is coauthor with Ken Blanchard and Jim Ballard of *Customer Mania!: It's Never Too Late to Build a Customer-Focused Company.* This book grew out of a study of Yum! Brands, the world's largest quick-service restaurant corporation, with 850,000 employees in more than 100 countries. He is also coauthor with Pat Stewart of Situational Frontline Leadership, a popular training programme for frontline leaders.

Susan Fowler

Ms Susan Fowler is coauthor with Ken Blanchard and Laurence Hawkins of *Self Leadership and the One Minute Manager*, published in 2005. With Ken Blanchard and Laurence Hawkins she created and is the lead developer of Situational Self Leadership®, a best-of-class self-leadership and personal empowerment programme.

Ms Fowler received the Lifetime Achievement Award for creative training designs from the North American Society for Games and Simulations. As a senior consulting partner with The Ken Blanchard Companies, Ms Fowler has consulted with Pfizer, Harley-Davidson, MasterCard, AMF Bowling, Dow Chemical, KPMG, Black & Decker, SC Johnson, TJX Retailers, the National Basketball Association, and dozens of other clients. Prior to that, she gained worldwide seminar presentation experience with CareerTrack.

Ms Fowler brings a unique perspective to her programmes from her extensive experience in advertising and television and radio broadcasting. She received her degree in marketing from the University of Colorado. As one of the world's foremost experts on personal empowerment, she has delivered training seminars, workshops, and keynote speeches to more than 50,000 people in over 20 countries and in all 50 states.

Her publications include *Overcoming Procrastination, Mentoring, The Team Leader's Idea-a-Day Guide* (coauthored with Drea Zigarmi), and *Empowerment* (coauthored with Ken

Blanchard). Ms Fowler also serves as an adjunct professor on the University of San Diego's Master of Science in Executive Leadership course.

Robert Glaser

Mr Robert Glaser is a regional consulting partner at The Ken Blanchard Companies and has been a member of the consulting partner group for 13 years. He has a 30-year track record of successfully facilitating leadership development, team development, strategic planning, performance consulting, organisational change, and organisational culture change.

Prior to joining Blanchard, Mr Glaser worked for more than 20 years in a Fortune 500 restaurant chain based in San Diego, where he was the director of management and leadership development.

Mr Glaser is an adjunct faculty member on the University of San Diego's Master of Science in Executive Leadership course. He is also coauthor of Blanchard's Gung Ho!® culture change programme and process.

He has extensive international and cross-cultural experience and served for four years in the Peace Corps in Ghana and Uganda.

Mr Glaser received his bachelor's degree in social science from California State University at Chico and his master's degree in leadership studies from the University of San Diego.

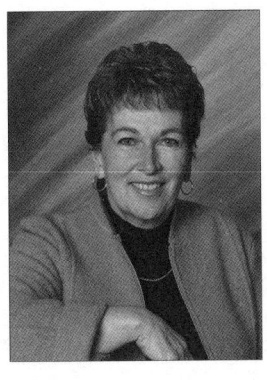

Lael W. Good

Ms Lael Good serves as a lead consultant on many of Blanchard's largest multinational client initiatives, including Coca-Cola, Diageo, Mars/Masterfoods, MTN South Africa, Nokia, Pfizer Pharmaceuticals, Royal Dutch Shell, SAP, and Skanska. She is one of the most requested and respected consulting partners because her unique skill set enables her to work with global organisations in places as diverse as Western and Eastern Europe, Central and Latin America, Africa, China, India, and the Middle East.

She is coauthor of two Blanchard programmes —Situational Team Leadership, with Don Carew and Eunice Parisi-Carew, and The Leadership Bridge: SLII® and MBTI®, with Tom Hill and Ken Blanchard. She also is an expert on the dynamics of high-performing teams.

Working with global clients, Ms Good provides customised design, delivery, and sustainability solutions. Her capabilities in and knowledge of organisational development and instructional design complement her natural ability to influence and involve people in solving their own problems.

Ms Good received her bachelor's degree in counselling from the University of Arizona and her master's degree in counselling psychology from the University of Wyoming.

Dr Vicki Halsey

Dr Vicki Halsey is a spirited speaker, author, coach, and trainer whose lively presentations promote learning and captivate audiences worldwide. Her mission of inspiring others to claim their greatness is achieved through blending solutions that meet the needs of all learners.

As vice president of applied learning for The Ken Blanchard Companies, Dr Halsey specialises in partnering with organisations to design, deliver, and coach people through interactive workshops, keynotes, webinars, and blended classroom and virtual trainings. She is the coauthor of Blanchard's Legendary Customer Service programme as well as the award-winning blended Situational Leadership® II training. Her clients include Fortune 100 companies such as Nike, Gap, Wells Fargo, Oracle, and Procter & Gamble. In addition, Dr Halsey is cocreator of the highly acclaimed Master of Science in Executive Leadership and EMBA degree courses for the University of San Diego and Grand Canyon University, respectively.

She is coauthor of the best-selling book *The Hamster Revolution: How to Manage Your Email Before It Manages You.* It contains strategies that cut e-mail time in half and improve the quality of the work environment by reducing stress and inspiring clarity. Her forthcoming book, *The Hamster Revolution for Meetings: How to Meet Less and Get More Done*, offers a simple system that helps keep meetings productive, on track, and engaging.

Laurence Hawkins

Dr Laurence Hawkins is one of the founding associates of The Ken Blanchard Companies, as well as an internationally renowned management consultant and motivational speaker. With Ken Blanchard and Susan Fowler, he coauthored the Situational Self-Leadership programme, which focuses on empowerment and taking initiative when you're not in charge. He is also the coauthor with Ken and Susan of *Self Leadership and the One Minute Manager*, published in 2005.

Dr Hawkins has concentrated much of his work on aerospace, particularly Lockheed Martin and McDonnell Douglas, and pharmaceutical giants such as Pfizer, Merck, and GlaxoSmithKline. He has focused his career on applying the Blanchard standards of Situational Leadership® II, Situational Team Leadership, and Situational Self-Leadership in the international arena, concentrating on Europe, South America, and Saudi Arabia. More recently, he has been teaching the tools, concepts, and philosophy of self-leadership to clients in China and Korea—countries where obedience is rapidly shifting to a culture of entrepreneurship and taking initiative.

Dr Hawkins received his bachelor's degree in American history and literature from Williams College and his master's and doctorate degrees in leadership and organisational behaviour from the University of Massachusetts Amherst.

Judd Hoekstra

Mr Hoekstra is one of Blanchard's experts in organisational change and is coauthor of its Managing a Change consulting methodology and training programme. His approach to change is based on a shared commitment to Dr Don Carew's principle that people have a right to be involved in decisions that affect their lives and the concept that those who plan the battle rarely battle the plan.

Mr Hoekstra's positive attitude, ability to work well with all people, and passion for "doing the right things right" help those he works with make great things happen.

Prior to joining Blanchard in 2001, Mr Hoekstra served as a strategy execution consultant with Fourth Floor Consulting. Before that, he was a change management consultant with Accenture. He was primarily responsible for helping client executives lead their organisations through large-scale changes. His experience crosses a number of industries; his clients have included The Dow Chemical Company, Allstate Insurance Company, Anheuser-Busch, and Commonwealth Edison.

Mr Hoekstra received his bachelor's in business management and marketing from Cornell University and graduated from the Advanced Business Management course at Kellogg Graduate School of Management. He and his wife, Sherry, live in the Chicago area and are the proud parents of Julia and Cole.

Fay Kandarian

Dr Fay Kandarian has worked as both an internal and independent organisational change consultant over the past 20 years. She has been a consulting partner with The Ken Blanchard Companies since 1998.

Her extensive line, staff, and executive experiences provide constant reference points that inform her consulting. Her areas of expertise include whole systems change, executive coaching, strategic planning, intervention design, leadership and team development, communications skills, and process consultation.

While doing doctoral research at Columbia University's Department of Organisation and Leadership, Dr Kandarian studied and developed proficiency in using large-group interventions as a new paradigm for organisation development and large-scale change. She researched Polarity Management (B. Johnson, 1996) as a training intervention to help teach systems thinking skills. She later introduced Polarity Management's "both/and" thinking to The Ken Blanchard Companies.

Working with fellow HPO team members Jesse Stoner, Eunice Parisi-Carew, and Don Carew, she helped create the HPO SCORES model and coauthored the article "High-Performing Organizations: SCORES."

She holds a bachelor's degree from George Washington University, a master's in business from the University of New Haven, and a master's and doctorate in education from Columbia University.

Linda Miller

Ms Linda J. Miller is an executive coach, trainer, and keynote speaker who has a passion for people taking effective, intentional action. She helped launch Corporate Coach U, a leader in organisational coach training. Since 2000, she has served as global liaison for coaching with The Ken Blanchard Companies. In 2002, Ms Miller coauthored Coaching Essentials for Leaders, a coach training programme that encourages leaders to use coaching skills to create strong business alliances.

Ms Miller also coaches executives and helps organisations establish internal coaching cultures. Her client list includes leaders and their teams from Adobe, Alltel, Boeing, Deloitte, Duke Energy, Franklin Templeton, KPMG, Nissan, Pfizer, SAP, Scotia Bank Wells Fargo, and the University of Washington. She co-led a team that moderated 13 of the Arizona state legislative debates in collaboration with the Arizona Clean Elections Commission during the 2008 election cycle.

As a founding recipient of the Master Certified Coach designation from the International Coach Federation, Ms Miller has been featured in numerous articles and television news segments on coaching. She is coauthor with Madeleine Homan Blanchard of *Coaching in Organisations: Best Coaching Practices* from The Ken Blanchard Companies.

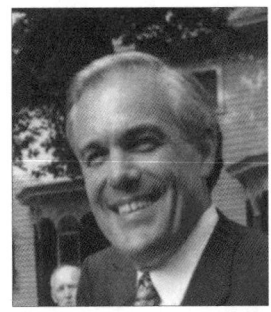

Alan Randolph

Dr Alan Randolph is an internationally respected and highly accomplished management educator, researcher, and consultant. His work focuses on empowerment, leadership, teamwork, and project management issues for both domestic and international organisations in the public and private sectors. He has worked in a variety of countries, including most recently Peru, Brazil, China, Germany, France, and Poland.

Dr Randolph is a professor of management and international business at the Merrick School of Business at the University of Baltimore. He also is a senior consulting partner with The Ken Blanchard Companies. He has developed a variety of leadership and empowerment educational products. He has also published numerous articles in practitioner and academic journals such as *Harvard Business Review* and *Sloan Management Review*.

Dr Randolph has written and coauthored a number of books, including *Go Team!: Take Your Team to the Next Level*, *Checkered Flag Projects: 10 Rules for Creating and Managing Projects That Win!*, *Empowerment Takes More Than a Minute*, and *The 3 Keys to Empowerment: Release the Power Within People for Astonishing Results*.

Jesse Stoner

Dr Jesse Stoner is widely known as one of the foremost experts on vision and leadership. A highly regarded management consultant and author, for more than 20 years Dr Stoner has helped leaders create organisations where people can thrive and make significant contributions. Her work in vision development has helped individuals, leaders, and companies create compelling visions, identify the strategies to capture them, and ensure that they are lived on a day-by-day basis.

She coauthored with Ken Blanchard the best-seller *Full Steam Ahead! Unleash the Power of Vision in Your Work and Your Life*. She is also coauthor of Creating Your Organisation's Future, a programme that helps leadership teams develop a shared vision for their department or organisation.

Dr Stoner was a member of the original research team investigating the characteristics of high-performing organisations. She helped create the HPO SCORES model and coauthored the article "High-Performing Organizations: SCORES" and the assessment The HPO SCORES Profile.

Additionally, she has contributed to the development of the Building High-Performing Teams programmes. She coauthored Team Development Stage Analysis (TDSA) and "The Team Member's Role in Building High Performing Teams."

Dr Stoner earned advanced degrees in psychology and a doctorate in organisation development from the University of Massachusetts.

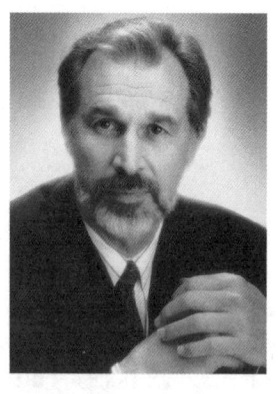

Drea Zigarmi

Formerly president of Zigarmi Associates, Inc., Dr Drea Zigarmi is the director of research and development for The Ken Blanchard Companies. His work has been critical to the company's success with its clients. Almost every product that has been developed at The Ken Blanchard Companies over the past 20 years has his mark on it. He coauthored with Ken Blanchard the well-known Leader Behaviour Analysis instrument and the Development Task Analysis form used in all Situational Leadership seminars.

He has coauthored three books: *The Leader Within: Learning Enough About Yourself to Lead Others*, *The Team Leader's Idea-a-Day Guide*, and *Leadership and the One Minute Manager*.

He received his bachelor's in science from Norwich University. He earned a master's in philosophy and a doctorate in administration and organisational behaviour from the University of Massachusetts Amherst.

Patricia Zigarmi

Dr Patricia Zigarmi is a founding associate of The Ken Blanchard Companies, where she serves as vice president for business development. She is a speaker, consultant, product designer, business developer, account strategist, trainer, and team builder for many of Blanchard's clients and is a mentor to many colleagues at Blanchard.

Dr Zigarmi is coauthor of *Leadership and the One Minute Manager*. She also designed Blanchard's premier product line, Situational Leadership® II. With her leadership, ongoing initiatives for Situational Leadership® II training and coaching have been negotiated with many global companies and most of the Fortune 500 companies. She is also the author of Blanchard's Managing a Change programme and a number of performance management products on giving feedback and monitoring and reviewing performance.

Dr Zigarmi teaches Managing a Change for the Masters in Executive Excellence course at the University of San Diego. She is also a member of the San Diego Women's Foundation.

She received her bachelor's in sociology from Northwestern University and her doctorate in leadership and organisational behaviour from the University of Massachusetts Amherst.

SERVICES AVAILABLE

The Ken Blanchard Companies® is a global leader in workplace learning, productivity, performance, and leadership effectiveness. It is best known for its Situational Leadership® II programme—the most widely taught leadership model in the world. Because of its ability to help people excel as self-leaders and as leaders of others, SLII® is embraced by Fortune 500 companies as well as mid- to small-sized businesses, governments, and educational and non-profit organisations.

Blanchard® programmes are based on the evidence that people are the key to accomplishing strategic objectives and driving business results. They help people develop excellence in leadership, teams, customer loyalty, change management, and performance improvement. The company's continual research points to best practices for workplace improvement. Its world-class trainers and coaches drive organisational and behavioural change at all levels and help people make the shift from learning to doing.

Leadership experts from The Ken Blanchard Companies are available for workshops, consulting, and keynote addresses on organisational development, workplace performance, and business trends.

Global Headquarters

The Ken Blanchard Companies
125 State Place
Escondido CA 92029
www.kenblanchard.com
1-800-728-6000 in the USA
+1-760-489-5005 international

UK Office

The Ken Blanchard Companies
Gateway Guildford
Power Close
Guildford, Surrey GU1 1EJ
United Kingdom
+44 (0) 1483 456300
Email: uk@kenblanchard.com

Keynote Speakers

Blanchard Keynote Speakers present enduring leadership insights to all types of management-related events, including corporate gatherings and celebrations, association conferences, sales meetings, industry conferences, and executive retreats. Our network of speaking professionals is among the best in the world at engaging audiences to new levels of commitment and enthusiasm.

Blanchard speaker topics include

- Coaching
- Customer loyalty
- Employee engagement
- Leadership
- Motivation and inspiration
- Organisational change
- Public-sector leadership
- Teambuilding
- Women in leadership

To book a Blanchard Keynote Speaker for your next event, please call:

United States: 1-800-728-6000

United Kingdom: +44-01483-456300

Canada: 800-665-5023

International: +1760-489-5005

Or visit www.kenblanchard.com/speakers to learn more and to book your speaker today.

Social Networking

Visit Blanchard on YouTube

Watch thought leaders from The Ken Blanchard Companies in action. Link and subscribe to Blanchard's channel, and you'll receive updates as new videos are posted.

Join the Blanchard Fan Club on Facebook

Be part of our inner circle and link to Ken Blanchard on Facebook. Meet other fans of Ken and his books. Access videos and photos, and get invited to special events.

Join Conversations with Ken Blanchard

Blanchard's blog, HowWeLead.org, was created to inspire positive change. It is a public-service site devoted to leadership topics that connect us all. This site is non-partisan and secular and does not solicit or accept donations. It is a social network, where you will meet people who care deeply about responsible leadership. And it's a place where Ken Blanchard would like to hear your opinion.

Ken's Twitter Updates

Receive timely messages and thoughts from Ken. Find out the events he's attending and what's on his mind.

Tools for Change

Visit www.kenblanchard.com and click "Tools for Change" to learn about workshops, coaching services, and leadership programmes that help your organisation create lasting behaviour changes that have a measurable impact.

Helping People Win at Work with Situational Leadership® II

Situational Leadership® II (SLII®) is the most widely taught leadership model in the world. SLII® provides leaders with a diagnostic approach for creating open communication and developing self-reliance in those they manage. It is designed to increase the frequency and quality of conversations about performance and development. As a result, competence is developed, commitment is gained, and talented individuals are retained.

SLII® is recognised as both a business language and framework for employee development because it works across cultural, linguistic, and geographic barriers. The foundation lies in teaching leaders to diagnose the needs of an individual or team and then use the appropriate leadership style to respond to the needs of the person and situation.

Based on 30 years of research and corporate adoption, SLII® is proven to help develop leaders who excel at goal setting, coaching, performance evaluation, active listening, and proactive problem solving. By creating the systems needed to track performance and partnering, it has allowed users to clarify individual goals and ensure alignment with the organisation's goals. In addition, SLII® has helped companies increase the retention of "star" employees, improve individual and organisational development, and improve job satisfaction and morale at all levels.

Contact The Ken Blanchard Companies at +1-760-489-5005 to find out how your company can develop competence, gain commitment, and retain talent.

INDEX

Index

U–V

W–Z